TACTICAL DECISION-MAKING IN SPORT

This book expands on the 'Developing Thinking Players' model across a wide range of team and individual sports, to explain how coaches can help athletes to learn how to make better decisions during play and to think for themselves. It provides an overview of game-centred and athlete-centred approaches to teaching and coaching in sport, combining essential theory with practical tips and guidance.

Written by an international team of coaching researchers and practising coaches, the book provides sport-specific instructions for coaching players in territory games, net games, striking games, target games, racquet games and combat sports, including netball, basketball, ice hockey, cricket, softball, football, rugby, volleyball, squash and karate. The book argues that the implementation of these student and athlete-centred approaches creates more opportunities for athletes to understand their sport and improves their ability to think for themselves and to learn to make better in-game decisions. Providing a theoretical underpinning for teaching tactical decision-making, it considers the development of players at all levels and age groups, from youth athletes to elite level. Thirteen sport-specific case studies offer real-world coaching insights.

This is essential reading for any student, researcher or practising teacher or coach working in sport, physical education and coach education.

David Cooper is Associate Professor, Teaching Stream in the Faculty of Kinesiology and Physical Education at the University of Toronto, Canada. He is a National Coaching Certification Program (NCCP) Course Facilitator and was Head Coach (1998–2015) of the successful University of Toronto Varsity Blues women's squash team.

Barrie Gordon is Associate Professor in Health and Physical Education at the Victoria University of Wellington, New Zealand. Barrie has been involved in playing fastpitch softball in the New Zealand national league and currently represents New Zealand in the over 55s TAG football team.

TACTICAL DECISION-MAKING IN SPORT

How Coaches Can Help Athletes to Make Better In-Game Decisions

Edited by David Cooper and Barrie Gordon

Routledge
Taylor & Francis Group

LONDON AND NEW YORK

First published 2020
by Routledge
2 Park Square, Milton Park, Abingdon, Oxon OX14 4RN

and by Routledge
52 Vanderbilt Avenue, New York, NY 10017

Routledge is an imprint of the Taylor & Francis Group, an informa business

British Library Cataloguing-in-Publication Data
catalogue record for this book is available from the British Library

Library of Congress Cataloging-in-Publication Data
A catalog record has been requested for this book

ISBN: 978-0-367-27523-5 (hbk)
ISBN: 978-0-367-27524-2 (pbk)
ISBN: 978-0-429-29648-2 (ebk)

Typeset in Bembo
by Wearset Ltd, Boldon, Tyne and Wear

This book is dedicated in memory of Dr Guido Geisler who sadly passed away after writing two of the chapters and agreeing to be a co-editor. His contribution to coaching, research and this project has been missed by many, especially his friends and colleagues at the University of Toronto, Canada and the University of Tsukuba, Japan.

CONTENTS

FIGURES

TABLES

CONTRIBUTORS

John Barrett is the Head Coach of the Varsity Blues Men's volleyball team programme since 2011. In the spring of 2018, he was voted President of the Canadian U SPORTS men's volleyball coaches association. John competed at the 1984 Olympic Games, the 1983 Pan Am Games and at the 1990 world championships for Canada. He played professional basketball in Europe for 14 seasons where he made history as the first volleyball player in the world to exclusively employ the spike serve in matches. He was head coach for both the men's and women's beach volleyball teams at the 2003 Pan Am Games and is currently the 2019 Canadian senior B men's team head coach.

Dave Brunner has served the United States Army for the past 10 years as a Human Performance Team manager in the field of sport and performance psychology. His team has developed and delivered holistic human performance training to Special Operators, Intelligence Analysts and Aviators. He holds a PhD from the University of Idaho in the Philosophy, Pedagogy, and Psychology of Sport. Before affiliating with the Army he spent 25 years as a football coach and teacher at the university and secondary school level. His career in coaching includes positions as a head football coach at three different high schools in North and South Carolina, and as an assistant coach and coordinator at two different NCAA Division I university football programmes.

John Campbell is the Head Coach Men's Varsity Blues basketball team at the University of Toronto. He has been a head coach in post-secondary basketball in Canada for over 25 years. John has been an assistant coach at the international level for both Canada and Great Britain. He attended the National Coaching

Institute at the University of Victoria, British Columbia, and is a Learning Facilitator for the NCCP course of "Train to Compete – Tactics and Strategies".

Greg Gary is the former Head Coach of the University of Toronto Varsity Blues football team (2010–2017) and a faculty member in Kinesiology and Physical Education at the University of Toronto, Canada. Greg attended California State University Fullerton (CSUF), Greg signed as a free agent with the Los Angeles Rams in the National Football League. After a short stay with the Rams, he came to the Canadian Football League and played four seasons with the Hamilton Tiger Cats and was a member of the 1986 Grey Cup winning team.

Guido Geisler was an Associate Professor at the Tsukuba International Academy for Sport Studies (TIAS) at the University of Tsukuba, Japan. Guido obtained his UEFA-B football-coaching licence from the German Football Federation (DFB) in 2016. He coached varsity soccer at the University of Toronto and at club level in Japan. He designed and conducted soccer coaching courses for the Sports Authority of India (SAI). Sadly, Guido passed away on October 26, 2018 after contributing two chapters to this book.

Karlene Headley-Cooper is a teacher at Crofton House School in Vancouver BC, Canada. Prior to moving to Crofton House School, Karlene was a Senior Instructor in the Faculty of Kinesiology and Physical Education at the University of Toronto where she taught fundamentals in fitness, exercise, physical activity and communication. Karlene is a recipient of a 2017 University of Toronto KPE Award of Excellence in Teaching. She was an Ontario University Association women's squash all star on six occasions and a member of the 2005 women's team that was inducted into the Varsity Blues Hall of Fame in 2018. Karlene was also a member of Great Britain women's softball team for ten years (2005–2014) playing in four World Cups and has coached various GB national teams from U13 to women's (2007–2016).

Gerard Lauziere is a Senior High Performance Coaching Consultant with the Coaching Association of Canada. He has also been the High Performance Director of both the Canadian Fencing Association (2010–2011) and Taekwondo Canada (2009–2010). Between 1985 and 1996, Gerard represented Canada in various international karate competitions around the world, including two Pan Am Championships (Brazil, 1985, and Curacao, 2000) and two world championships (Peru 1990 and Spain 1992).

Darren Lowe is the former Head Coach of the University of Toronto Varsity Blues men's ice hockey team (1995–2016). He represented Canada at the 1984

Winter Olympics and played in the NHL for the Pittsburgh Penguins during the 1983–1984 season. Darren was the OUA Coach of the Year in 2000–2001, 2002–2003 and 2011–2012. A full time member of the Faculty of Kinesiology and Physical Education, Darren is currently involved in the development of a Master's of Coach Education course.

John M. McCarthy is the Director of the Boston University Athletic Coach Education Institute. He is a clinical associate professor in the Wheelock College of Education and Applied Human Development, and oversees the Coaching Specialization in Counseling and Applied Human Development programme. His area of engaged scholarly work includes coach development, positive youth development through physical activity and trauma-informed coaching. He is a strong advocate for designing socially just sport systems that are equitable, diverse and inclusive. As a former high school and college football coach for 15 years and a father who has coached children in youth basketball, he places a high value on the importance of the role of the coach in society.

Tabitha McKenzie is a lecturer in Te Kura Māori at Victoria University of Wellington, New Zealand. Tabitha has represented New Zealand in the Open Women's touch team as well as the Open Mixed touch team where she was also captain.

Kaleigh Ferdinand Pennock is a PhD candidate in the Faculty of Kinesiology and Physical Education at the University of Toronto. She completed a double Master's degree from the European Masters in Sports and Exercise Psychology (EMSEP) programme, earning a Master of Sports Science in Sport Psychology from Lund University, Sweden, and a Master of Science with a specialisation in Diagnostics and Intervention from Leipzig University, Germany. Her dissertation addresses sport-related concussion under-reporting and how adolescent athletes make concussion-related decisions. Her research interests include sport and performance psychology, psychology of athletic injury and perfectionism in sport and dance.

James Wallis is a Principal Lecturer in Sport, Coaching and Exercise Science at the University of Brighton, UK. He started his career as a PE teacher before completing his MSc in Sport and Exercise Science and doctorate in education. He has worked for many years in youth performance and in international sport for development settings where he specialises in the design and delivery of age-appropriate and ecologically valid coaching practice. His University teaching commitments focus on pedagogy in sport coaching, youth sport programmes and reflective practice. He has numerous publications in the field, including the 2016 Routledge text, *Becoming a Sport Coach*.

Mike Way is the Head Squash Coach of the men and women's Harvard University squash teams. His women's team has won the USA national university squash championship for five successive years (2015–2019). In 2019 his men's team won the national championships for the first time since 2014. Mike was the coach of squash world champion and Commonwealth gold medallist Jonathon Power from 1995–2005. More recently, Mike coached Ali Farag at Harvard who is currently the world squash champion.

Nathalie Williams is a lecturer in the Faculty of Kinesiology and Physical Education at the University of Toronto, Canada. She earned her qualified teacher status in Physical Education at Loughborough University, UK, and has been in the profession for nine years. She represented the U16 and U18 Welsh netball squads, Welsh colleges field hockey and Welsh schools track and field.

Tom Williams is the Head of Strength and Conditioning at Toronto Football Club (TFC). In 2017, TFC won the Major League Soccer Championship. Tom was also with Leicester City Football Club during the 2015–2016 season when they surprised everyone by winning the English Premier League. Tom also has his UEFA B licence in coaching. He coached at Derby County FC and Nottingham Forest FC while studying Sport Science at Loughborough University, UK. Tom holds a Masters in High Performance Sport from the Australian Catholic University (ACU)

PREFACE

Every coach at some point must have wished that their athlete or athletes had made a better in-game decision. Listening to interviews of coaches after a loss, many have wished that if only their players had made better choices in various important situations, the result might have been different. In every competitive event, match or game, once the event begins, the coach's ability to influence the outcome of in-game play may be limited.

In some sports, the coach can try to change the game by calling a timeout or making a substitution. In sports that have significant breaks between action, such as basketball, volleyball, and hockey, the coach has a chance to communicate tactical changes to the players, if the game has not been going according to plan. In soccer and rugby, there is a considerable period of game play before and after half-time happens, so players must be able to make their own in-game tactical decisions without being influenced by the coach.

In other sports, such as squash, the coach may only get a few seconds to talk to their athlete. In sports that consist of races, such as athletics and swimming, once the race begins, the coach cannot speak to their athletes until the end of the event. Regardless of how many opportunities a coach may have to talk to their athletes during breaks in the event, the reality is that once the referee, umpire or official starts the contest, the athlete is left to their own decision-making ability to navigate the event.

The purpose of *Tactical Decision-Making in Sport: How Coaches Can Help Athletes Make Better In-Game Decisions* is to address the complex challenge of how to encourage athletes to become better in-game tactical decision-makers. When using an Athlete Centred-Coaching approach, the coach views their athlete more holistically and tries to empower them to become an active participant in the development of their athletic career. Traditionally, coaches have been responsible for enhancing the physical abilities, technical skills, and tactical knowledge of their athletes. Athlete-centred coaches are committed to involving their athletes in the development process. The pursuit of performance excellence is enhanced when coaches and athletes work together to learn how to make better in-game decisions. This book encourages coaches to create a practice environment where the athlete can learn how to make better in-game tactical decisions.

The book is divided into five parts. Part I, Chapter 1 written by David Cooper, serves as an introduction to the book. He examines and explains the close links between Athlete-Centred Coaching and Game-Centred Approaches to teaching and coaching that encourage the practice of empowering athletes to make in-game decisions.

In Part II, Tactical Decision-Making – Ideas, Theories and Thoughts, Chapter 2 written by Barrie Gordon explains his theory behind the concept of Developing Thinking Players, which has its roots in Teaching Games for Understanding, Play Practice and Game Sense. Chapter 3 by Kaleigh Ferdinand Pennock examines the theoretical considerations of athlete decision-making. Research in this area stems from a complex, interdisciplinary perspective with roots in neuroscience, economics and psychology. Sport is an ideal setting in which to examine decision-making behaviours and processes. Chapter 4, written by the late Guido Geisler explores the common considerations within the four pillars of coaching with reference to territory games. These four pillars of coaching are the technical, tactical, physical and psychological foundations upon which coaching is founded. Guido introduces the concept of the "tactical triangle" that players try to develop. These are reading the play, acquisition of the required knowledge to make appropriate tactical decisions and the application of the player's decision-making ability to solve the problem. In Chapter 5, Karlene Headley-Cooper draws on her own playing, coaching, research and teaching experiences to present some of the challenges that coaches face in empowering athletes to "think for themselves". Rounding out Part II is Chapter 6, written by Tom Williams, which examines the question "Can game data measure the effectiveness of the athlete's decision-making process?" Tom's position as Head of Strength of Fitness at Toronto Football Club brings him into daily contact with all types of data collected from the players. It is up to him to evaluate these data and plan the training accordingly.

In Part III, 13 coaches from a variety of different sports share their insight as to how they encourage their athletes to think for themselves. Chapters 7 to 13 focus on Territory games as described in Teaching Games for Understanding. Chapter 14 focuses on Over the Net games. Chapters 15 and 16 looks at Striking and Fielding games. Chapter 17 is a generic chapter about Strategies for Target games. Chapter 18 examines Individual Sports that are Wall and Racquet games and Chapter 19 is about decision-making in Combat sport.

Chapter 7 focuses on soccer (North America) or football (rest of the world) and is written by Guido Geisler and James Wallis. Chapter 8 is written by Tabitha McKenzie and Barrie Gordon and introduces touch rugby. Chapter, written by

Darren Lowe, is about the fast-moving sport of ice hockey, Chapter 10 is written by John Campbell and is about basketball. Nathalie Williams, in Chapter 11, shares her insight into how netball players can be encouraged to make their own in-game tactical decisions. In Chapter 12, John McCarthy and Dave Brunner explain how the seemingly coach-controlled sport of football (in North America) can become a game where players have an input into the decision-making process. In Chapter 13, David Cooper shares some of the ways "End Zone Games" can be played as small-sided games within the Game Centred Approach model of teaching and coaching Territory games.

Chapter 14, written by John Barrett, looks at the way an outside hitter in volleyball can be coached to be able to recognise different plays and decide where is the best court location is to attack. Barrie Gordon, in Chapter 15 looks at decision-making scenarios faced by baseball and softball players as to where to hit the ball and when to run the bases. Chapter 16, written by David Cooper, focuses on the sport of cricket and how making poor in-game decisions can change the game and how coaches can work with their players to avoid such poor decisions. Barrie Gordon, in Chapter 17 describes generic decision-making strategies that feature in a number of Target games such as golf, archery and bowls. In Chapter 18, Mike Way explains how he coaches his squash players to become better in-game tactical decision-makers. Gerard Lauziere closes out Part III of the book with Chapter 19, which focuses on the combat sport of karate.

Part IV is called Through the Lens of a Coach. Greg Gary writes about his journey in Chapter 20, from being a professional football player with the Los Angeles Rams in the National Football League (in America), to the Hamilton Tiger Cats in the Canadian Football League, to the head coach of the University of Toronto Varsity Blues. In Chapter 21, David Cooper reflects on a lifetime of coaching from club, high school, county and university teams. He shares experiences that have shaped his philosophy as a coach and seen him change from being a coach who focused on developing the technical ability of his athletes using skills and drills to an athlete-centred coach who has seen the benefit of a Game Centred Approach to teaching and coaching.

Part V of the book provides insight into how coaches can translate decision-making theory into practice, thereby empowering athletes to become better in-game tactical decision-makers. In Chapter 22 Barrie Gordon provides a summary of the previous chapters and draws some conclusions that should help coaches develop new ideas that will help them encourage their players to become more independent and think for themselves.

ACKNOWLEDGEMENTS

David Cooper would like to acknowledge the support and encouragement from his wife Arlene and his daughter Karlene. He would also like to thank his colleagues in the Faculty of Kinesiology and Physical Education at the University of Toronto, Canada, and those around the world who have written chapters contributing to the success of this project. Guido was a friend and colleague for over 20 years. We are all very glad that his work lives on in this book.

Barrie Gordon would also like to acknowledge the loss of Guido and his disappointment at never having had the opportunity to meet and work with him. While Guido's work is included in this book his role as co-editor would have allowed him to offer a greater contribution. Barrie would also like to thank his family for their support and acknowledge his colleagues from around the world who have all contributed to this work.

PART I

Introduction

1

LINKING ATHLETE-CENTRED COACHING, GAME-CENTRED APPROACHES AND DEVELOPING THINKING PLAYERS TO IN-GAME TACTICAL DECISION-MAKING

David Cooper

Coaches who wish to develop a player's ability to become a better in-game tactical decision-maker need to coach in ways that facilitate this growth. It is important that the coach creates an environment where athletes are empowered to be active participants in their coaching and learning experience. This is a fundamental pillar of all Athlete-Centred Coaching (ACC) approaches, as outlined by Miller and Kerr (2002), Kidman (2005), Kidman and Lombardo (2010), Headley-Cooper (2010) and Pill (2017). An important aspect of the athlete empowerment process is developing a supportive and non-threatening practice environment where athletes take responsibility for their decision-making and find answers to the challenges that are presented to them. A supportive environment means that making, and learning from mistakes in practice becomes an integral part of their development. It is only after athletes become comfortable with this process in practice, that they will begin to feel confident about making their own decisions in the in-game environment.

One method of teaching and coaching sport that will be discussed in this chapter, and throughout the book, is the Game-Centred Approach (GCA).

This method focuses on the coach or teacher creating in-game or in-practice learning situations that help athletes and students understand what choices they have in solving challenges which arise in any game or practice situation. Coaches using GCA believe that athletes learn best when game situations are simplified and explained, using small-sided games or activities where the normal rules and playing dimensions have been adapted to focus on a certain skill or tactical play.

This chapter will consider the following four well known models:

- Teaching Games for Understanding (Bunker & Thorpe, 1982, 1986)
- Play Practice (Launder & Piltz, 2013)

- Game Sense (Light, 2013; Light & Harvey 2018)
- Developing Thinking Players (Gordon, 2015)

Teaching Games for Understanding

The Teaching Games for Understanding (TGfU) model was initially created by David Bunker and Rod Thorpe from Loughborough College of Education (now Loughborough University) in the 1980s. TGfU was developed in response to strong criticism of school Physical Education (PE) programmes. This criticism was based on the belief that PE concentrated largely on teaching technical sport skills which students were then unable to apply when playing in actual games. It was also felt that students developed a limited sense of 'the game' and only a rudimentary knowledge of the tactics and strategies.

TGfU has taken nearly 30 years to become internationally accepted by health and physical education teachers and coaches as one of the most effective ways of teaching and coaching sports. This book will use "PE" as the designation of teachers of physical education for all teachers involved in the practice of teaching health and physical education

For many years PE teachers preferred the traditional model of a skill-based games teaching curriculum. But as PE and Games became an increasingly optional school subject, students who had not been successful or did not enjoy sport chose other subjects and the PE teacher was faced with developing a new student-friendly approach to encourage pupils to choose PE. TGfU fitted this description perfectly. Subsequently, colleges and universities who were tasked with training the next generations of PE teachers embraced this new approach. There is now an extensive body of research into TGfU, with works by Linda Griffin and Joy Butler (2005; Butler & Griffin 2010) leading the way. Other respected authors have contributed to this scholarly body of work, such as Launder and Piltz (2013), Light (2013) and Light and Harvey (2017)

Game Sense

The first reference to Game Sense is attributed to den Duyn (1997) but it has taken until 2013 for Richard Light in his book *Game Sense: Pedagogy for Performance, Participation and Enjoyment* to bring this model out of the shadows of TGf U. However, the use of "game sense" has become a synonym for an athlete who regularly demonstrates good decision-making in moment-to-moment times in games play. In the teaching and coaching content, it has come to mean an approach using modified sport games that engage the participant in an activity that develops both skill learning and strategic games playing. It is often described as "making the best play at the most appropriate time". This requires the athlete to observe and understand what is going on around them, and then based on their experience of playing the game, make the best choice to solve that problem or challenge. This has been called Game Intelligence.

Play Practice

Similar to Light's description of Game Sense is the model described in *Play Practice* (Launder & Piltz (2013). Fundamental to the philosophy of all GCA models is the use of small-sided games rather than the full game as a teaching and coaching tool. The teacher or coach designs a practice or game that is relevant or similar to the full game but is played in a smaller area (sometimes called a grid) with fewer players on each team (3 v 3) or even unbalanced teams (4 v 2). Here the actual game play is reproduced on a much smaller level, which allows the players the time and opportunity to solve their own in-game scenarios.

The role of the teacher or coach is to "design" these games so that the players can find ways of solving the problem without the teacher or coach telling them the answer. This practice is described as "deliberate practice" by Ericsson and Starks (2006). This is a major fundamental of GCA and is also a classic example of ACC or student-centred learning. By encouraging the player(s) to engage their cognitive decision-making processes as well as their physical and motor skills, coaches can develop a more holistic approach to learning, teaching and coaching.

Many international associations including the United States Soccer Federation use a version of the Play Practice model in their grassroots coaching schemes. In this GCA, the game is the focus. In the first stage, practice starts by playing the game or a modified version of the game in a safe and enjoyable environment, usually in small-sided games played in grids. The coach or teacher observes the players and guides them towards finding their own solutions to a particular challenge. For example, how can four attackers best keep possession of the ball against two defenders?

In the second stage, based on the teacher or coach's observation of the first stage, specific practices are designed to develop the challenges posed in the first stage. This could be either a skill-based practice designed to improve the players' ball control and retention, or a strategy-based practice where players are encouraged to understand the concept of creating space and giving alternative pass options to the person who has the ball.

The third stage is a return to the game in either the full game or a larger version of the modified game (such as 6 v 6). The teacher or coach can also add a new dimension to the practice where the players have to keep possession but move the ball forward into the attacking zone. Defenders are tasked with delaying them or taking the ball from them. In this final game the teacher or coach tries to keep their technical or tactical comments to the bare minimum and provides only positive words of encouragement to all the players. This process can be called "Progressing the Game". The teacher or coach uses this opportunity to observe the game, to evaluate their success at communicating ideas to the players, assess how much the players have learned (or not learned) and plan for next session. In summarising this "Play–Practice–Play" approach, the teacher, or coach designs the practice for a specific skill or game purpose. The game is played by athletes in a safe, enjoyable, and positive environment where it is acceptable to make mistakes without being criticised by the coach.

Historically, TGfU has been associated with teaching PE to children aged 5–12 mostly at the primary or elementary school level. Game Sense requires the athlete to have developed a background of experiences upon which to draw and is often associated with more developed players. As the title of the Launder and Piltz (2013) book suggests, *Play Practice: Engaging and Developing Skilled Players from Beginners to Elite* can be used for all levels of abilities. It is more prescriptive and develops pedagogical concepts that help to create situations that maximise learning and positively influence the attitude of learners.

Launder and Piltz (2013) break the process of teaching activities into four sequential stages. These are:

- Simplifying activities
- Shaping activities
- Focusing activities
- Enhancing activities

The role of the teacher or coach has changed to becoming the learning facilitator or game designer rather than the person who is telling their students and athletes what to do. Concepts of enjoyable and meaningful play are developed so that athletes enjoy the learning experience and will be keen to continue and develop mastery of their game-playing skills and strategies.

Developing Thinking Players

The most recent of the four GCAs to learning, teaching and coaching is the Developing Thinking Players model as developed by Barrie Gordon (2015). This approach uses modified equipment and rules to introduce and develop tactical understanding and decision-making. This approach can lead to advanced tactical understanding and decision-making for players with a wide range of skills and experience. A full explanation of the Developing Thinking Players model can be found in Part II, Chapter 2, Developing Thinking Players written by Barrie Gordon.

Although each GCA has its own teaching and learning principles, there is a large area where they overlap in approach and demonstrate non-linear pedagogy. In Figure 1.1 the "inner core" represents this area where we find the student or athlete as the primary focus of these approaches. As such we can demonstrate how the GCA to learning, teaching and coaching are an integral part of both student-centred teaching and athlete-centred coaching models. Each one of the four models suggests practice situations in which athletes develop, learn, and successfully perform

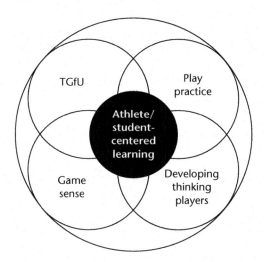

FIGURE 1.1 The nonlinear relationships that exist between teaching games for understanding, play practice, game sense and developing thinking players

plays demonstrating that they understand what is required. The more times they practice these plays, the better they become at recognising what they should do in different in-game situations and making better decisions on their own.

For more information relating to this topic refer to Chow, Davids, Button, and Renshaw's (2015) description of nonlinear pedagogy in skill acquisition. In this book the authors address the complexity of learning movement skills in a constraints-led approach as it is applied to sport skill acquisition.

Making better in-game choices or decisions

An athlete's ability to make successful in-game choices or decisions has been described by Launder and Piltz (2013) as a four-step process. These steps are:

Step 1. Read the display by scanning what is going on around you.
Step 2. Process what you have scanned – the brain has to determine what the athlete has seen.
Step 3. Make the best decision (based on steps 1 and 2) about what you are going to do.
Step 4. Perform the skill or activity that you have decided is the most appropriate choice and perform it at the optimum time.

Sounds simple. But if it were, a lot of athletes and coaches would be more successful. So how do we teach athletes to become proficient in taking these four steps? The specific demands of each sport will influence how the four steps are performed, but research has shown us that the basic process remains the same regardless of the sport. In fact, solving problems in a real-life situation could follow this process. Each step is more complicated than it sounds. This is central to what this book attempts to answer. This book gives coaches, in a variety of sports, some ideas to use with their own athletes.

Basic explanation of the traditionally accepted four-step process

1 Read the display by scanning what is going on around you

How do we know what to look for? How do we learn to focus on what is important in the display, and what is irrelevant? Improving an athlete's attentional focus will help once the athlete knows what to focus on and what to ignore. How does an athlete become proficient in looking for and finding the most important cues? Experience will play a part in narrowing down what is important, but how does an athlete gain this experience? An example of this process can be seen by closely observing the routine of a baseball pitcher at the start of an inning:

- Walks out to the mound. Starts to ignore the crowd and noise.
- Positions him or herself on the pitching rubber. Focuses on the batter, catcher and umpire.

2 Process what you have scanned – the brain has to determine what the athlete has seen

How long does the athlete take to process the information that has been transmitted to the brain? What part does an athlete's choice reaction time play in this process? Depending on how many choices are presented to the athlete, this will complicate the process. In sports where deception is considered to be an important part of the game, how do athletes learn not to be deceived? Returning to our pitcher:

- Focuses on the catcher's signs.

3 Make the best decision or choice (based on steps 1 and 2) about what you are going to do

This is the most important part for the athlete. Having completed steps 1 and 2, the athlete decides on what is the most appropriate choice based on all of the information that the brain has processed. This can be the most difficult part. Often when working with beginners, the coach will simplify the process and tell the athlete what the correct response is. The coach will then create practices in which the athlete learns to recognise the cue and initiate the correct response. However, in coach-controlled situations, the coach will tell the athlete what to do and when to do it, thereby removing the opportunity for athletes to learn how to make decisions themselves. Our pitcher:

• Decides on which pitch to throw.
• Finds the appropriate grip on the ball. Focuses in on the catcher's glove.

If the coach is athlete-centred and believes in empowering athletes to be engaged in the decision-making process, then the coach will choose to allow the athletes to make their best decisions. This choice may be successful or it may not. If it is not successful, the coach will then intervene to help the athlete discover why the choice did not bring about the desired outcome. During this process, the athlete is totally involved in learning how they could have made the correct decision.

The athlete must be placed in this situation frequently and must meet with a reasonable amount of success in order to become more confident and experienced. Eventually they will learn how to make the correct choice. In every sport, the athlete will always be faced with making decisions. How the athlete learns to make more good choices than bad choices will influence the progress of the athlete from beginner to advanced. The time it takes for the athlete to make a good decision is also crucial. A coach expects that through meaningful practices, the athlete will learn how to make good decisions faster.

4 Perform the skill or activity that you have decided is the most appropriate choice and perform it at the optimum time

Once the brain has processed all of the information, it sends signals to the relevant muscle groups to perform the movement. This part of the process is known as movement time. Thus, the applicable equation can be written as "choice reaction time + movement time = total response time". To be successful in responding to the challenges that athletes face, i.e. to make appropriate choices and plays in real game situations, they must learn the specific techniques to counter particular challenges. Our pitcher:

• Begins the wind up and releases the ball towards the catcher's glove

Beginners may not yet have mastered the technique required. The coach must then teach the athlete the required technique using a variety of practices that the coach has learned. This may take many hours of careful deliberate practice to bring athletes to the stage where they can perform the required technique in a correct manner. Coaches may use a direct teaching method to hone the technique and then introduce the athlete to a sequence of drills where the difficulty of executing the technique is gradually increased.

Another method used by coaches who favour the GCA is to place the athlete into a small-sided game or activity, which is shaped to encourage them to use the learned technique. By creating a game, the athlete can be introduced to teammates and opposition. This multiplies the complexity of the technique, and the athlete is introduced to the reality of decision-making in real game situations.

At this point, the learned technique can become a skill if the athlete can put the four steps together and meet the challenge that the coach has created within a small-sided shaped game. The introduction of other athletes into the small-sided shaped game can be done in such a way that the outcome to the challenge is likely to be successful if the teams are not equal. In Territory Games, for example, where the challenge is to maintain possession, playing 5 v 1 initially will improve the chances of athletes making good decisions and demonstrating skilful play. Once the five athletes can show that they can keep possession, the coach can increase the difficulty of the small-sided shaped game by making it 4 v 2 and eventually to an equal-sided 3 v 3 game.

What abilities do athletes need to have to become good in-game decision-makers?

- Athletes must become "students of their game". They must understand all aspects of the game and their abilities. They must clearly demonstrate Game Intelligence.
- Athletes must be able to "play their game" in respect to how they "read the game". They must be aware of what is going on around them. They must concentrate on the game and not be distracted.
- Athletes must "know themselves" in respect of knowing what their strengths and weaknesses are in action. They must play within and up to their limits.
- Athletes must "know their teammates" and what they are capable of doing and achieving.
- Athletes must "know their opponents". Meticulous game preparation is essential and is the responsibility of both the coach and athlete.
- Athletes must "appreciate the state of the game". During in-game play, athletes must be aware of the game objective, the score, the timing of the game (is the game in the first or last five minutes), the environment and the rules or laws of the game.

Elite coaches such as Sir Clive Woodward, former coach of the 2003 England Rugby World Cup winning team, and more recently the current 2019 England rugby team coach, Eddie Jones, are now mentioning the concept of Game Intelligence.

Game Intelligence can be seen as the collective outcome of correct in-game tactical decision-making. The question for the coach then becomes "How can I teach my athlete Game Intelligence?"

Lennartson, Lidström and Lindberg (2015) in "Game Intelligence in Team Sports" discuss the concept of Game Intelligence and state;

> Game intelligence in team sports is usually regarded as something very incomprehensible, and excellent players are often praised for how they "read the game". Even though most would agree on what constitutes good skills – technique, strength, agility, endurance, etc. – it is less obvious what characterises a good player in terms of game intelligence.
>
> *(Lennartson et al., 2015, p. 1)*

It is the responsibility of the coach to ensure that their athletes have the skills, strategies, physical and mental preparation along with the criteria listed above and are ready to play!

In Part III of this book, the focus is on case studies of specific sports. Coaches will explain how they develop thinking players and encourage them to make their own in-game tactical decisions.

Useful links

United States Soccer Federation, www.ussoccer.com/stories/2018

References

Bunker, D., & Thorpe, R. (1982). A model for the teaching of games. *Bulletin of Physical Education, 18*, 5–8.

Bunker, D., & Thorpe, R. (1986). *The Curriculum Model: Rethinking Games Teaching.* Department of Physical Education and Sports Science, University of Technology, Loughborough, UK.

Butler J., & Griffin L.L. (Eds.) (2010). *More Teaching Games for Understanding.* Champaign, IL: Human Kinetics.

Chow, J.Y., Davids, K., Button, C., & Renshaw, I. (2015). *Nonlinear pedagogy in Skill Acquisition.* New York: Routledge.

den Duyn, N. (1997) *Game Sense: Developing Thinking Players Workbook.* Canberra: Australian Sport Commission.

Ericsson, K.A., & Starkes, J.L. (2003). *Expert Performance in Sports: Advances in Research on Sport Expertise.* Champaign, IL: Human Kinetics.

Gordon, B. (2015). *Developing Thinking Players: Baseball/Softball Edition.* New Zealand: ETNZ Ltd.

Griffin L.L., & Butler J.I. (Eds.) (2005). *Teaching Games for Understanding.* Champaign, IL: Human Kinetics.

Headley-Cooper, K.J. (2010). *Coaches' Perspectives on Athlete-centred Coaching.* Master's Thesis, University of Toronto.

Kidman, L. (2005). *Athlete-centred Coaching: Developing Inspired and Inspiring People.* Christchurch, NZ: Innovative Communications.

Kidman, L., & Lombardo, B. (Eds.) (2010). *Athlete-centred Coaching: Developing Decision Makers.* Worcester: IPC Print Resources.

Launder, A.G., & Piltz, W. (2013). *Play Practice: Engaging and Developing Skilled Players from Beginners to Elite.* Champaign, IL: Human Kinetics.

Lennartson, J., Lidström, N., & Lindberg, C. (2015). Game intelligence in team sports. *PLoS ONE, 10*(5): e0125453. doi:10.1371/journal.pone.0125453.

Light, R. (2013). *Game Sense: Pedagogy for Performance, Participation and Enjoyment.* New York: Routledge.

Light, R., & Harvey, S. (2017). *Positive Pedagogy for Sport Coaching.* New York: Routledge.

Miller, P.S., & Kerr, G.A. (2002). Conceptualizing excellence: Past, present and future. *Journal of Applied Sport Psychology, 14*, 140–153.

Pill, S. (Ed.) (2017). *Perspectives on Athlete-centred Coaching.* New York: Routledge.

PART II
Tactical decision-making – ideas, theories, and thoughts

2

DEVELOPING THINKING PLAYERS

Barrie Gordon

All coaches and players want to be involved with teams that are successful both on and off the field.

Achieving success, however, is not always easy and usually requires a range of different factors to come into alignment. The coach can influence some of these factors, while others such as injuries and the calls that officials make are outside of the coach's control. One area where coaches can make a difference is in the way they choose to run their team practices. There is of course no right way to coach, and good coaches will implement a range of approaches based on their own knowledge and background and what they perceive to be the team's needs.

The Developing Thinking Players (DTP™) coaching approach is one option that coaches can draw on to help generate success both for the team and for individual players. It is based on the belief that appropriate coaching can encourage every player to develop a greater understanding of the game and that developing this deeper understanding will bring an extra dimension to their play.

We all know of players who have a real feel for the game, who understand it in ways that lead to them making good decisions and making great plays at crucial times. But how do they develop this understanding? Are they born with a special level of interest that leads to them becoming "students of the game" or can this understanding be developed through good coaching and game experience?

The DTP™ approach is designed to encourage players to think about their game and to make smart decisions in a range of scenarios. It is not a silver bullet that will magically transform all players into truly great ones. What DTP™ does offer, however, is an opportunity to help all players to reach their real potential as athletes. This is a potential not limited to players' physical skills but includes their "feel" for the game and their subsequent ability to play better and smarter.

DTP™ is based on well-established coaching principles supported by a robust research base (Aspasia, Chrysoula, Panagiotis & Georgios, 2017; Gordon, 2015, Griffin and Butler, 2005). The programme owes much to the Teaching Games for Understanding (TGfU) model that has become popular within coaching and the teaching of physical education in recent years (Bunker & Thorpe, 1982). Like TGfU, the DTP™ model has an emphasis on participant empowerment and game-based learning. While firmly focused on these two principles, it also has a distinct emphasis on two other areas; tactical understanding and developing good decision-making.

Tactical understanding

There is an intrinsic interest and enjoyment in understanding the tactical require-ments of games and in being able to react successfully to tactical situations as they arise. Tactical understanding is an important aspect of learning to be a successful player, and coaches often have limited expectations of what players can understand tactically. These limited expectations are often related to the players levels of skills, with coaches believing they are not ready to develop advanced tactical under-standing until they are highly skilled. The DTP™ approach encourages coaches to have very high expectations of what players are capable of learning tactically, independent of their levels of skill and experience, and for this reason the DTP™ approach keeps tactical understanding at the forefront of coaching sessions.

Decision-making

Strongly associated with developing an understanding of tactics is the need for players to become good decision-makers so that they can successfully act on that understanding. To become good decision-makers, players need to have opportu-nities to practice making decisions in authentic contexts. While this may sound obvious, players are seldom placed in realistic scenarios that are designed to give them practice at reading situations, making appropriate decisions, and then con-sidering the subsequent results of their actions. When this does happen, it pre-pares them to make better decisions in later game situations. In order to develop good decision-making, it is important that players, having made the play, are then given the opportunity to analyse their decision-making in relation to the con-sequences that result. It is the process of observing and thinking about what has occurred that generates true learning for the players.

Modified equipment and rules

We want the players to be able to concentrate on developing a good level of tactical understanding and decision-making, so the activities and games make extensive use of modified equipment and rule changes. This overcomes the prob-lem where players are restricted in their ability to concentrate on tactics and enact decision-making because of their inability to use equipment skilfully or because the rules are too advanced for their present level of ability. A player in a baseball game may, for example, decides that to throw the ball to home is a good tactical decision. If, however, they are unable to successfully field a hit ball, then the opportunity to put such decision-making into practice is lost. The use of modified equipment and rules allows relatively low-skilled players to develop advanced tactical knowledge and to experience authentic decision-making.

For this reason, there can be a number of differences from the official game in the equipment used and, in the ways, that the activities and games are played. In the case of developing the thinking of baseball/softball players (Chapter 15), soft balls that are easily caught can be used in the scenarios if the skill level of the players is such that this is appropriate. For other activities, the "batter" can throw the ball, with a single bounce, directly to a fielder or into space. At times, the skill level of the fielding players is such that the batters could hit off of a batting tee or hit a pitched ball. At all times, though, the intention is to set the required skill at a level that allows students to concentrate fully on tactics and to physically implement their decisions.

Skill development

The use of modified equipment and reduced expectations of game-specific skills can appear to be a non-skill based model. This is certainly not the case. One principle that underpins the DTP™ approach is that the motivation to learn physical skills is enhanced when players fully understand why they are important within the game context. Players who know that they need to spike a ball into the open area of the opposition court in volleyball, for example, but fail to do so successfully in a modified game scenario, will then be highly motivated to learn how to execute the skill. This motivation will be higher than if the skills were taught in isolation, with no context in which to place them.

Questioning and discussion

A central requirement of this model is the need for the coach to question players and hold discussions in a way that supports the learning process. The skilful processing of the experience is crucial and the player's decision-making, and general play will offer numerous opportunities on which to base these discussions. If, for example, a player in a basketball activity dribbles past their marker rather than choosing to pass to an unmarked player and subsequently loses the ball, this will offer a stark illustration of why it is important to make good decisions. The resulting discussion will be strengthened by the authentic context in which the mistake was made. Examples of questions that could be asked include:

- Can you explain why you decided to …?
- Why did you choose that option?

- What were the options that were available to you?
- What would you choose next time?

It is also important to always take the opportunity to reinforce good tactical decision-making when it occurs by focusing on situations in which players have made good decisions such as:

- Why was that such a good decision?
- What was so good about that last play?
- In that last play we got exactly what we wanted; what did players do to achieve it, and how can we make sure it happens again?

DTP™ in practice

The DTP™ approach can be applied in most sports and games. Chapters 8, 15 and 17 on touch, target games and softball are all based specifically on DTP™ and offer examples of the approach in practice. It is of course also acknowledged that all the coaching chapters are based on encouraging players to become thinking players. Another example of the DTP™ can be seen in the following modified game of volleyball. I have used this game many times for physical education classes and for volleyball teams where players skills levels are still developing. When skills are not fully established, players can often struggle to consider tactics and decision-making because they are concentrating on executing the skills.

DTP™ Volleyball Game

The game is set up with six players per side and the net at a lower height. This game is played with the normal rules of volleyball in regard to scoring, rotations etc. The modification is that at any time players can chose to use either the correct or modified skill techniques. When serving for example, a player can choose to either serve underhand, use an overhand or jump serve or simply throw the ball over. If the player serves and it is a fault, they get a second attempt, but the ball must be thrown. The receiver of the serve can either forearm pass the ball or catch and throw the ball up high to the setter. The setter may then decide to set the ball or catch and throw to the spikers. No player is committed to using either approach and a setter, for example, may catch and throw up to the spikers until one arrives that is 'just right' and attempt a full set. In the same game another more experienced player may set each time unless they receive a poor ball at which time they catch and pass to the spiker.

The tactics employed by the teams can be very sophisticated with extensive use of blockers, fake and backcourt spikers and a lot of movement around the court. There is no real limit to how far the games can be developed tactically with the students developing very sophisticated decision-making.

Assessment

For coaches who have committed to teaching tactical awareness and good decision-making as an integral part of their coaching one area of difficulty can be assessment. As in other areas of coaching, coaches need to be able to assess players in order to identify areas for future development and as a way to measure progress (Light, 2012). Traditionally coaches have assessed players around skill and results either in practice situations or during game play. A volleyball coach may test a player to see how many jump serves they can land in a specific area or a baseball coach may consider a player's batting average as one form of assessment. If coaches are working to develop tactical awareness and good decision-making, then these traditional types of assessments are less relevant. It seems to make little sense to coach for game tactics and decision-making and then when it comes to assessing the learning that has occurred to assess other aspects of game play.

One assessment approach that is useful for assessing tactical understanding and decision-making is the Game Performance Assessment Instrument (GPAI) (Oslin, Mitchell & Griffin, 1998).

The GPAI can be used in modified or full games at practice or during competition games and it offers coaches an opportunity to assess a player's ability to play games in an authentic context. It also considers a player's ability to contribute to the game with or without possession of the game object.

The GPAI is based on the concept that there are seven components that can be used as a basis for assessment in the full range of sports and games:

- Base – Appropriate return of performer to a "home" or "recovery" position between skill attempts.
- Adjust – Movement of the performer, either offensively or defensively, as required by the flow of the game
- Decisions made – Making appropriate choices about what to do with the ball (or projectile) during the game.
- Skill execution– Efficient performance of selected skills.
- Support– Off-the-ball movement to a position to receive a pass (or throw).
- Cover –Defensive support for a player making a play on–the–ball or moving to the ball (or projectile).
- Guard/mark –Defending an opponent who may or may not have the ball (or projectile).

There are two main ways of using the GPAI in practice. The first, which is illustrated by the soccer example below, involves individual assessment of players. The second method involves observation of a small group followed by an assessment being given based on a general impression of a player's ability and decision-making in a game situation.

Developing and using the GPAI

Step 1 - Game components are selected for the assessment. In making your decision you need to be aware of the practicalities of assessment. While there may be five or six components that are applicable for your sport, it may be a more effective to select only one or two.

Step 2 - For each of the components selected create specific criteria. The criteria should be clear and observable. In the soccer example the criteria for the decision-making component are:

- Player chooses to pass to an open teammate.
- Player chooses to shoot when appropriate.

Step 3 – Complete the assessment. As mentioned previously, there are two main options – observation of an individual player either by the coach or other players, or assessments of groups of players at the same time.

Observation of an individual player

During a game a running record is kept of their play using a grid as shown in Table 2.1. If a coach is assessing decision-making using the soccer example below every time the player made an appropriate decision, it would be recorded under the (A) appropriate column. When they made an inappropriate decision, it would be recorded under the (IA) or inappropriate column. The same process is used when the player executes a skill effectively (E) or ineffectively (IE) and when the player moves into an appropriate supporting position (A) or an inappropriate position (IA).

The usual way of doing this is to use a simple scoring system of dashes. For example, at the end of the assessment a record is available of the number of appropriate and inappropriate decisions made by the player. This offers data from which comments can be made about the player's decision-making ability under game conditions.

During game play the assessor records the individual's performance for all the components selected. Some activities can involve multiple components. A player who shoots unsuccessfully at goal for instance could receive an appropriate coding for decision-making and an ineffective coding for skill from the same action. In Table 2.1, the observed player, Becky, has made two appropriate decisions, one effective and one ineffective skill attempts and has moved appropriately into position three times to receive a pass.

TABLE 2.1 Example of GPAI for soccer – Individual assessment of players

GPAI: Soccer

Coder: Barrie   Player: Becky

Category – criteria for appropriate/effective rating:

1. Decisions made: Player chooses to pass to an open teammate.
                    Player chooses to shoot when appropriate.

2. Skill execution: Reception – control of pass and set up of the ball.
                     Passing   – ball reaches target.
                     Shooting   – ball stay below head height and is on target.

3. Support: The player appeared to attempt to support the ball carrier by being
                     in/moving to an appropriate position to receive a pass.

Decision made		Skill execution		Support	
A	IA	E	IE	A	IA
II		I	I	III	

Key: A = appropriate; IA = inappropriate; E = effective; IE = ineffective

An alternative to the teacher/coach doing the assessment is to use players to assess each other. By using peer assessment, you lower the amount of time needed and the process of assessing requires that the player completing the assessment understands the concepts. This brings about a deeper level of understanding in all the players. If time is given for players to discuss the assessments with the person they have been observing, I have found that the level of discussion can be very impressive.

Group Assessment using GPAI

A second method is to make group judgements, rather than following individuals, as shown in Table 2.2. In this method, the assessor watches a small group of players. After observing for five to six minutes the assessor fills in a number against each player next to the component(s) that have been selected. The judgement is made at the completion of the observation and is based on an overall impression of the players' play.

In the example given below, the assessor Barrie, after observing six players in a game for five minutes, recorded his assessment. It shows that Becky was assessed as having an effective performance in offering support (4) and a very effective performance when guarding or marking her player (5). David was less successful and was recorded as weak (2) in offering support and very weak (1) in guarding/marking players.

While this method may not offer the same degree of accuracy as the first it does have the advantage of being more time effective. In trials, I have found that this method offers a surprising degree of consistency between assessors.

TABLE 2.2 Example of group assessment GPAI

Coder: Barrie

Date: May 1ˢᵗ 2019   Game: Soccer: (6 v 6)

Data sheet scoring key:

5 = very effective performance

4 = effective performance

3 = moderately effective performance

2 = weak performance

1 = very weak performance

Components observed with criteria:

Support – Player moves to an open position to receive a pass

Marking – Player marks an opponent when ball comes into the defensive half of the field.

Name	Base	Adjust	Decision Making	Skill Execution	Support	Cover	Guard or Mark
Becky					4		5
David					2		1
Carolyn					5		4
Shelia					2		3
Susan					3		2
Larry					2		1

Conclusion

This chapter examined the DTP™ approach to coaching, an approach is based on the belief that tactical understanding and good decision-making are fundamental to developing thinking players and that these can be developed through appropriate coaching. While specific sporting examples are given in this, and other chapters within the book, this approach can be implemented with a wide range of other sports and games. The chapter also introduced the GPAI which is closely aligned with the DTP™ approach. As stated, it makes little sense to coach for game tactics and decision-making and then assess physical skills. The GPAI is a useful addition to the tools available for any coach wanting to assess a player's broader contribution to game play and to develop thinking players. Readers who are interested in game-based assessment may also like to consider the Team Sport Assessment Procedure (TSAP) (Richard & Griffin, 2002) another well-known assessment instrument.

Discussion Questions

What would be the best way to move players, who were well developed tactically, into skill learning?

Select a sport and identify what the three most appropriate components would be to include in a GPAI assessment.

What would be the positives and negatives of including players in developing GPAI criteria?

References

Aspasia, D., Chrysoula, N., Panagiotis, S., & Georgios, L. (2017). Physical education teachers' action research on teaching games for understanding. *Mediterranean Journal of Social Science*, *8*(2), 105–112.

Bunker, D., & Thorpe, R. (1982). A model for the teaching of games in secondary schools. *Bulletin of Physical Education*, *10*(1), 9–16.

Gordon, B. (2015). *Developing Thinking Players: Baseball/Softball Edition*. New Zealand: ETNZ Ltd.

Griffin, L., & Butler, J. (2005). *Teaching Games for Understanding; Theory, Research and Practice*. Champaign, IL: Human Kinetics.

Light, R. (2012). *Game Sense. Pedagogy for Performance, Participation and Enjoyment*. New York: Routledge.

Oslin, J., Mitchell, S. & Griffin, L (1998). The Game Performance Assessment Instrument (GPAI): Development and preliminary validation. *Journal of Teaching in Physical Education*, *17*, 231–243.

Richard, J., & Griffin, L. (2002). Assessing game performance: an introduction to the team sport assessment procedure (TSAP). *Physical and Health Education Journal*, *68*(1).

3

THEORETICAL CONSIDERATIONS OF ATHLETE DECISION-MAKING

Kaleigh Ferdinand Pennock

As Sarah, a professional soccer player, receives the ball at her feet, she can hear her coach shouting instructions from the sidelines and the roar of the crowd. She dribbles forward, moving over the midfield centreline. She can see the opposing team's goalie shift her position in net, and two of her own teammates streaking up opposing wings. With the defender moving in to challenge her, Sarah touches the ball from her left foot to her right and kicks it to where she thinks her teammate will be in the next five seconds.

From the perspective of the casual observer, Sarah's action of passing the ball to her teammate may seem relatively straightforward. However, for Sarah, passing the ball to that specific player, rather than shooting, dribbling around the defender or passing to a different teammate required numerous split-second calculations. Her ability to consider multiple factors – the speed of her teammates, her own passing precision, the environmental conditions of the pitch, the skill of the defender, and so on – contributed to her decision-making process.

The purpose of this chapter is to provide a starting point for understanding the theoretical decision-making literature by first defining decision-making and identifying characteristics that bound decision-making in sport. Next, an overview of key theoretical approaches to decision-making are highlighted, and two theories, simple heuristics and ecological dynamics, are explored. Finally, considerations for implementing decision-making training as part of athlete development are addressed.

Characteristics of decision-making

Decision-making is a complex, heavily researched field that draws from a variety of disciplines, including economics, psychology and neuroscience (Raab, Bar-Eli, Plessner, & Araújo, 2019). Bar-Eli and colleagues define *decision-making* as "the process of making a choice from a set of options, with the consequences of that choice being crucial" (Bar-Eli, Plessner & Raab, 2011, p. 6). In sports, decision-making can involve various *agents*, such as players and coaches, various *tasks*, such as passing or calling a play, and various *contexts*, such as during a single play or during half-time (Johnson, 2006). Thus, decision-making serves as adaptive behaviour for athletes to function under a variety of stressors and demands, and is often dependent on the environment, temporal factors, and the rules of the specific sport (Tenenbaum & Filho, 2017). Although the specific agents, task and contexts may vary, there are features that extend across numerous domains.

Johnson (2006) identified four core features that characterize decisions in sport. First, decisions in sport are considered *naturalistic*, in that the agents involved are familiar with both the tasks and the environment. Second, sport decisions tend to reflect *internal* and *external* dynamics, both temporal processes. Internal dynamics reflect how an athlete may obtain and process information over time, whereas external dynamics refers to how the situation itself may change (Johnson, 2006). For example, if we refer back to our hypothetical scenario with Sarah, her decision to pass to a particular teammate may be influenced by the changing information she has gathered (e.g. she perceives her opponent is growing more and more fatigued), and by the changing situation (e.g. her teammate trips and is no longer open to receive the ball). Third, sport decisions tend to be made *online*, in that athletes are making decisions live, or while the task is occurring (Johnson, 2006). Decisions can also occur in a reflective manner, such as a coach using previous game information to decide which athletes will start the subsequent game. Fourth, decisions in sport often have an element of *variability*, which describes the unpredictable nature when factoring in multiple decision-makers and situations (Johnson, 2006). Team sports, in particular, may offer unique and complex decision-making scenarios, as players need to strike a balance between attacking, defending, and cooperating with teammates to effectively oppose the competition (Gréhaigne, Godbout, & Bouthier, 2001).

Theories of decision-making

The breadth of decision-making theories and models is staggering; from an overarching perspective, Bar-Eli et al. (2011) identified nearly 300 theories that span decision-making, judgement, risk taking, reasoning and behavioural science. From a subject-specific level, however, there are approximately a dozen theories that have sport-related application (Bar-Eli et al., 2011). A recent review paper by Raab and colleagues (2019) distinguished many of these theories into four streams of decision-making research in sport: (1) economic, (2) social cognition, (3) ecological and (4) cognitive approaches. Within these approaches, there are a number of specific decision-making theories, including subjective expected utility theory (SEU; Edward, 1954), decision field theory (DFT; Busemeyer & Townsend, 1993) and prospect theory (Kahneman & Tversky, 1979), among others. Given the scope of this chapter, we will look more closely at two theoretical frameworks for decision-making in sport that have been widely implemented: simple heuristics and ecological dynamics.

Simple heuristics

Gigerenzer and Gaissmaier (2011, p. 454) defined heuristics as a "strategy that ignores part of the information, with the goal of making decisions more quickly, frugally, and/or more accurately than more complex methods". Simply put, heuristics allow for faster and more efficient decision-making (de Oliveira, Lobinger, & Raab, 2014). Heuristics have been demonstrated to be as effective and accurate for decision-making as more 'rational' thinking strategies founded in logic and statistics, despite requiring less processing information and occurring very quickly (Gigerenzer & Gaissmaier, 2011). Drawing on the foundational work of Nobel Laureate Herbert Simon (1956, 1982), heuristics allow athletes and other decision-makers in sport to make quick and efficient decisions under internal and external constraints (Raab, 2012).

Heuristics are structured on three building blocks that dictate how an individual is able to make decisions. The first block is *search rules*, in which one searches for information cues and searches for alternatives (de Oliveira et al., 2014; Gigerenzer & Gaissmaier, 2011). Second, *search-stopping rules* address when to stop searching for information or alternative approaches. Compared with novice athletes, expert athletes are better equipped to determine when to stop searching, and to use the procured information to make a decision (de Oliveira et al., 2014). Finally, *decision rules* identify how the decision is made after stopping the information search. These building blocks help describe an athletes' behaviour and the process of deciding between two or more options (Raab, 2012). For example, a common simple heuristic is the *take-the-first* heuristic, which describes athletes selecting the first identified option (Raab, 2012; Raab et al., 2019). Using Sarah's soccer play again as an example, Sarah would search for information on what to do with the ball, would stop searching after two or three options (e.g. passing, dribbling, or shooting), and would select the first option (e.g. passing to a teammate).

In a study using eye-tracking data to infer search strategies and deliberation in handball players, Raab and Johnson (2007) found athletes often selected the first option that came to mind, with the sample of expert athletes selecting the first option 60 per cent of the time. Although these findings help demonstrate the usefulness of a streamlined heuristic approach to decision-making in sport, it is important to consider the *ecological rationality* of heuristics. Ecological rationality refers to the appropriateness of the selected heuristic within a particular environment (Gigerenzer & Gaissmaier, 2011; Raab, 2012). In this sense, consideration is given to which heuristics athletes may use, and the effectiveness of said heuristic within the constraints of the environment (Bennis & Pachur, 2006).

Ecological rationality may also support how expert athletes select an appropriate heuristic depending on the type, availability and validity of available cues (Marasso, Laborde, Bardaglio, & Raab, 2014).

Ecological dynamics

Ecological dynamics offers an alternative perspective to simple heuristics for understanding decision-making in sport. Ecological dynamics considers how and why athletes regulate performance and how in-game decisions are a reflection of athletes' relationships with teammates, opponents, and space and time constraints (Travassos, Davids, Araújo, Esteves, & Esteves, 2013). Araújo, Davids and Hristovski (2006) describe the performer–environment relationship as central to decision-making behaviour, which is viewed as "emerging from the interactions of individuals with environmental constraints over time towards specific goals" (Araújo et al., 2006, 656). This performer–environment system considers perception and action as embedded in the decision-making process, which is linked to the ongoing interaction between athlete and the dynamic environment (O'Connor, Wardak, Goodyear, Larkin, & Williams, 2018; Raab et al., 2019). Thus, behavioural changes occur as a function of the dynamic environment and reflect ongoing and emergent decision-making processes, as athletes direct their actions and interactions with the environment to achieve a goal (Araújo et al., 2006). From a training perspective then, improving decision-making may be predicated on exposing athletes to practice environments where contextual information and cues are needed for superior decision-making abilities (Gréhaigne et al., 2001; O'Connor et al., 2018).

An ecological dynamics approach has been argued as an ideal perspective for performance analysis. Traditional methods of performance analysis, such as notional techniques, have been useful for describing behaviours and tendencies of athletes and teams and can provide important data on the sequential processes that occur during sport performance (Vilar, Araújo, Davids, & Button, 2012). However, a notional analysis approach tends to lack a theoretical perspective to explain the *how* and *why* of athlete behaviour (Travassos et al., 2013). In contrast, an ecological dynamics approach allows coaches and researchers to better understand how athletes' adaptive behaviours may be constrained by the given performance environment (Vilar et al., 2012). Further, an ecological dynamics perspective allows for performance to be examined at various levels or subsets (Travassos, Araújo, Correia, & Esteves, 2010; Travassos et al., 2013). This approach may be useful for coaches to develop specific training simulations that replicate game scenarios for identified subsystems (Travassos et al., 2013). Thus, coaches can address tactical decision-making at a particular systems level and within certain environmental settings, such as an entire offensive unit or a dyadic defence pairing.

From theory to practice: key considerations

Applying theoretical concepts of decision-making to training or competition scenarios requires reflection on the unique characteristics of the agents involved and the sport-specific environment. One potential area of exploration is examining the decision-making of experts versus novices, and how deliberate practice may contribute to their decision-making abilities. Deliberate practice is a well-studied model in sport for the development of expertise levels and is founded on the principles of systematic and long-term practice (Ericsson, 2006; Ericsson, Krampe, & Tesch-Romer, 1993). Experts may have an increased knowledge base that contributes to their judgement and decision-making abilities, and Gréhaigne and colleagues (2001) have noted that experts in sport make faster and more accurate decisions than novice players. Thus, if deliberate practice is considered essential for expert performance, and if expert performers are shown to have improved decision-making skills with respect to speed and accuracy, de Oliveira and colleagues (2014) contend that talent detection and development should be framed towards assessing and developing heuristics in athletes. To do so, athletes can seek to improve the efficiency of a particular heuristic by calibrating the heuristic to more valid cues, or learning which heuristic makes sense in the given environment or situation. When experts and novice decision-makers use heuristics, experts may be more skilled at parsing out valid information during the first building block of search rules, compared with novice athletes who may struggle to identify information cues. From a heuristic perspective, therefore, athletes should be trained for functional rather than optimal decision-making (de Oliveira et al., 2014).

With respect to athlete development, Marasso and colleagues (2014) argued for the need for a developmental perspective on decision-making, and to consider the age, experience, and maturation level of athletes. A developmental perspective could improve on the heuristics models by acknowledging the maturation required to balance and assess different heuristic models and make effective decisions. Age may impact how individuals contextualise the consequences of their behaviours, and the value they ascribe to certain decisions (Boyer, 2006; Bruine de Bruin, 2012; Furby & Beyth-Marom, 1992). For coaches of youth athletes, failure to consider maturation and development may lead to deeming certain decisions as poor or risky, when in fact adolescents are using sound decision-making processes (Furby & Beyth-Marom, 1992). Ultimately, these seemingly poor decisions just may not align with the preferred decision-making of the coach or trainer, despite the age-appropriateness of these decisions.

Crone and Dahl (2012) suggested that socio-affective processes should be examined to help explain adolescent decision-making. A shift throughout adolescence from self-oriented to more prosocial behaviours supports socio-affective developmental changes (Crone & Dahl, 2012). These pro-social behaviours become evident in experiments designed to elicit risk taking behaviours in the presence of peers. For example, Albert and colleagues (2013) found adolescents take more risks when peers are present in a decision-making task compared with when completing the task alone. Their findings suggest that adolescents are reward-focused and sensitive to the effects of social stimuli, which may also suppress the ability to inhibit impulsive responses. For example, as a junior soccer player, Sarah may have been more inclined to shoot the ball rather than pass if she perceived the acclaim from fans or peers due to scoring a goal as more rewarding than an assist to a teammate. In light of this perspective, athletes may choose to behave in ways to enhance their social rewards. Here, an ecological dynamics approach to decision-making may help both coaches and athletes contextualise decision-making behaviours to the given environment; this can be further reinforced when coaches provide opportunities for athletes to practice plays or tactics that model live-game scenarios.

A final point of consideration is the translation of scientific findings into tangible, measurable and specific principles or cues for coaches, athletes and others in the sport community. There is a need to take theoretical concepts and apply them to improving decision-making in athletes, and to understand whether athletes and coaches are in agreement with what defines and constitutes 'good' decision-making. For example, O'Connor and colleagues (2018) explored perceptions of decision-making in a phenomenographic study of 25 soccer coaches, all of whom had played soccer professionally and had a minimum of 20 years' experience coaching or playing. Findings highlight considerable variation between coaches on what constitutes 'good' decision-making, ranging from simple conceptualizations to more sophisticated and holistic perspectives (O'Connor et al., 2018). The authors recommend coaches create opportunities for athletes to be creative and practice their decision-making behaviours. For example, chapters in Part III of this book offers suggestions for how coaches may create scenarios for athlete decision-making. This work speaks to the need for there to be ongoing work bridging theory and practice, and for the provision of practical solutions for coaches and athletes to use in training.

Overall, the sport decision-making literature is a dynamic, ever-changing field, blending theory and application. Drawing from various disciplines invites a unique and collaborative perspective for studying decision-making theory and practices. For athletes, coaches, and other participants in sport and athlete development, improving decision-making skills needs should be approached with regard for age, stage of development, experience and the sport environment. Decision-making research in sport offers tremendous opportunity to advance our understanding of how athletes such as Sarah and others are able to make effective and timely decisions in sport. Thus, continued facilitation and reinforcement of athlete decision-making may have positive implications for the development and well-being of athletes of all ages.

Discussion questions

1   How do simple heuristics explain athlete decision-making in sport?
2   How do ecological dynamics explain athlete decision-making in sport?

3   Given some of the key characteristics of decision-making, what should coaches consider when developing decision-making training scenarios for their athletes?

Useful links

For further reading on theoretical aspects of decision-making in sport, please see: Bar-Eli, M., Plessner, H., & Raab, M. (2011). *Judgement, Decision Making and Success in Sport*. Chichester, UK: Wiley-Blackwell.

References

Albert, D., Chein, J., & Steinberg, L. (2013). The teenage brain: Peer influences on adolescent decision-making. *Current Directions in Psychological Science, 22*(2), 114–120. https://doi.org/10.1177/0963721412471347.

Araújo, D., Davids, K., & Hristovski, R. (2006). The ecological dynamics of decision making in sport. *Psychology of Sport and Exercise, 7*, 653–676. https://doi.org/10.1016/j.psychsport.2006.07.002.

Bar-Eli, M., Plessner, H., & Raab, M. (2011). *Judgement, Decision Making and Success in Sport*. Chichester, UK: Wiley-Blackwell.

Bennis, W.M., & Pachur, T. (2006). Fast and frugal heuristics in sports. *Psychology of Sport and Exercise, 7*, 611–629. https://doi.org/10.1016/j.psychsport.2006.06.002.

Boyer, T.W. (2006). The development of risk-taking: A multi-perspective review. *Developmental Review, 26*(3), 291–345. https://doi.org/10.1016/j.dr.2006.05.002.

Bruine de Bruin, W. (2012). Judgement and decision making in adolescents. In M.K. Dhami, A. Schlottmann, & M.R. Waldmann (Eds.), *Judgment and Decision Making as a Skill: Learning, Development and Evolution* (pp. 85–112). Cambridge, UK: Cambridge University Press.

Busemeyer, J., & Townsend, J. (1993). Decision field theory: A dynamic-cognitive approach to decision making in an uncertain environment. *Psychological Review, 100*(3), 432.

Crone, E.A., & Dahl, R.E. (2012). Understanding adolescence as a period of social – affective engagement and goal flexibility. *Nature, 13*(9), 636–650. https://doi.org/10.1038/nrn3313.

de Oliveira, R.F., Lobinger, B.H., & Raab, M. (2014). An adaptive toolbox approach to the route to expertise in sport. *Frontiers in Psychology, 5*, 709–712. https://doi.org/10.3389/fpsyg.2014.00709.

Edward, W. (1954). The theory of decision making. *Psychological Bulletin, 51*(4), 380.

Ericsson, K.A. (2006). The influence of experience and deliberate practice on the development of superior expert performance. In K.A. Ericsson, N. Charness, P.J. Feltovich, & R.R. Hoffman (Eds.), *The Cambridge Handbook of Expertise and Expert Performance* (pp. 685–705). New York: Cambridge University Press.

Ericsson, K.A., Krampe, R.T., & Tesch-Romer, C. (1993). The role of deliberate practice in the acquisition of expert performance. *Psychological Review, 100*(3), 363–406.

Furby, L., & Beyth-Marom, R. (1992). Risk taking in adolescence: A decision-making perspective. *Developmental Review, 12*(1), 1–44.

Gigerenzer, G., & Gaissmaier, W. (2011). Heuristic decision making. *Annual Review of Psychology, 62*, 451–482. https://doi.org/10.1146/annurev-psych-120709-145346.

Gréhaigne, J.-F., Godbout, P., & Bouthier, D. (2001). The teaching and learning of decision making in team sports. *Quest, 53*(1), 59–76. https://doi.org/10.1080/00336297.2001.10491730.

Johnson, J.G. (2006). Cognitive modeling of decision making in sports. *Psychology of Sport and Exercise, 7,* 631–652. https://doi.org/10.1016/j.psychsport.2006.03.009.

Kahneman, D., & Tversky, A. (1979). Prospect theory: An analysis of decision under risk. *Econometrica, 47*(2), 263–292.

Marasso, D., Laborde, S., Bardaglio, G., & Raab, M. (2014). A developmental perspective on decision making in sports. *International Review of Sport and Exercise Psychology, 7*(1), 251–273. https://doi.org/10.1080/1750984X.2014.932424.

O'Connor, D., Wardak, D., Goodyear, P., Larkin, P., & Williams, M. (2018). Conceptualising decision-making and its development: A phenomenographic analysis. *Science and Medicine in Football, 2*(4), 261–271. https://doi.org/10.1080/24733938.2018.1472388.

Raab, M. (2012). Simple heuristics in sports. *International Review of Sport and Exercise Psychology, 5*(2), 104–120. https://doi.org/10.1080/1750984X.2012.654810.

Raab, M., & Johnson, J.G. (2007). Expertise-based differences in search and option-generation strategies. *Psychological Association, 13*(3), 158–170. https://doi.org/10.1037/1076-898X.13.3.158.

Raab, M., Bar-Eli, M., Plessner, H., & Araújo, D. (2019). The past, present and future of research on judgment and decision making in sport. *Psychology of Sport and Exercise, 42,* 25–32. https://doi.org/10.1016/j.psychsport.2018.10.004.

Simon, H. (1956). Rational choice and the structure of the environment. *Psychological Review, 63,* 129–138.

Simon, H. (1982). *Models of Bounded Rationality.* Cambridge, MA: MIT Press.

Tenenbaum, G., & Filho, E. (2017). Decision-making in sports: A cognitive and neural basis perspective. *Reference Module in Neuroscience and Biobehavioral Psychology,* 1–9. https://doi.org/10.1016/B978-0-12-809324-5.05526-7.

Travassos, B., Araújo, D., Correia, V., & Esteves, P. (2010). Eco-dynamics approach to the study of team sports performance. *The Open Sports Sciences Journal, 3,* 56–57. http://dx.doi.org/10.2174/1875399X010030100056.

Travassos, B., Davids, K., Araújo, D., Esteves, T.P., & Esteves, P.T. (2013). Performance analysis in team sports: Advances from an ecological dynamics approach. *International Journal of Performance Analysis in Sport, 13*(1), 83–95. https://doi.org/10.1080/24748668.2013.11868633.

Vilar, L., Araújo, D., Davids, K., & Button, C. (2012). The role of ecological dynamics in analysing performance in team sports. *Sports Medicine, 42*(1), 1–10. https://doi.org/10.2165/11596520-000000000-00000.

4

COMMON CONSIDERATIONS WITHIN THE FOUR PILLARS OF COACHING WITH REFERENCE TO TERRITORY GAMES

Guido Geisler

Research suggests that elite soccer players have 40–50 interactions with the ball per 90-minute game. They average no more than two touches of the ball per interaction and spend less than two minutes in possession overall (McGreskin, cited in deVos, 2013). This means that approximately 98 per cent of match time is spent on perception (mental appraisal of input) and decision-making (mental processing), and only around 2 per cent is spent on physical skill execution. Thus, games can largely be seen as a series of problems to be solved – and once the training week has ended and the match starts, the coach plays a considerably smaller part. It is the players who must solve those problems and implement the corresponding solutions.

With only subtle differences, the points noted above can easily be applied to a wide range of territory or team invasion games. Accordingly, effective and modern coaching requires training methods that facilitate the development of thinking players who can make quick and appropriate decisions in a variety of game situations. Stated otherwise, one of the coach's responsibilities is to help players develop each corner of the "tactical triangle" – reading of the play or situation, acquisition of the requisite knowledge to make appropriate tactical decisions, and application of one's decision-making skills to the problem. The tactical triangle is a construct that echoes the importance placed in Chapter 1 on giving players opportunities to practice reading situations, making appropriate decisions, and considering the subsequent results of their actions. As also stated in Chapter 1, however, players are seldom placed in realistic training scenarios that provide such opportunities.

A well-developed tactical triangle naturally functions best alongside an equally strong set of technical and physical abilities. Moreover, it functions alongside teammates in territory games, which adds communication (both verbal and non-verbal) to the sequence. When training for better game actions, then, players must learn to process information quickly before executing those actions, with concordant decision-making and communication that takes various factors into account – in which position, at which moment, in which direction, at which speed? Therefore, all game-related actions are reliant upon perception, communication, decision-making, and technical execution, the logical extension of which is that training actions must involve those features as well. Coaches who fall short in that respect will slow down player development

Overlapping training dimensions

Coaching is thus a multidimensional endeavour, and to develop thinking players whose game performances are consistently at an optimal or near-optimal level, coaches should make deliberate efforts where possible and appropriate to frame the four main pillars of training (technical, tactical, physical, and psychological) not as independent entities but, rather, as overlapping dimensions. To that end, approaches such as Game Sense (Light, 2004), Play Practice (Launder, 2001), and the Tactical Games Model (Mitchell, Oslin, & Griffin, 2006) were outlined in Chapter 1 as contemporary methods of blending technical and tactical training. Furthermore, increasing numbers of teams now recognize the value of sport psychology programmes, and there is a growing understanding today that physical training can incorporate technical development by adding the ball or game implement.

However, despite the many merits of game-centred models of coaching, the combination of technical and tactical emphasis during training activities sometimes fails to incorporate the full extent and complexity of a game's physical demands; demands that can affect cognitive processes once fatigue sets in. It can be argued that most players of territory games actually fatigue mentally before they fatigue physically. Similarly, mental skills programmes are often portrayed as something that is done away from the training site, administered by external consultants who are sometimes presumed (rightly or wrongly) to know relatively little about the nuances of the particular sport, its specific demands, or the experiences of competitors. The underlying implication is that there is room for greater emphasis on the design of training content that purposefully merges two, three, or even all four components into specific training activities.

This is not to say that simple technique practice, tactical patterns, physical training, or mental skills development should never be conducted independently. Indeed, there are times when a singular focus is warranted, and training cannot and should not be based on blended approaches only. Top clubs and national team programmes naturally include specialised or isolated practice in different domains where necessary, and it is important to state unequivocally that the premise behind this chapter is not to eliminate or disregard such approaches entirely. However, it must also be stated that the complete separation of training components should be predicated on specifically defined outcomes.

It should not be the everyday norm simply because of coaches defaulting to the methods that they were exposed to during their playing careers; i.e. coaches merely repeating what their own coaches did. Such methods are not usually up to date, nor are they informed by modern research findings.

There are coaches, of course, who do manage to utilise both isolated training emphases and blended training activities in a manner that optimises player development, but in many cases such overlap is the product of chance. In contrast, coaches who proactively develop thinking players through interwoven training dimensions typically do so via deliberate planning and clearly laid out focus points. For territory game players to evolve and hone their problem-solving abilities, they must learn to merge physical output, technical skill, and tactical awareness efficiently, both when attacking and defending, while free of mental interference (i.e. with full concentration on the relevant "game moments", allowing them to block out non-pertinent thoughts that can compromise performance). And all of this must occur while fitting into the on-field/on-court/on-ice team dynamic. The best coaches stand out for their ability to develop players in just such a manner.

From conscious to subconscious: the formation of good habits

A key point in the development of thinking players is the notion that training should not be done on "autopilot". Instead, coaches must ensure that players understand the context and meaning of each training activity, as noted in Chapter 1, so that they execute the required actions in a conscious mode. This is especially true in the initial stages, with the goal of internalising various good decisions for an array of game situations. Players then gradually develop subconscious decision-making processes through conscious repetition, which should eventually teach them to perform on autopilot in real game contexts and in a manner that is consistent with their roles and personalities as players.

Another way of describing the conscious-to-subconscious or autopilot transition is that, through a conscious understanding, players eventually acquire a set of appropriate habits for different game moments. Each game or training situation thus constitutes a trigger for a set of appropriate actions, and players learn to quickly choose one of those actions in a "best fit" manner. This removes much of the randomness from performance contexts, which means that excellence need not be regarded as a series of independent acts or episodes. Rather, it can be seen as the result of repetition of a set of good habits. Nevertheless, it bears repeating that such habit formation is accelerated through a conscious understanding of various training contexts in the early stages of development.

Against the backdrop of the preceding discussion points, the planning of training sessions is typically done with consideration of common territory games
principles within the four pillars of coaching. From there, coaches who wish
to develop thinking players can then devise training content that addresses and
blends those considerations as appropriate for the themes they wish to cover in
the session or sequence of sessions. A partial outline of some of those main games
principles is given below.

Technical training emphases

To practice and develop a given technical skill (e.g. passing in most territory
games), coaches need to design activities in a way that overloads that skill – e.g.
frequent situations must arise in which passing is necessary.

Another aspect of overloading a technical skill is to make the skill difficult,
through adaptations such as a reduced number of allowable touches, a smaller grid,
more defenders, etc. (this increases players' mental engagement with the activity).

Different positions in territory games entail different priorities with regard
to technical training – thus, position-specific technique training is also necessary
if players are to eventually perform on autopilot in real game contexts and in a
manner that is consistent with their roles.

As a simple example, the centre or power forward position in basketball requires
the development of good rebounding technique, whereas the point guard position demands more frequent practice of dribbling and perhaps 3-point shooting.

Tactical training emphases

One of the primary tactical emphases – and one upon which many other tactical
considerations rely – is the maintenance of team shape. In both attacking and
defending situations, players must be taught to always consider the position and
movements of:

- The player on the ball/game implement;
- The player(s) in support of the player on the ball/implement
- Cover for player(s) supporting the player on the ball/implement.

Spatial connections and understanding between players (e.g. different positional
lines stay connected) must also become internalised, which is largely dependent
upon verbal and non-verbal (e.g. gestures, eye contact) communication.

The manner of creating space and using space is a training point that falls
under individual tactics (at all times, especially in build-up play and attack, players
must either be using space or creating space, not merely occupying space).

Another individual tactical consideration in attack is decision-making when
in possession of the ball/implement. For example, when to pass forward, when

to dribble and move forward, when to pass wide, or when to pass back can be dependent on the state of the game as outlined below:

- An understanding of horizontal and vertical zones makes the preceding tactical considerations easier to train.
- Creating overload situations when both attacking and defending is a tactical priority in territory games.
- Training for effective counter-attacks is related to overload training.
- Pressing (offensive/full pressing, half pressing, false pressing, line of confrontation).
- Ball/implement recovery and counter-pressing must also be trained systematically.
- Transition play in attack and in defence.
- Switching the point of attack/playing out of the pressure zone.
- Establishment and management of width and depth.
- Controlling play between the positional lines (exploiting such spaces in attack, closing the gaps when defending).

Physical training emphases

Developments in training science are such that coaches need to understand the contemporary principle of better training versus more training in territory/invasion games. Using soccer as an example:

- Soccer is primarily an intensity sport, not an endurance sport as some believe – therefore, it is necessary to maintain a high level of intensity in training sessions (often achieved through HIIT [high intensity interval training] principles applied in soccer contexts).
- Similarly, a higher speed of actions should be one of the main training objectives (at higher levels of play, there is less time and less space for each interaction with the ball).
- Accordingly, modern approaches to youth training recommend slightly fewer training sessions per week (e.g. three sessions at some European youth academies), but they are conducted at high intensity as opposed to four to five sessions per week at medium/lower intensity.
- Training sessions should last 60 minutes, 75 minutes, or 90 minutes; generally speaking, none should be longer than 90 minutes, especially at the youth level.
- Just like tactical and technical training, soccer fitness sessions must also include communication, decision-making, and executing those decisions.
- For soccer fitness training, the ball should be included whenever possible. When the focus is simply on conditioning, the ball is not necessary.

Psychological training emphases

Many coaches see mental training as something esoteric that should be left to specialised consultants. In reality, though, a large number of teams do not have access to a recognized mental trainer. This means that there are too many coaches who pay little or no attention to this coaching dimension themselves. However, simple mental considerations can actually be integrated into the normal training routine, and in a manner that gradually makes the process habitual for players. The following provides a general outline of ways in which coaches or assistant coaches can make the mental side of preparation a part of their regular coaching practice.

Before training begins

- Set group/team goals for the training session; the coach could also ask players about personal goals that they might have set previously for the session.
- Privately elicit new/additional personal goals from two to four players for the session based on the team goals above and/or the players' own needs (this allows coaches to interact with each player over the course of the season about their personal goal setting).
- When possible, provide a visual of activities that will be done during the main part of the training session so that the players can begin to form their own visual images (mental rehearsals) of themselves performing the activities.

During the technical warm-up

- Set cue words for selected activities of the session.
- When appropriate, include an activity that changes frequently in order to both simulate and stimulate shifts in attentional focus (e.g. modified-game warm-up activities, such as a simple handball possession activity).

During the main part of the session

- Tell the players to visualise the successful performance of a training activity before execution or while recovering from a round/sequence.
- As coach, articulate the selected cue words before each round of an activity; encourage players to do the same mentally (either the same word or one they select themselves if another is more personally relevant).
- Tell the players to refocus and visualise after each round/sequence, especially to re-instil a successful image after a failed attempt.
- Make a video of the players to show them their performances – this is helpful in creating mental images of good execution and in creating new (corrected) images for less successful attempts.

After the session

- Check if group/team goals were met for the training session.
- Ask the players what they thought was done well (team "maintain" points) and what could have been done a little better (team "improve" points) during the session.

- Based on the above, set team goals for the next training session and, when applicable, for the next game.
- Check with the two to four players (selected earlier) about whether they met their goals for the session, then elicit/discuss individual "maintain" and "improve" points as well as associated personal goals for the next training session or game.

Within the psychological dimension, there are also certain initiatives that coaches (in the absence of mental trainers) can make use of away from the training site. This is in addition to the in-training suggestions above.

- Train players to always focus on the next game moment (to become clear/calm thinkers, regardless of what happened previously).
- Train players to develop and use in-game coaching patterns with each other (content-directed and informational commentary, not unfocused venting or criticism).
- Game and training-related video can be used during team meetings – various situations/moments are presented, and the players in the relevant area of the field/court/ice (e.g. positional groups) give input on applicable in-game instructions and comments that they can use with each other when such moments occur again in the future (this can include specific and agreed-upon cue words to trigger appropriate behaviours and actions for the particular situation).
- Train players to understand that outcome is not controllable – what can be controlled are process (performance and preparation), such that players give themselves the best chance for a successful outcome.
- Train players to focus on the present. Focusing on the past (e.g. mistakes) increases negative emotions such as anger and frustration; focusing on the future (i.e. game outcome, as opposed to anticipating performance situations) can increase nervousness/tension – a present-internal focus (the present moment) while training and playing will lead to more controlled actions.

References

deVos. J. (2013). Day three of the UEFA "A" license. Retrieved June 21, 2013 from www.tsn.ca/.

Launder, A.G. (2001). *Play Practice: The Games Approach to Teaching and Coaching Sports.* Champaign, IL: Human Kinetics.

Light, R. (2004). Coaches' experiences of game sense: Opportunities and challenges. *Physical Education & Sport Pedagogy, 9*(2), 115–131.

Mitchell, S.A., Oslin, J.L., & Griffin, L.L. (2006). *Teaching Sport Concepts and Skills: A Tactical Games Approach* (2nd edn). Champaign, IL: Human Kinetics.

5

CHALLENGES THAT COACHES FACE IN EMPOWERING ATHLETES TO "THINK FOR THEMSELVES"

Karlene Headley-Cooper

As a former international softball player, graduate school researcher and current Physical and Health Education teacher who is pursuing my next opportunity to coach softball, I often find myself reflecting on my previous experiences, learnings and challenges. My lived experiences form my personal, academic and athletic story. Sporting autoethnographies draw on personal experiences to extend sociological understanding of sporting cultures (Holt, 2003; Sparkes, 2000). Autoethnography will be used to connect my lived experiences and perspectives to the social world of sports coaching (Cooper, Grenier, & Macaulay, 2017; Ellis, 2004; Holman Jones, 2005). As a self-proclaimed life-long learner, my background and past experiences continue to inform my own decision-making and thinking processes as a coach and teacher. The goal of this autoethnographic chapter is to share perspectives on the challenges that coaches face that are powerful, emotive, and self-reflexive for the writer, as well as engaging and thought-provoking for the reader (Holt, 2003). Taking a few moments to consider "how do I ...?" or "how could I ...?" may enhance the overall sports experience in many different ways for each person involved. Given the widespread nature of challenges in sport coaching, this chapter will not provide specific solutions or answers; however, instead, my hope is that this chapter sparks a motivation to pause, think, consider, plan, change, overcome, and improve.

When I begin to reflect on the challenges that coaches face in empowering their athletes to think for themselves, I am reminded of one of the best quotes from my favourite movie, *A League of their Own*: when Coach Dugan (the character played so eloquently by Tom Hanks) says, "it's supposed to be hard. If it were easy, everyone would do it." And while I may disagree with his first statement, Coach Dugan is not completely wrong. Most challenges are hard. Many worthwhile pursuits are difficult. As a result, even though the process of facing, solving and overcoming obstacles can be tough, it can also be a rewarding learning experience. Coaches will undoubtedly face a variety of challenges throughout their coaching endeavours, far too many to list here; however, this chapter will present several key challenges that previous experiences as an athlete, coach, teacher and researcher have exposed as valuable learning opportunities. The importance of the coach–athlete relationship, the connection between coaching research and practice, the value of using case studies, and three sport-specific challenges will be discussed.

The coach–athlete relationship

Within an athlete-centred approach to sport, coaches act as leaders, partners and facilitators in the coach–athlete relationship, and therefore, this relationship is considered to be one of the most important interpersonal interactions in sport (Clarke, Smith, & Thibault, 1994; Jowett, 2005). The coach–athlete relationship is at the heart of the coaching process and is significant because of the impact it can have on the athlete's development, satisfaction, self-esteem, confidence, decision-making and performance (Jowett & Cockerill, 2003; Jowett, 2005; Lyle, 1999). From an athlete-centred perspective, coaches play a crucial role in helping their athletes pursue personal and performance excellence, on and off the playing field (Miller & Kerr, 2002). This empowering style of coaching enables athletes to gain and take ownership of the knowledge, development and decision-making processes that will help them to maximize personal development and physical performance (Kidman, 2005).

These findings, which are grounded in academic research, are akin to the experience-based words of John Wooden, widely considered one of the greatest American National Collegiate Athletic Association (NCAA) basketball coaches of all time. His teaching background and successful coaching career at the University of California, Los Angeles (UCLA) from 1948 to 1975, earned him the unofficial title of a coaching legend (Gilbert, 2010). In addition to publishing, *You Haven't Taught Until They Have Learned: John Wooden's Teaching Principles and Practices*, Coach Wooden once famously said, "a good coach can change a game. A great coach can change a life." This quote highlights that life is bigger than a game, and that additional skills and knowledge are required to be a great coach who can influence their athletes' lives within an empowering coach–athlete relationship.

As a coach, one consideration to make is the answer to the question: given the circumstances, are my athletes in the best possible position to succeed? Recent elite sport experiences have shown me that when the answer to this question is 'no' (therefore the athletes are not in the best condition or place), that achieving success is extremely difficult and rarely occurs. Within a holistic approach, this 'best' could be physically, mentally, socially, emotionally, and/or nutritionally. Recognition is also given to sporting systems and cultures that a coach may be required to work within. There may be specific protocols, decisions, or values that the team management or sport federation have put into place that limit the potential influence that the coach has on their athletes' well-being, development, and success. This is a significant challenge for any coach to overcome.

Building and maintaining a strong and respectful coach–athlete relationship takes time and effort. Appreciating and getting to know the athletes as more than physical performers is one of the cornerstone tenets of the athlete-centred approach to coaching (Headley-Cooper, 2010, 2017; Miller & Kerr, 2002). Developing an appropriate coach–athlete relationship requires effective communication habits. This can be a challenge for some coaches. Communication is an important skill that needs to be practised. As shared in my chapter in Shane Pill's book, *Perspectives on Athlete-Centred Coaching*,

> coaches need to reflect on their words, body language, and tone with the same dedication that they analyze video and scout opponents. As a coach, it is essential to be aware of not only what you are saying, but also how you are saying it.
>
> *(Headley-Cooper, 2017, p. 152)*

Many individuals in all professions struggle with this; however, it is of vital importance for sport coaches who strive to build a coach–athlete relationship that empowers their athletes to be their best and think for themselves.

The combination of previous coaching research and lived experiences have highlighted the importance of understanding and implementing strategies that empower athletes to be active participants within their own development, and more specifically within the decision-making process of being able to think for themselves; however, that is often easier said than done. A focused and respectful coach–athlete relationship can serve as a solid foundation from which to work from. As part of this relationship, the coach has many questions to consider, such as: are my athletes physically, mentally, socially, emotionally, and nutritionally ready? Have I taught and have my athletes learned the necessary skills and tactical plays? Do they understand when it may be most advantageous to do a particular skill or play? Have I effectively communicated sufficient encouragement, instruction, feedback? These are only a few challenging questions that may cause the coach to pause and think about the quality of the coach–athlete relationship and more specifically the preparedness of their athlete. Feeling competent, confident and comfortable to make the correct decision in the right moment leading to a successful outcome is a much more complicated process to complete within an ever-changing sporting field, court, pitch or arena.

In addition to working on addressing the challenge of developing and fostering a strong coach–athlete relationship that leverages the benefits of open two-way communication, coaches may also feel challenged to keep up-to-date with recent coaching research findings. Sport coaching research is constantly being conducted and published; however, the worlds of academic writing and active coaching often do not intersect. This challenge will be discussed next.

Coaching research and practice

Sport is multifaceted and complex. Research in sport has many broad areas to cover, from psychology to history to sport science to coaching, and so many more. According to the Coaching Association of Canada (2019, para 1), "coaching research is an essential component of athlete and coach development. Our athletes need coaches who can apply the theoretical models and important findings of research to the practical reality of day-to-day coaching." This can often be challenging for coaches, even the most experienced and educated coaches may find it difficult to implement the strategies and philosophies that they are knowledgeable about and aware of.

Previous experiences in academic research and sport coaching have combined to highlight the need for both researchers and practitioners (e.g. coaches) to do their due diligence to engage in the development and implementation of coaching knowledge and behaviours. Several analyses conducted by sport scientists and psychologists have targeted addressing the gap between research and practice (Halperin, 2018; Holt et al., 2018). According to Reade, Rodgers, and Hall (2008, p. 319), "coaches are most likely to consult other coaches, or attend coaching conferences to get new information. Sport scientists and their publications were ranked very low by the coaches as a likely source of sport science information." The challenges of researcher knowledge dissemination, information translation and coach access are not new; however, there is not an overwhelming number of resources available that have been able to bridge this gap.

Studies have identified the challenge of this gap for many years, and therefore it is a little disconcerting that such a well-documented gap still exists. Lyle (2018, p. 433) invites us to:

> Imagine a context in which coaches are familiar with coaching theories and their purpose, have access to academic papers, understand research methodologies and their limitations, are required to reflect on their practice, are held accountable for being up to date, have a clear personal theory of expertise, have sufficient breadth of knowledge and experience to interpret findings and identify relevance.

After all these years, experiences, and studies, why do we have to imagine this situation? How can researchers and coaches reduce the gap and achieve the practices that Lyle suggests in order to enhance the overall sporting experience for everyone involved?

There are many factors that combine to make coaching research dissemination, translation and implementation a significant challenge for researchers and coaches. Recommendations have been made for researchers to use lay language to make coaching knowledge more understandable to the diverse coach audience and to find ways to transfer information through direct communication (e.g. coaching clinics) to increase the opportunities for coaches to access information (Reade et al., 2008; Williams & Kendall, 2007). Next, after the information has been received, the coach is encouraged to actively implement or adopt the new information or best practices into their coaching sessions with their athletes. All of this requires the buy-in from researchers and coaches to synergistically engage in this process of learning and behaviour change. For everyone to achieve success in their own areas of expertise, research or coaching, all researchers, coaches and athletes need to be playing the same game.

In addition, Halperin (2018) suggests that researchers and coaches could both benefit from using more case studies;

> Case studies can serve as a potent communication strategy to nonscientist coaches if presented as narratives, … loosely defined as examples, anecdotes, and stories consisting of at least 1 person experiencing at least 1 event. Narratives are easier to process, comprehend, and recall and are more engaging and persuading. Since coaches commonly acquire knowledge through informal discussions with peers, they are familiar with narrative format and thus are more likely to be influenced by and receptive to case studies.
>
> *(Halperin, 2018, p. 824)*

Recognising the challenges of language and access, the second part of this chapter attempts to tap into a case studies approach as a method for coaches to share strategies they have used to develop thinking players.

Sport-specific challenges

The process of empowering athletes to think for themselves is fraught with challenges. Sport-specificity will be the next challenge to consider. Each sport has different timings, etiquette norms, rules, and procedures. Each player has varied skills, abilities, and motivations. As a result, there is no one-size-fits-all answer to solving any of the challenges discussed in this chapter. Again, the combination of experiences and research will continue to present ideas for you, the reader, to consider.

Using the recommendations of Halperin (2018), two case studies will be used to present three sport-specific challenges that coaches face in empowering athletes to think for themselves. The first case study will include two examples from the fantastic sport of softball. For those of you who are not familiar with softball (or baseball), one of the basic hitting techniques is a bunt. Many hitters prefer to take a full swing at the incoming pitch (ball); however, using a short placed hit, such as a bunt, may be the most advantageous planned or surprise play a batter can make. The purpose of the bunt is to hit the ball close to the batter within the diamond (fair) field, thereby causing the defence to move a greater distance to pick up the ball. To defend this play, the defence needs to move quickly, pick up the ball, and make a strong and accurate throw to a base (usually first base) all before the batter-runner gets to the base. This can be a challenging physical play for everyone involved. In addition, this play requires a lot of decision-making, especially from the batter and/or the batting team coach.

On many occasions, batters will only attempt to bunt after their coach has given them the signal to bunt; however, from my perspective as a coach who encourages the development of my athletes as thinking players, I want my players to be able to 'read the defence' and confidently know when (and how, because we have previously practised the skill in isolation and in game-like training) to put down a bunt based on what they are seeing from their vantage point in the batter's box. If the batter sees that the fielder is playing a long way back from the spot where they would aim to put the bunt (e.g. the third base fielder is beside the base and therefore approximately 55 feet from where the bunt will be placed), then I, as an encouraging and athlete-centred coach, would support my athlete in their decision-making to try to put down a bunt and get a safe hit single in that situation.

In practice situations prior to the game, I would have previously educated my athletes on how to read the defensive positioning. I would have also taught them to recognize their skill sets in being able to execute this play, and communicated with them that this preparation has given them the understanding and skill necessary to implement this play in a game situation, even if I did not give the signal for it. As coach, I need to trust the preparation as well as trust my athletes. If the execution of the play is successful, my athletes will learn from the experience, and if the play is unsuccessful, they will also learn from the opportunity.

The conversations between myself (as coach) and the athlete(s) following this decision-making scenario would likely involve some questioning. Recognizing the importance of the coach–athlete relationship, the tone of my verbal communication would be calm and inquisitive. I am talking *with* the athletes and not *at* them to find out more about their thought-processes that led to the decision that they made. Regardless of the outcome of the bunt play, this is a learning opportunity. I would ask my players: What did you see or feel that sparked your thought to bunt in that situation? How confident did you feel that you could successfully execute the play? Why might you make the same or different decision if you were in that situation next game? These open-ended questions facilitate a discussion about the process of decision-making. It is not about whether the decision was right or wrong, or if the execution was good or bad. Rather it is an opportunity to understand, teach, and empower athletes to think for themselves leading to a decision to make a particular movement, in this case to bunt, or not to bunt. These questions can be edited to apply to any other sport-specific situation.

A second softball example highlights the presence of "thinking players" who are making real-time decisions on the field in comparison to "doing players" who are performing the skills signalled in by the coach. My international softball playing career spanned ten seasons (2005–2014) and overlapped with my coaching career from 2007 onwards. I continue to follow international softball coaches, and I recently had the honour of supporting the South African junior women's softball team at the World Baseball Softball Confederation (WBSC) Under 19 Women's Softball World Cup in Irvine, California. Throughout this tournament, I was able to observe the technical and tactical changes that softball has undergone over the years. One of the biggest changes is how some coaches relay signals to their athletes. The process of communication and decision-making has significantly changed within several teams.

When I was a player (and that was not that long ago; I retired in 2014), there seemed to be two approaches of deciding which pitches a pitcher would throw. One process was as follows: the catcher would relay the signal to the pitcher, and the pitcher could shake off the signal to say no, and the catcher would give another signal until they agreed which pitch to throw. This was often based on a scouting report that the coach had reviewed with the pitcher and catcher prior to the game. The second method was: the coach would give the signal to the catcher and the catcher would then relay the signal to the pitcher, which usually limited the pitcher's option to shake off the signal because she knew that it had come from the coach. The first process enabled the catcher and pitcher to think for themselves (based on observations and/or the scouting report), make the decision to call a particular pitch, communicate via hand signals, and throw the agreed upon pitch. The second method maintained the communication path of catcher to pitcher and removed the decision-making of the players of which pitch to call in the ever-changing game situations.

Based on observations from the 2019 WBSC U-19 Women's Softball World Cup and recent years of watching NCAA college softball, I have noticed that a third system has come into play. Some coaches are now relaying signals directly to the pitcher and catcher. This communication process has been enhanced by the use of an arm-band that contains computer-generated printouts of numbers sequences that the coach and players have as a playbook or script to which skill or play to execute. Using this system, the coach looks at their arm-band and sees that the particular pitch and location (e.g. a curveball outside low and away) is communicated with a three number sequence (e.g. 1–2–3), they give that signal with their fingers or verbally, the players look on their arm-band, and know exactly which pitch and location to throw. This system eliminates all decision-making by the catcher and pitcher, as well as all communication between catcher and pitcher, inevitably turning athletes into doers instead of thinkers.

The game of softball has not changed; however, in this example, the process of empowering decision-makers has changed. This is where I pause to reflect. As a softball coach who values my coach–athlete relationship and keeps updated on recent coaching research, I have another challenge to consider. Do the benefits of controlling the game by signalling the pitch selection to my pitcher and catcher outweigh the value of teaching my catcher and pitcher to call their own game and therefore think for themselves to make their own decisions? I hope that you also pause and consider your own sport now. Is there a situation in which you, as coach, need to choose between controlling the game versus teaching and empowering your athletes to think for themselves and make their own decisions? What do you do? Again, this is a challenge that many coaches face, and therefore, this chapter has likely prompted more questions than answers because we as coaches need to think and make our own decisions too.

The second case study will focus on an example from the healthiest sport to play, squash. Squash is a fast-paced racquet sport that consists of "repeated, short, high-intensity, intermittent bouts" and at the elite level is considered an anaerobic-aerobic activity (Girard et al., 2007, p. 909). At the competitive level, the sport of squash consists of a best-of-five-game series, with the winner being the first player to win three games, in which each game is played to 11 points (unless 10–10, and then one player must win by two clear points). According to the 2019 World Squash Singles Rule 7.1, "A maximum of 90 seconds is permitted between the end of the warm-up and the start of play, and between each game" (World Squash, 2018, p. 3). This 90 second interval is the only time in which coaching is permitted, as it is a conduct violation to receive coaching during the game play. As a former University of Toronto squash player and coach, I can attest from previous lived experiences that the 90 second break often feels extremely short. Unfortunately, the difficulty of this challenge is how best to communicate effective coaching information in such a short time period. This challenge may be similar in other sports that may have similar game restrictions that limit the time a coach has to communicate with their athletes during game play.

The 90 second break in between games serves two different purposes for the athlete and the coach. The athlete usually wants to sit down, rehydrate, catch their breath, towel off, and, depending on the outcome of the previous game, possibly listen to some coaching advice. On the other hand, also depending on the game situation or their coaching approach, the coach usually wants the player to take a few seconds to compose themselves, and then use the remaining time to receive specific and detailed coaching information about strategy changes, skill modifications, and (hopefully) positive reinforcement. This is a lot for the coach to communicate and for the athlete to process in 90 seconds.

Generally, squash coaches may use one of two or a combination of two methods of giving feedback during the short 90 second break. Coaches who wish to use a developing thinking players and empowering thinking for themselves approach, may ask their athlete questions such as: What strategy did you find successful in that previous game? What strategy did you find least successful in that previous game? Is there a particular shot or shot location that you think has been working well for you? These questions will facilitate a brief conversation with the athlete and coach in which the athlete will need to think about their game play in order to answer the questions. This will encourage the athlete to think about which strategy worked, and therefore allow the athlete to recognize what shot and shot location they need to continue to use in the next game.

Alternatively, given the short period of time, coaches who want to be more direct in their communication might choose to say to their athlete: "Your opponent has trouble retrieving balls that you hit with power deep into the back-hand corner. You have won 80 per cent of the rallies when you drive the ball into the backhand corner. You are using shot location very well; continue to use the backhand corner to your advantage in the next game." This second approach is quick and specific, but removes their athlete's need to think for themselves. Instead, this direct approach focuses on having the athlete follow the coaching instructions that the coach feels will best lead to winning the game.

Once again, I pause and consider this example. Which is the most appropriate method of communication? Which do I use most often? Is one method better than the other? As the coach, my decision to ask questions or give directive instructions will depend on many factors. Playing sports is situational, and so is coaching. There are many factors that influence game play, and coaching practices may vary in different situations and with different people.

The flow and timing of sports action can significantly influence the coach's ability to provide coaching assistance to their athletes during game play. Every sport has different timings of stoppages, allowance of time-outs, and in-between sets or period breaks. While this adds to the uniqueness of each sport, it also creates different challenges for coaches who wish to coach, teach, or instruct during the game play.

Conclusion

Challenges are difficult because they are often multifaceted, complex, situational, interpersonal, and unpredictable. Coaching is more than agreeing to coach for a season, being a nice person, having a level and age-appropriate coaching philosophy, or being able to find enough people to play the game. These are all necessary parts of being a coach. Coaching is full of challenges that may cause some coaches to question their involvement or push others to continue to use the same methods that they have been using their entire coaching career. Change is also hard. Building and maintaining a quality coach–athlete relationship, engaging in opportunities to learn about recent coaching research developments, and recognizing the sport-specific challenges are only a few of the challenges that coaches face when empowering their athletes to think for themselves. Using a growth mindset approach, great coaches can approach challenges as an opportunity to grow, think, ask questions, consider different options, plan for change, improve, and pursue success.

I hope this chapter has motivated you to reflect on your own challenges, ask questions of yourself, and encourages you to keep improving your own coaching practices in order to continue to empower your players to develop as athletes who can think for themselves.

References

Clarke, H., Smith, D., & Thibault, G. (1994). *Athlete-Centred Sport: A Discussion Paper.* Federal/Provincial/Territorial Sport Police Steering Committee.

Coaching Association of Canada. (2019). Coaching research. Retrieved August 20, 2019, from https://coach.ca/coaching-research-s16562.

Cooper, J.N., Grenier, R.S., & Macaulay, C. (2017). Autoethnography as a critical approach in sport management: Current applications and directions for future research. *Sport Management Review, 20*(1), 43–54.

Ellis, C. (2004). *The Ethnographic I: A Methodological Novel about Teaching and Doing Autoethnography.* Walnut Creek: AltaMira.

Gilbert, W. (2010). The passing of a legend: Coach John Wooden. *International Journal of Sports Science & Coaching, 5*(3), 339–342.

Girard, O, Chevalier, R., Habrard, M., Sciberras, P., Hot, P., & Millet, G.P. (2007). Game analysis and energy requirements of elite squash. *Journal of Strength and Conditioning Research, 21*(3), 909–914.

Halperin, I. (2018). Case studies in exercise and sport sciences: A powerful tool to bridge the science–practice gap. *International Journal of Sports Physiology and Performance, 13*(6), 824–825.

Headley-Cooper, K. (2010). Coaches' perspectives on athlete-centred coaching (Master's Thesis). University of Toronto.

Headley-Cooper, K. (2017). The autoethnographic journey of athlete-centred experiences, research and learning: Athlete to researcher, now coach, and beyond. In S. Pill (Ed.), *Perspectives on Athlete Centred Coaching* (pp. 150–160). Abingdon, UK: Routledge.

Holman Jones, S. (2005). Autoethnography: Making the personal political. In N.K. Denzin & Y.S. Lincoln (Eds.), *Handbook of Qualitative Research* (3rd edn, pp. 763–792). Thousand Oaks: Sage.

Holt, N.L. (2003). Representation, legitimation, and autoethnography: An autoethnographic writing story. *International Journal of Qualitative Methods, 2*(1), 1–22.

Holt, N.L., Camiré, M., Tamminen, K.A., Pankow, K., Pynn, S.R., Strachan, L., ... Fraser-Thomas, J. (2018). PYDSportNET: A knowledge translation project bridging gaps between research and practice in youth sport. *Journal of Sport Psychology in Action, 9*(2), 132–146.

Jowett, S. (2005). The coach-athlete partnership. *The Psychologist, 18*, 412–415.

Jowett, S., & Cockerill, I.M. (2003). Olympic medalists' perspective of the athlete-coach relationship. *Psychology of Sport and Exercise, 4*, 313–331.

Kidman, L. (2005). *Athlete-Centred Coaching: Developing Inspired and Inspiring People.* Christchurch, NZ: Innovative Communications.

Lyle, J. (1999). Coaching philosophy and coaching behaviour. In N. Cross & J. Lyle (Eds.), *The Coaching Process: Principles and Practice for Sport* (pp. 25–46). Oxford, UK: Butterworth Heinemann.

Lyle, J. (2018). The transferability of sport coaching research: A critical commentary. *Quest, 70*(4), 419–437.

Miller, P.S., & Kerr, G.A. (2002). Conceptualizing excellence: Past, present and future. *Journal of Applied Sport Psychology, 14*, 140–153.

Reade, I., Rodgers, W., & Hall, N. (2008). Knowledge transfer: How do high performance coaches access the knowledge of sport scientists? *International Journal of Sports Science & Coaching, 3*(3), 319–334.

Sparkes, A.C. (2000). Autoethnography and narratives of self: Reflections on criteria in action. *Sociology of Sport Journal, 17*, 21–43.

Williams, S.J., & Kendall, L. (2007). Perceptions of elite coaches and sports scientists of the research needs for elite coaching practice. *Journal of Sports Sciences, 14*, 1577–1586.

World Squash Federation (2018). World squash singles rules 2019. Retrieved from www.worldsquash.org/wp-content/uploads/2018/11/190101_Rules-of-Singles-Squash-2019-V1-1.pdf.

6

CAN GAME DATA MEASURE THE EFFECTIVENESS OF THE ATHLETE'S DECISION-MAKING PROCESS?

Tom Williams

Introduction

Data analysis has come to play a fundamental role within the sporting world, with a great deal of emphasis placed on athlete monitoring pre, during and post competition. The key outcome is to gain performance knowledge in movement, tactical statistics and physical workloads. These technological developments are staples amongst youth, professional and amateur sport, as coaches and athletes aim to objectively analyse performance to support their decision-making efficiency and productiveness in competition. This chapter will look to assess the current advances in technology that affect an athlete and coach's decision-making abilities.

The quest for excellence in sport today ensures multiple physical and technical avenues are constantly examined with a great deal of emphasis placed on the marginal gains surrounding sports performance. Athletes who endeavour to break world records, score more points and be remembered as all-time greats, are the reality of modern-day sports. The outcome, however, has never changed, as the capability to win the game, race or competition is the fundamental and only measure of success. Therefore, in an age of technology and analysis, the ability to enhance an individual's skills or physical abilities whilst seeking the smallest performance gains against competitors is undoubtedly paramount.

Data are now readily available, as coaches, athletes, and fans crave additional information in relation to team and athlete successes. Television broadcasters, social media, and smart applications can provide a detailed analysis of an athlete's performance at the click of a button. Many sporting organisations utilise statistical data to influence the recruitment of athletes and coaches. It is evident that twenty-first century athletes and coaches are data driven, where sport science, and data analysis have become driving forces within professional sporting organisations.

The current ability to objectively quantify many performance outcomes, providing further context to subjective technical, tactical, and physical decisions or opinions, is key in sports. This context can be created through an accumulation of multiple sources of information such as video tracking, internal and external physical workload monitoring and real-time tactical statistics. These factors aim to enable coaches to draw objective conclusions and observations to support their experience in their desired sporting field.

Many of these developments in technology can assist youth, amateur and professional coaches and athletes, as affordable iOS and Android applications and programs are now available to enhance the development of decision-making in sport. Conversely, the effectiveness of the technology must be reliable with a high-level environmental validity, as the application of data to inform decisions is paramount. This chapter will focus on analysing key technological developments for applied coaching through assessing performance and decision-making in sports. The key factors examined include observation monitoring of youth athletes, in-game physical tracking, and tactical analysis. In addition, this chapter will offer an insight into the effectiveness of systems to be applied into day-to-day coaching practices.

Longitudinal maturation and growth monitoring

As athletes mature and develop from youth to adolescent to senior levels, many factors are present that affect decision-making both from an athlete and coach's perspective. These factors vary significantly between each individual, as physiological and cognitive functions, including growth and maturation, are developing. Maturation in youth sport is now a prime factor for talent identification and recruitment of athletes in many sport academy systems, with longitudinal analysis conducted to predict athletes' future characteristics and growth patterns whilst aiming to reduce the onset of growth-related injuries.

It was once stated that age is merely a number; however, in modern sport this statement is not the case, most coaches that have taken a team photo will see the variability in athletes' heights, weights and muscle mass, even within athletes of the same age. Age is categorised into biological age, which is defined as the athlete's measure of years since birth, and most commonly used, whilst biological age is a measurement of that athlete's physiological maturation status. This is certainty more problematic to assess, as inter-athlete variability occurs resulting in differences in the time and speed of growth. An assessment of biological age will categorise aspects such as skeletal and sexual characteristic development, along with rapid increases in growth. These factors are essential to monitor to assess an athlete's status from a recruitment and injury prevention standpoint.

Coaches must pay close attention to the maturing athlete as an overload in training volume during periods of rapid growth, known as the Peak Height Velocity (PHV), may severely impact the athlete's health status and hinder their future physical and psychological development. PHV commonly occurs in females around the age of 12, and around 14 for male athletes. Whilst male athletes' PHV occurs later, it lasts significantly longer and is far more intense. Therefore, utilising an analysis system that encompasses long-term maturation tracking ensures athletes are given the optimal attention during stages of development.

A simple and effective method is to measure height and weight every three months, this enables coaches to assess significant changes in growth over a short period of time. If changes occur, the coach can plan to reduce training volume to limit growth-related injuries such as Sever's disease, Osgood–Schlatter disease, and stress fractures. Whilst these data may not directly affect in-game decision-making, they are an important area of concern for athlete health and physical development. Research by Mirwald, Baxter-Jones, Bailey and Beunen (2002) indicated specific equations to determine an athlete's predicted height and time from PHV where growth-related injuries can occur. These equations are based on athlete's height, weight, leg length and parents' heights. These equations are utilised regularly in many sporting organisations to determine PHV. It is vital to plan a well-thought-out process of physical development during PHV. Focus must be given to multiple cognitive skills and multi-sports to develop cognitive function, which will aid the athlete's development as they reach adulthood. Therefore, enforcing strategies to limit excessive volume and intensity during PHV, such as reducing on-field training time and game minutes, provides a simple and effective strategy to reduce the risk of growth-related injuries and ensures athletes fulfil their maximum future potential.

For example, in Little League Baseball, pitch count is closely monitored and the amount of time between a pitcher's outings is clearly stated to reduce the risk of overuse injury (Pytiak et al., 2017). PHV applications and spreadsheets are readily available to aid coaches in quantifying growth and maturation in adolescent athletes

Additional practices such as video-based movement assessments to assess joint angles and asymmetries can be accessed through many iOS or Android applications such as Hudl Technique®, Coach's Eye®, and CoachNow®, which may provide further context to analysing movements of the maturing athlete. Selecting sport-specific movements, such as jumping, landing and running, whilst comparing an athlete's baseline test videos to their latest test encapsulates an ongoing video library of analysis into an athlete's movement capabilities during PHV. Techniques such as a landing from a jump can be a determining factor for knee injuries due to the high eccentric forces associated with landing, especially in female athletes due to changes in hip angle during puberty (Silvers-Granelli, Bizzini, Arundale, Mandelbaum & Snyder-Mackler, 2017). This key factor is where video-based movement data can assist in addressing movement and strength deficiencies during phases of PHV. Young athletes' ability to function and make good in-game tactical decisions may be compromised by ignoring the effect of human development. Coaches must pay close attention to these hormonal adaptations in athletes' growth and maturation.

Physical in-game monitoring

Physical workload monitoring is one of the most examined aspects when quantifying performance across multiple sports. Research has been conducted in team territory sports, such as football, rugby and Australian rules football (Bangsbo, 1992; Lago & Martin, 2007; Lago-Peñas, Lago-Ballesteros, Dellal, & Gómez, 2010; Wisbey, Montgomery, Pyne, & Rattray, 2010). Much of this research is used to determine the physical demands of the sport and quantifying the most critical periods throughout a game or training session. This enables coaches and fitness staff to create a periodised training model to optimise the physical characteristics of each athlete.

The ability to sprint, change direction and jump are regular and decisive physical factors in many team sports. Therefore, it is paramount to create a strategy to assess physical performance within the coaching framework. Coaches must aim to develop a plan to allow for fluctuations in training, such as increasing training volume early in the week, which leads to amplified physical gains, known as loading. Reducing the load closer to competition is known as tapering. This strategy aims to evenly distribute workload without leaving athletes fatigued for competition, which could enhance injury risk and diminish performance.

Research has been carried out into the effects of workload and performance through dividing time into training and recovery periods to ensure an optimal physical outcome is developed in a well-balanced setting (Bannister, MacDougall, Wenger, & Green, 1991; Chiu & Barnes, 2003). Imagine weighing scales: one side holds training and the other holds recovery. Should the training aspect be carried out with limited tapering, the recovery will suffer, indicating the need to taper and reduce volume. Likewise, should insufficient training occur, the athletes' fitness will suffer, which inevitably leads to decreased performance levels. Physical monitoring is directly correlated to coaches and athletes' decision-making skills, as, when athletes are fatigued, their cognitive function and ability to perform the required technical and tactical skills will decline, leaving the team or individual athlete at a disadvantage (Rampinini, Impellizzeri, Castagna, Coutts, & Wisløff, 2009; Tomporowski 2003).

Team performance has been seen to become less effective in the final stages of a game due to the onset of muscle fatigue and the emotional stresses that surround winning and losing. Therefore, ensuring athletes are in peak physical condition to carry out their individual responsibilities is fundamental for a coach. Utilising reliable and valid measures of objective data from wearable technology, such as Global Positioning Systems (GPS) and Heart Rate (HR) monitors, have yielded great success in allowing coaches to quantify the demands of each athlete during competition and training (Malone, Di Michele, Morgans, Burgess, Morton, & Drust 2015). Many wearable technologies can be expensive due to the amount of information and speed of the data they process, but they are necessary as in professional sports gaining even a minimal advantage in physical development is vital. GPS companies such as Catapult Sports® have developed a hierarchy of GPS systems, from professional sports to youth club teams, the latter which are much more affordable and simple to use due the lower levels of data collected. Nevertheless, key metrics such as distance covered, speed, and change of direction can be quantified across all GPS systems, and are vital physical aspects to develop as they impact decision-making.

GPS technology is classified as external load as it impacts the working muscles and joints, whereas HR is categorised as internal load. This involves the response of the body to the training or game demands. This enables coaches to assess the fitness levels of athletes and quantify how they respond to training drills. For example, an athlete who has a high HR response, may have difficulty executing cognitive decisions owing to impaired fitness levels. A simple analogy is to compare the human body to a motor car, the internal load which can be measured in HR is equivalent to the engine of the motor car. While the external load, is the equivalent to the tyres, wheels, suspension and drive shaft of the motor car.

Additionally, a simplistic method also exists that is a combination of both internal and external load called Session Rate of Perceived Exertion (sRPE). sRPE has been shown to be the most cost-effective monitoring tool, that can be used in daily training to inform coaches' decisions and planning sessions based on how the athlete has responded. The athletes will report their individual perceived difficulty on a scale of one to ten (1 = Easy, 10 = Game Like) for each training activity and for a total rating of the session. A supplementary time variable is added, where an athlete's score is multiplied by the duration to create an arbitrary unit of workload.

Table 6.1 details an example of a single athlete reporting their response in relation to training activities. This provides coaches with a physical cost of each activity, on which they can base future predictions and allow sufficient planning and workload distribution throughout a training week.

Table 6.2 details an example of each athlete's response to the entire session. As each training activity occurs a totally different response will be present amongst the athletes.

Utilising physical workload data in coaching practices is simple and effective to implement to ensure training and fatigue are balanced correctly. This enhances planning to ensure each athlete is able to efficiently carry out their position-specific demands during competition.

TABLE 6.1 Example of an individual athlete's response to training drills

Athlete	Total training time (mins)	Athlete score (1–10)	Total sRPE (score*time)
Athlete A	70	7/10	490
Athlete B	70	5/10	350
Athlete C	70	9/10	630

TABLE 6.2 Example of an individual athlete's response to total session

Training drill	Time (mins)	Athlete score (1–10)	sRPE (score*time)
Passing	10	2/10	20
Dribbling	15	4/10	60
5v5 Game	25	7/10	175

Tactical analysis

Along with the quantification of the physical demands of performance, both technical and tactical analysis are central principles in team and individual organisation and decision-making processes. The ability of an athlete to carry out a desired skill or movement in a manner in which the training and preparation has been coached is vital to success.

A team's vision or philosophy is generally implemented through the goals and relationships of the athletes and coaches to create a holistic model for success. The coach in many individual sports can support the athletes' goals. Preparation is based around peaking for competition and coaching the technical and tactical deficiencies within the athlete's game whilst catering for challenging environmental conditions such as heat, altitude or course difficulties in sports such as cycling, skiing, and golf. The tactical preparation in individual sports is somewhat less chaotic than in team sports where multiple uncontrollable factors present difficulties in executing a tactical plan.

Territory game coaches desire to tactically analyse opponents and athletes to combat their style of play and to enhance the team's ability to exploit weaknesses in the opposing team's system. Many coaches use video analysis, including observing footage of themselves and opponents, which is subsequently carried out in applied scenarios on the training field to enhance the athletes' learning ability. Software such as Dartfish®, Performa Sports®, and Sportstec Gamebreaker® and Hudl® are readily available for coaches to utilise. However, a large portion of time is devoted to manually editing video and data, which fundamentally limits influence in practice.

Software developments must be made that aim to reduce the time burden associated with manual editing and to create a seamless workspace for coaches to affect decision-making that is both cost and time effective. Whilst many of these systems are extremely coach friendly and simple to use, it is vital that using this software does not take time away from the coaching process. Systems such as Sportstec Gamebreaker® and Hudl® are generally utilised by a video analyst, who supports the coach, owing to the specialist skills involved in video clipping and tagging. Nevertheless, utilising tools such as Dartfish® and CoachNow®, that are accessible through iOS and Android systems can ensure coaches can organise and store data to share with athletes and communicate key messages and instructions. However, systems such as Metrica® utilise game footage and provide a pre-clipped analysis on the game based on the key technical aspects and physical data. This is a vital time-efficient system to utilise; however, it is generally more accessible to professional teams because of cost.

A coach must understand the learning requirements of athletes as some may be visual learners and video technology is extremely helpful to help them clearly understand the tactical requirements. Other athletes may be kinesthetic learners and must be able to practise the style of play through application and repetition to understand the game plan. Therefore, to enhance an athlete's decision-making skills, the coach must first understand each athlete's learning capabilities. Sports technology enables an interactive approach for both coaches and athletes to assess performance and direct future performance.

Video-based tracking is a process where game recordings are taken and broken down into specific clips which represent the team's style of play and the technical goals. The level of analysis provided in these systems can be extremely detailed as certain systems, including Metrica®, are able to recognise specific actions and automatically create video clips based on a predetermined tactical requirement. For example, for a soccer coach who wants the defensive line to remain no more than 10 m apart to ensure large spaces are minimal for the opposition to move into, a live video tracking system placed around the stadium can sound an alarm and create a clip of the playing phase should one player be more than 10 m from his or her co-defender. This enables specific tactical knowledge to be utilised in an extremely effective manner whilst allowing for a high level of objectivity in decision-making. Likewise, the ability of athletes to study video of themselves, along with objective tactical feedback based on the coach's philosophy, can enhance the coach–athlete learning process. As technology is constantly developing, virtual reality can be used such that athletes can visualise key decision moments in the game and relive the experience in a controlled environment, which can cater for both visual and kinesthetic learners.

The team's identity and coaching philosophy is a key factor in the analysis process and the information must guide athletes to make the correct decisions based on how the coach wants the team or athlete to perform. Two important tactical principles in team territory sports that require effective decision-making are the transitions that occur between attacking and defending of the offensive and defensive team, and each individual's organisation. These principles aid coaches in their analysis of the tactical details that are developed within coaching philosophy, and to utilise video technology to quantify the effectiveness of an athlete's decision in relation to the game scenario. Video feedback can be utilised as an assessment tool in the days preceding a game. However, software such as Hudl® Performa Sports®, and Sportstec Gamebreaker®, can provide coaches with live information, which can be relayed to the athlete during intervals or half-time. This enhances the communication levels between coach and athlete whilst assisting in controlling emotional decisions that can be reactive and do not support the coaching philosophy.

As the athletes begin to understand the key principles and their roles and responsibilities within the tactical framework, the coaching model begins to

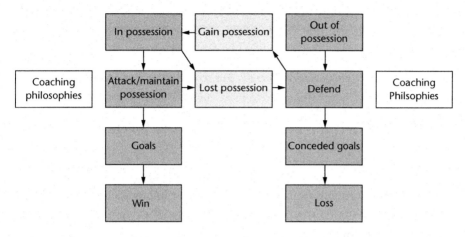

FIGURE 6.1 Decision tree of the transition periods of a team

expand and provide further detail. Many coaches have developed decision trees that assist the athlete's decisions when certain patterns occur during a game. These charts ensure a simple communication tool can be implemented based on the coaching philosophy (Farahnakian & Mozayani, 2008; Kasaei, Kasaei, Kasaei & Taheri (2010). Figure 6.1 details a decision tree of the transition periods of a team and how to implement the correct strategy.

Conclusion

Currently, coaches, teams and individuals have access to a lot of performance-related data due to objective technologies such as GPS and in-game monitoring systems such as Metrica®, Pro-Zone® and Hudl® providing coaches with technical and physical analysis. These systems can create key video clips, tactical statistics and physiological information, including distance covered in territory games, both with and without possession, and the maximal speeds achieved by the players.

However, a lack of contextual tactical data exists or is diluted through the excessive physical data research. Therefore, a reliance on published tactical decision-making data may provide prove problematic in terms of tactical modelling. Creating multiple tactical plans based on coaching philosophy through the use of decision trees may be a proactive method of implementing key tactical information, where decision-making can be assessed. Decision trees are a simple and effective method to ensure athletes understand their roles in given situations. This, however, reduces autonomous decision-making and improvisation, although it ensures emotional and reactive judgements are kept to a minimum, whilst maximising athlete responsibilities. It is important to maximise athlete decision-making skills without creating a paint-by-numbers approach. Conversely, coaches must be aware that environmental factors and human relationships are key facets in athletic performance.

Data is vital within professional and youth sport, with many high-profile organisations utilising data to implement performance strategies. It is important to note that data are not used to drive decisions but to aid in providing context through intuition and creating an ongoing education process to supplement a coach's or athlete's experience. There is a misconception that using data is a negative factor in sports, and that coaches are losing sight of athletes' development due to an over-reliance on data. However, utilising systems such as PHV monitoring, tactical analysis and physical tracking ensures a holistic and objective view of the demands of the sport, whilst assessing the effectiveness of the coaching philosophy and athlete learning capabilities.

Having reliable and effective data that can be applied to performance is a requirement for coaches and athletes. In an age of information technology, it is important that the twenty-first century coach is comfortable with technology, as athletes are using it in every facet of their lives.

Therefore, as coaches, we must aim to coach to the level of the athlete and direct them through avenues they are comfortable with. There is no single method that can objectively assess an athlete or coach's decision-making skills. It is the collaboration of coaching philosophy through integrating objective data into an ecologically valid framework. A great deal of research and emphasis is placed on supporting the coaching process, and multiple authors and bloggers aim to dive deeper into the intricacies surrounding athlete analysis. Further information is available in the following websites.

Useful websites

Growth and maturation

www.scienceforsport.com

Physical analysis

www.catapultsports.com/resources
www.scienceforsport.com
https://martin-buchheit.net/
http://sportperfex.com/the-concept/

Technical and tactical analysis

https://statsbomb.com/
www.agilesportsanalytics.com/
www.coach-logic.com/blog/
http://blog.isportsanalysis.com/
www.performasports.com/blog

References

Bannister, E.W., MacDougall, J.D., Wenger, H.A., & Green, H.J. (1991). Modeling elite athletic performance. In: *Physiological Testing of the High-Performance Athlete* (pp. 403–424). Champaign, IL: Human Kinetics.

Bangsbo J. (1994). The physiology of soccer with special reference to intense intermittent exercise. *Acta Physiologica Scandinavica. 619*, 1–55.

Chiu, L.Z., & Barnes, J.L. (2003). The fitness-fatigue model revisited: Implications for planning short and long-term training. *Strength and Conditioning Journal, 25*(6), 42–51.

Farahnakian, F., & Mozayani, N. (2008). Learning through decision tree in simulated soccer environment. *International Conference on Computational Intelligence and Security, 2*, 68–70.

Kasaei, S.H.M., Kasaei, S.M.M., Kasaei, S.A.M., & Taheri, M. (2010). Design of an action selection mechanism for cooperative soccer robots based on fuzzy decision-making algorithm. *Broad Research in Artificial Intelligence and Neuroscience, 1*(3), 5–18.

Lago, C., & Martín, R. (2007). Determinants of possession of the ball in soccer. *Journal of Sports Sciences, 25*(9), 969–74.

Lago-Peñas, C., Lago-Ballesteros, J., Dellal, A., & Gómez, M. (2010). Game-related statistics that discriminated winning, drawing and losing teams from the Spanish soccer league. *Journal of Sports Science and Medicine, 9*(2), 288.

Malone, J.J., Di Michele, R., Morgans, R., Burgess, D., Morton, J.P., & Drust, B. (2015). Seasonal training-load quantification in elite English Premier League soccer players. *International Journal of Sports Physiology and Performance, 10*(4), 489–497.

Mirwald, R.L., Baxter-Jones, A.D., Bailey, D.A., & Beunen, G.P. (2002). An assessment of maturity from anthropometric measurements. *Medicine and Science in Sports and Exercise, 34*(4), 689–694.

Pytiak, A.V., Stearns, P., Bastrom, T.P., Dwek, J., Kruk, P., Roocroft, J.H., & Pennock, A.T. (2017). Are the current Little League pitching guidelines adequate? A single-season prospective MRI study. *Orthopaedic Journal of Sports Medicine, 5*(5), 2325967117704851.

Rampinini, E., Impellizzeri, F.M., Castagna, C., Coutts, A.J., & Wisløff, U. (2009). Technical performance during soccer matches of the Italian Serie A League: Effect of fatigue and competitive level. *Journal of Science and Medicine in Sport, 12*(1), 227–233.

Silvers-Granelli, H.J., Bizzini, M., Arundale, A., Mandelbaum, B.R., & Snyder-Mackler, L. (2017). Does the FIFA 11+ injury prevention program reduce the incidence of ACL injury in male soccer players? *Clinical Orthopaedics and Related Research, 475*(10), 2447–2455.

Tomporowski, P.D. (2003). Effects of acute bouts of exercise on cognition. *Acta Psychologica, 112*(3), 297–324.

Wisbey, B., Montgomery, P.G., Pyne, D.B., & Rattray, B. (2010). Quantifying movement demands of AFL football using GPS tracking. *Journal of Science and Medicine in Sport, 13*(5), 531–536.

PART III

Tactical decision-making and sport-specific coaching for a variety of sports

7

SOCCER (NORTH AMERICA) OR FOOTBALL (REST OF THE WORLD)

Guido Geisler and James Wallis

This chapter begins with a brief recap of the opening section of Chapter 4. As mentioned, elite-level soccer players typically spend around 98 per cent of match time on mental appraisal and mental processing – in other words, perception and decision-making – while only 2 per cent of a 90-minute game involves the physical execution of technical skills (McGreskin, cited in deVos, 2013). This emphasis on cognitive processes necessitates a well-developed tactical triangle that is, reading the situation, acquiring skills to meet the situation and making decisions in their application. Furthermore, the majority of players' decisions must take position, moment, direction, and speed into account. Thus, to bring everything together, coaching content must be suitably holistic by acknowledging and incorporating the typical technical and tactical content as well as diverse physical, cognitive, emotional and social dimensions of play. This chapter will make regular reference to the concept of 'holistic coaching' which demands that coaching interventions take the whole player into account when attempting to enhance performance.

In this regard, non-linear and game-centred approaches, which are underpinned by more ecologically valid coaching content, have received increasing endorsement in the research literature (e.g. Grehaigne, Wallian, & Godbout, 2005; Launder, 2001; Light, 2004; Mitchell, Oslin, & Griffin, 2006). This has included the value of overlapping training dimensions that are outlined in Chapter 4. An extension of this premise is the physical training practice of 'fitness with the ball'. This is another relatively modern approach that combines physical conditioning with technical development through maximal ball contact (ideally, 500–1000 touches per 90-minute training session), whilst simultaneously building fatigue through increasing physical demands on players. Mental skills training offers a further set of tools that are at the modern coach's disposal, but despite these research-led innovations within the broad approach of holistic coaching, gaps still remain in their concurrent application. One example is that technical–tactical games or conditioned practices sometimes fail to challenge players' physical capacities.

Conversely, fitness with the ball does not always demand simultaneous technical, tactical and cognitive considerations. Mental skills initiatives are often divorced from the specific training context and focused on the education of psychological factors (for example motivation, anxiety regulation, attention control) impacting performance, but they have little application in the training environment. Constructing training activities which adopt holistic and nonlinear approaches, for example games-based methodologies, offer the coach and players a more valid and beneficial use of training time, whilst avoiding the decomposition of games into drills which only challenge one dimension of player development.

Breaking training sessions down into segments where each has a separate emphasis on technical skills (e.g. ball mastery exercises), team tactics (e.g. team shape shadow play), physical capacity (e.g. strength or agility training), or mental preparation (e.g. arousal regulation) is common amongst many of the most celebrated clubs around the world. As discussed previously, specialised practice in different domains has its time and its value. However, it should not be the only way that training is conducted if the goal is to develop well-rounded, thinking players. Furthermore, players must understand the game-related meaning of training activities so that they are executed in a conscious mode rather than one in which they are cognitively disengaged. Over time, as players internalise a variety of good decisions for different game situations, they gradually develop subconscious decision-making processes (through conscious repetition) and ultimately develop the ability to perform on autopilot in real game contexts.

More advanced or more experienced players can shift their available cognitive resources away from basic decisions, for example which foot to use, how to control the ball, where to place their first touch, and onto more challenging time-constrained decisions that are common in game play. Players may eventually develop a wider perceptual field, deriving more useful and abundant information on which to base decisions. Players also learn to perform in a manner that is consistent with their roles and personalities as players (e.g., as artists, such as creative midfielders, or as soldiers, such as ball-winning or holding midfielders), hence decisions can be guided by role, position or match situation.

With the preceding recap as a brief theoretical foundation, this chapter will address and exemplify how to create and adapt coaching content that integrates the holistic training dimensions from some well-known football training tasks. It addresses both individual- and team-oriented considerations and encourages players to make situation-appropriate decisions on a quick, continuous, and frequently changing basis that is more representative of game contexts than drills alone.

Small-sided games and training activities (versus drills)

As this chapter progresses, we will be using a variety of football terminology. For example, the words "advantaged team" and "disadvantaged teams" are used. An "advantaged team" is one that has more players than the "disadvantaged team". The tactical reasons for doing this in football and many Territory games is to create game-like scenarios when teams find themselves with more or less players than the opposing team. For technical or skill development, using an "advantaged team" will give that team more opportunities and time to learn a skill such as receiving a pass without the defending team closing them down so quickly.

Speed of play is a major training objective in soccer, since players have less time and less space with the ball as the level of play increases. Moreover, a high speed of action is necessary during training in order to develop high speed decision-making. In fact, one aspect of "football fitness" that receives less attention than physical markers is the ability to make decisions and execute those decisions at a high tempo, as frequently as possible, and as long as possible during matches to simulate decision-making under fatigue (especially into the late phases of games).

Again, consider that players often fatigue mentally before they fatigue physically – mental fitness is an important part of football fitness, but one that is sometimes overlooked. From that perspective, effective training content to develop thinking soccer players can be divided into small-sided/modified games and technique-oriented practice that incorporates tactical considerations (decision-making situations). For the latter, the term "activities" is a more accurate description than the word "drills". Drills are mechanical sequences detached from real game play and real game pace; they require little or no interpretation, as all of the associated decisions are made by the coach beforehand and reflected in the drill's instructions. Activities, on the other hand, are much less constrained and can contain elements of randomness that are characteristic of higher-tempo game situations. Activities require players to make decisions, and at times, to solve problems. Redesigning commonly used drills into more open-ended activities and games that require greater cognitive involvement is highly recommended to all practising coaches

The first set of sample training content is comprised of small-sided/modified game situations, with gradual increases in playing area. The second set of training scenarios can be classified as activities since they require players (within defined grids) to execute technical skills cleanly, at a high speed and intensity of play, and with an awareness of specifically selected tactical considerations. It should quickly become clear that even the training activities, which have a strong technical focus, can incorporate tactical thinking and decision-making in the absence of (competitive) small-sided games. To that extent, it should also be emphasised that holistic training activities play an important role in overall development – training sessions cannot merely be one long series of small-sided competitive games. That being said, small-sided games should form part of every session, with selected and well-designed training activities (as opposed to drills) enlisted to exploit the important technical and tactical abilities that are required for success in those modified games which are typically done in games-based coaching methods.

With respect to cognitive skills, most of the scenarios require quick shifts in attentional focus (from narrow to broad and back) and a maintained level of concentration, both of which are essential for good decision-making. Moreover, objectives for the activities and small-sided games can be set within a motivational climate that promotes the motive to succeed (see Arkes & Garske, 1982). That is, players are meant to become comfortable and confident on the ball. They are encouraged to attempt specific actions, including difficult ones, such that they are not afraid to have the ball or to use it positively. Possible increments in confidence can come from increasingly successful replication at an increasingly consistent (and high) standard. This contrasts with motivational climates that foster the motive to avoid failure (i.e. playing it safe through the fear of making mistakes, which hinders task mastery). Players need to understand that failure is not problematic of and by itself. Rather, it should be seen as a form of "payment" that is necessary to achieve success. To explain, successful players are not the ones who make the fewest mistakes; they are the ones who deal best with those mistakes by learning from them and making the necessary adjustments. From the holistic perspective adopted for this chapter, dealing with and reinterpreting 'failure' and developing player capacity to 'bounce back' from adverse experiences is an example of the incorporation of the emotional dimensions of player development.

The following samples of training content, both small-sided games and training activities, are designed with a view to exemplifying holistic approaches by blending two, three, or even four training dimensions into the small-sided game or activity. Following each game or activity are some possible holistic adaptations that could be employed to add dimensions and validity. Adaptations suggested are most often manipulations made to the task or on the performer.

It should also be mentioned that each training session begins with a game-like warm-up exercise (e.g. handball, soccer with a rugby ball, among others). Such warm-up games counter the common and misguided view that a warm up is merely a physical process by engaging players both physically and mentally while fostering foundations such as communication, support movements, balance, and agility. Warm ups should provide players with the opportunity to prepare for all dimensions that follow in the main session. Whilst, various elite programmes, including the youth national teams of the French Football Federation (FFF) and multiple youth academies use this approach, it should be strongly advised that coaches are made acutely aware of the needs to use age-appropriate approaches to training that take into account the physical, emotional and social stage of development of players, and do not impose adult training on youth performers as 'mini adults'.

Sample small-sided games – based on keeping possession and quick transitions

Possession game #1 – focusing on technical skill development

Making quick transitions between overload and numerical disadvantage situations within a small grid involving two teams of two players each (total of four players) v one team of two players. If the disadvantaged team of two wins the ball, the team that lost it counter-presses to regain it quickly. Multiple decisions are demanded of players. For example, the advantaged team is required to make decisions concerning their position and support play, how long to retain the ball, their execution of passing skills and decisions concerning how and when to make their pass. The disadvantaged team must make decisions concerning how, when and who to press, how to close the space, when to drop off and conserve energy.

Consider that 60–70 per cent of all goals are scored in the transition phase. In the moment after a team has won possession through an overload action, the opponents are typically out of position and vulnerable to a counter-attack, and in such situations it takes an average of 11.6 seconds to score a goal. Developing team decisions based on the moment of transition, whether defending or attacking is a key feature of football and is developed in this small-sided game.

Possible holistic adaptations

Physical – adapt the size and dimensions of the grid or place a time constraint on recovering the ball to increase intensity demand on the disadvantaged pairing.

Social – limit the verbal communication between players, both overload and disadvantaged groups. This demands greater use of visual information and players 'getting their head up' when receiving the ball.

Cognitive – create a scoring system for successful first touch or second touch passes. This condition adds a further decision to be made when receiving the ball.

Emotional – keep score of the system used above. Scores can be recorded and recalled in future sessions to be used as targets for personal improvement.

Possession game #2 – focusing on technical skill development

This is played at high physical intensity using reduced grid size. One team has a numerical advantage via a neutral player inside the grid. If the disadvantaged team recovers the ball, their aim is to play the ball out of the crowded pressure zone to any one of the three neutral players outside of the grid. After which that neutral player joins them inside for a new overload situation while the previous neutral player now assumes one of the outlet/support positions outside of the grid (see Figure 7.1).

Possession game (with overload)

Black vs **White** inside grid

Grey Player A plays with Black team – thus it's 6v5 (Black overload)

Once White wins the ball, they must play to any of the 3 Grey players outside the grid (live play inside the grid until they can do that) – e.g., **White Player 1** wins the ball, passes to a teammate who plays to **Grey Player B**

Once that happens, **Grey Player B** enters the grid with the ball and **Grey Player A** steps outside to replace him/her; **Yellow Player B** now plays with the White team – thus it's now 6v5 for the White team (White overload)

Process continues – the overload situation keeps changing (sometimes in White's favour, sometimes in Black's favour)

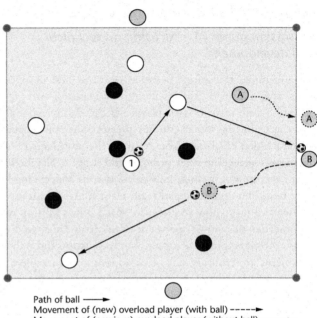

Path of ball ⟶
Movement of (new) overload player (with ball) ----▶
Movement of (previous) overload player (without ball) ·······▶

FIGURE 7.1   Possession game #2 – focusing on technical skill development

Possible holistic adaptations

Cognitive – by changing the grid dimensions the players in possession will be afforded differing amounts of time on the ball, this impacts the number of touches they can take to move the ball. Placing a smaller grid, using different colour cones, inside the original grid with coach changing the size of the grid frequently will add a further cognitive dimension to the game. For even further demand, three of four different grids can be added, this will increase the range and type of passes afforded to players.

Physical – the above adaptations will increase the physical demand on the team without the ball. They will need to make decisions concerning the timing and intensity of their press or when to close, intercept or attempt to tackle. The game will continue to evolve as players fatigue (an intended performer constraint) which again may change the decisions of players in possession as they may be under less pressure due to fatigued opponents.

Emotional – loss of possession is recorded and presented at the end of the session. Players know that every possession is important and their passing decisions and execution have consequences beyond the team losing the ball in a training exercise. Having made decision or execution errors it is an opportunity to see which players continue to seek the ball and which ones "hide". This provides an insight into their growth or fixed mindset.

Possession game #3 – focusing on technical skill, physical training and tactical development

Played at high-intensity within a defined space with one or two neutrals – as the ball is won and lost, the team in possession tries to open up quickly to the outside edge of the space ("open fist" to create width and depth) and play the ball out of pressure to the width of the grid; the team that lost the ball tries to counter-press quickly (through an immediate "closed fist" to become compact and deny space through the dangerous central playing channel/middle); the neutral player(s) must always stay central to serve as a midfield link (tactical). At the moment of transition players must communicate to act immediately "as one" to close or open out depending on whether they have won or lost the ball (social) (see Figure 7.2).

- 6+1 v 6 (black vs. white, + grey neutral player)
- Team in possession has an **open fist** shape via players positioned around the edge of the grid while also keeping 1 or 2 players inside for support (positions are interchangeable according to the run of play)
  → **objective is to continuously switch the point of attack and pass to teammates over 3 different sidelines within the same possession sequence (= 1 goal)**; players step out over the line to receive, then step back in

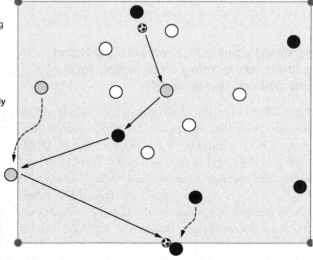

- Upon losing possession, that team **closes the fist** by **immediately** converging upon the ball **as a group** (**counter-pressing** to win back **quickly**)
- After re-gaining possession, 1ˢᵗ pass/dribble should **play the ball away from pressure** while **quickly opening the fist again** to create passing options over 3 sidelines
- Neutral player stays inside the grid and supports the team in possession so that the team with the ball is aleays in an **overload** situation

Emphasis is on the **continuous process** of opening up (after winning possession), converging/counter-pressing as a group (to win the ball back, and **switching play**

FIGURE 7.2 Possession game #3 – focusing on technical skill, physical training and tactical development

Sample modified games – focusing on attentional focus shifts and ball-oriented defending

Modified game #1 – 8 v 8 with goals and goalkeepers focusing on technical, tactical and physical skills

Periodically the coach puts a new ball into play to create a new game moment; players must focus on the new ball and ignore the previous one. This can begin to train quick attentional shifts and quickly re-establishing a disciplined team shape under the new circumstances. From the holistic perspective there is a social demand on players to communicate quickly and clearly to respond to the new game situation. To enhance complexity the coach may introduce a ball to a completely different point on the pitch to challenge the speed of transition and communication. Numerous individual, paired and team decisions need to be made under time pressure, with effective communication. Further extension of this activity can include "random refereeing" where the coach makes calls which accentuate a particular objective, for example; regaining defensive shape when caught offside, or counter pressing when losing the ball in the defensive third.

From a technical perspective, occupying and controlling the central playing area is key to having a team that is sound defensively (difficult to penetrate) and potent in attack (having many options going forward), for example central midfielders and centre backs staying central, holding midfielders and centre backs staying connected are two features of team shape that can be coached through the open-ended decision-making games exemplified here.

Modified game #2 – 8 v 8 with goals and goalkeepers focusing on technical, tactical, physical and cognitive skills

After a fixed time, the coach stops play and uses a Game Sense approach to elicit positive patterns and responses to specific match situations. For example, match form tactical training on a 2/3 pitch to address specific phases of play (typically 6 v 6 plus goalkeeper such that there is a "focus team" and a "sparring partner") – the focus team attempts to implement a selected tactical theme (e.g. counter-attack) from a position on the pitch that represents a designated game moment (e.g. where the ball was recovered); following several rounds without comment, the coach can create an open dialogue with players based on decisions made and outcomes elicited. Players can be asked questions on which to build a bank of suitable responses to the selected tactical theme according to a range of specific situational determinants such as, match situation, ability of opponents, position of opponents or level of fatigue. The coach can then allow players to construct a range of personal responses based on the affordances of their bodies, their perceived abilities and on the situation. Ultimately, there will be multiple correct responses to a given situation. Players need to be given scope to construct a bank of suitable responses and then to apply the most suitable to the specific game moment.

Sample training activities

Combined aerobic/anaerobic activity (physical) in which two players on opposite sides dribble continuously around a rectangular grid (technical) with a teammate situated at the midpoint of each long side, a little inside the rectangle. The first phase simply involves a wall pass with the teammate around the cone, this is the base of the 'drill' and requires no decision-making. The coach must build a more robust and useful training activity from this commonly used drill. Potential, but by no means the only possible adaptations, are to add a second phase which involves a decision to either use the wall pass or perform any type of feint, dodge or trick to keep the ball (cognitive). A possible third phase has a defender situated at the cone and requires tactical decision-making (a wall pass with the teammate versus a feint/move to beat the opponent.) The player's decision may be based on a range of situational factors such as; perceptions of their own skill and speed, perceptions of the ability and speed of the defender, perceptions of the passing ability of their teammate, available space. Through the coach changing some of the situational factors above, the player is required to continually adapt decisions made.

Consider the very typical and traditional shooting 'drill' where the coach lays the ball either left or right for the forward to run onto the ball to strike first touch at the goal. This drill is a commonly used practice that is fun and generates a degree of isolated technical challenge, but offers very little in terms of game-skill development or execution when applied on its most basic level. Building the scenario by adding defenders starting from the apex either side of the six-yard box, one of whom closes the attacked down before they have taken their first touch creates a more open training activity which requires a greater degree of decision-making. The attacker must now take their first touch to take into account a defender closing them from the right or the left, adding in a cognitive dimension to the activity. The task can be further developed by adding a third defender who begins their recovery run from behind the attacker which opens up the affordance to take their first touch to either side and to either shoot or dribble around the keeper. Levels of difficulty can be added with two of the three defenders closing the attacker, which again places pressure on the speed of decision-making of the attacker. The coach is able to continually create cognitive challenge by changing the defenders and their respective distances and starting position relative to the attacker.

Passing pattern practice (technical) between players inside and outside of a grid, requiring anaerobic bursts (physical) by both the inside and outside players as well as spatial awareness to maintain shape/balance inside and outside of the grid when not on the ball (tactical). See Figures 7.3, 7.4, 7.5 and 7.6, which progress this theme of players moving to make and receive short and long passes.

- 5 Players (3 outside, 2 inside).
- Players inside the grid alternate supporting (with lay-off) the outside player in possession.
- Outside players hit a diagonal ball in either direction after the lay-off from the player inside the grid.
- At the same time, the outside player not involved in the sequence must run to the open side in support (to give a new diagonal pass option [i.e., form a trangle] for the outside player who's now in possession).

- **Continuous** and **quick**.
- Players can vary between 1-touch and 2-touch ... is 2-touch, the 1st touch should se the ball purposefully to the side for an explosive step before the 2nd touch.

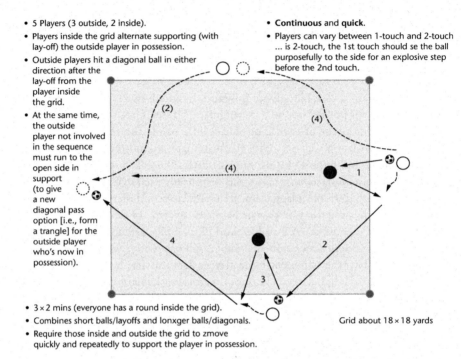

- 3 × 2 mins (everyone has a round inside the grid).
- Combines short balls/layoffs and lonxger balls/diagonals.
- Require those inside and outside the grid to zmove quickly and repeatedly to support the player in possession.

Grid about 18 × 18 yards

FIGURE 7.3 Sample training activity #1 – passing and moving

- Now with 6 Players (4 outside, 2 inside)
- Players inside ther grid continue to alternate on who plays the lay-off
- Again, players outside the grid play a diagonal ball in either direction after the lay-off from the player inside the grid

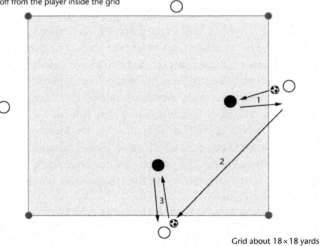

Grid about 18 × 18 yards

FIGURE 7.4 Sample training activity #2 – passing and moving – enhancing decision-making

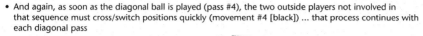

- And again, as soon as the diagonal ball is played (pass #4), the two outside players not involved in that sequence must cross/switch positions quickly (movement #4 [black]) … that process continues with each diagonal pass
- The inside player not involved in the lay-off moves quickly into a support position for the next lay-off with the new outside player (movement #4 [grey])

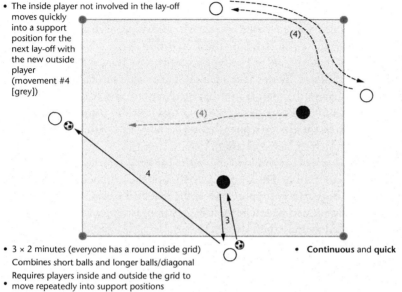

- 3 × 2 minutes (everyone has a round inside grid) Combines short balls and longer balls/diagonal
- Requires players inside and outside the grid to move repeatedly into support positions
- **Continuous** and **quick**

FIGURE 7.5   Sample training activity #3 – passing and moving – increasing the difficulty of decision-making

The activity in itself is capable of enhancing the technical reproduction of isolated passing skills and, in time, add the physical demand of testing technical execution of passing skills under fatigue. However, the task in this format is divorced from the game environment as it becomes routine with little in-game decision-making.

The training activity, as presented here, offers opportunities for players in possession to make some basic decisions concerning the direction of the diagonal pass. Aside from this, there is little additional decision-making demanded of players. In this respect, in its current format, it can be considered a highly technical 'drill' which has the potential to enhance passing skills under minimal cognitive load. The challenge for the coach is to construct additional dimensions of the 'drill' to engender further holistic challenge in either the cognitive, emotional or social dimensions of the players.

A common progression is to add a further player on the outside of the grid. This increases the number of options open to the player in possession, particularly if supporting players move laterally to create different angles and length of pass. However, these minor adaptations alone do not create sufficient holistic demand on the player with the ball that would enhance their 'in-game' decision-making.

A further common adaptation to the drill is to create the added technical challenge of passing to a player in motion. The movement of the two players not involved in the current passing sequence requires the receiving player to process additional visual information about the exact location of their target.

In their own right these three progressive practices offer quick, repetitive and engaging activity. They have the added benefit of demanding high technical and physical competence for successful execution. However, each of these activities should be viewed as the base, or the foundation from which to construct more meaningful, holistic and game-representative coaching content. Example enhancements to these activities may include (but not be limited to) any intervention that challenges the players to think on their feet and make time-limited decisions. For example, players inside the grid may call the name or colour bib of the next receiver, the passer is then having to take on board external, audial information on which to base a decision.

Using the same activity as outlined above, the players can be also be challenged to take in visual information. The second player inside the grid not involved in the lay-off makes an early run to support one of the diagonal passes. The passer must make a visual search to see which of their pass options is supported before taking their first touch and making their pass.

An alternative, which also requires the search and use of visual information, is that one of the outside options makes themselves unavailable to receive a pass by turning their back or by folding their arms. The passer must search for this information before taking their first touch and setting up their next pass.

The second player inside the grid could now be made an opponent, their role is to run to mark one of the supporting players on the outside of the grid. This demands that the passer must decide which of the pass options have been closed off before taking their first touch. This adaptation may be advanced further by adding another opponent thereby affording two 'closed' options and one 'open' option to the passer.

Summary

The sample activities and small-sided games might seem similar to what some coaches already do. The difference lies in the extent to which particular training themes or points of focus are deliberately "exploited" or accentuated in the activity or game, which is a function of the coach's ability to identify the necessary patterns and make those patterns arise frequently through the instructions and feedback that are given. Conditioning the game in this way enhances opportunities for the coach to manipulate their practices in order to enhance player decision-making within specific situations.

By adapting practices using the holistic approach advocated, the coach can move training activities towards more valid and supportive training content which more closely embodies challenges and situations that players will experience within the game context. When done systematically, the players will be practising technical elements of the game in combination with multiple other demands, including decision-making. By reviewing coaching content, specifically 'drills', in this way, it can create meaningful practice through intention rather than the product of chance – the models provided here are meant to help coaches emphasise their target points and to design activities and modify games accordingly.

In this respect, this chapter has attempted to achieve dual roles. First, to help coaches understand a more holistic view of coaching and, second, to use the indicative examples as a means to help coaches to continue to construct content that can add deeper value to their sessions.

Discussion questions

1 Adapting practices
   Based on the examples of adaptations from possession games 1 and 2 above, consider the ways in which this possession game could be adapted to increase differing holistic dimensions.
   - How could further emphasis be placed on the decision-making of players?
   - Could emotional pressure be applied by placing constraints on players?
   - Could physical demands be manipulated for teams when in and out of possession?
   - Are there any further person or task constraints that could add even further value to this possession game?

2 Using a Game Centred Approach
   Pick a selected tactical theme that you wish to develop. Construct a modified game using suitable pitch and player constraints. After playing the modified game consider questions you could ask of individual players and teams that could develop their decision-making in specific situations. For example, a centre forward in a ball retention game has multiple options of what to do with the ball but must make decisions based on a range of situational factors. Through the coach adapting situational factors (e.g. score, overload, opponent, team formation) the player is encouraged to construct different responses. No one response is 'right' in all situations. Players must make decisions based upon a range of factors, often under time and situation pressure.

References

Arkes, H.R., & Garske, J.P. (1982). *Psychological Theories of Motivation*. Monterey, CA: Brooks/Cole.

deVos. J. (2013). Day three of the UEFA "A" license. Retrieved from www.tsn.ca/

Grehaigne, J.F., Wallian, N., & Godbout, P. (2005). Tactical decision learning model and students' practices. *Physical Education & Sport Pedagogy*, *10*(3), 255–269.

Launder, A.G. (2001). *Play Practice: The Games Approach to Teaching and Coaching Sports*. Champaign, IL: Human Kinetics.

Light, R. (2004). Coaches' experiences of game sense: Opportunities and challenges. *Physical Education & Sport Pedagogy*, *9*(2), 115–131.

Mitchell, S.A., Oslin, J.L., & Griffin, L.L. (2006). *Teaching Sport Concepts and Skills: A Tactical Games Approach* (2nd edn). Champaign, IL: Human Kinetics.

8

TOUCH RUGBY

Tabitha McKenzie and Barrie Gordon

An introduction to the game of touch

Touch rugby, or touch as it is commonly known, is a six-a-side territory game played on a rectangular shaped field of 50×70 metres without goal posts. The game of touch is derived from rugby and rugby league but does not feature tackling or hard physical contact. Instead players simply touch an opposition player, who is in possession of the ball, with their hand(s). This action is called a 'touch' and the team in possession has six touches to advance the ball to the opposition's goal line. When they reach the goal line they attempt to score a 'try' or touchdown by placing the ball on the ground on or behind the line. If a team receives six touches without scoring a try, possession is given to the defensive team.

A relatively simple game, touch promotes the fundamental skills of running, passing, evasion and support play, while developing the basic principles of attack and defence. The ball may be passed to on-side players (behind the ball carrier) of the attacking team, who may in turn run or otherwise move with the ball in an attempt to gain territory and to score. No kicking is allowed. Defending players try to prevent the attacking team from gaining territory by touching a player in possession of the ball. Either defending or attacking players may initiate the touch. For readers interested in finding out more about the game, rules can be accessed at www.touchnz.co.nz and there are numerous examples of the game in action on YouTube.

Touch is played in a number of countries internationally, with Australia and New Zealand being the strongest nations. Touch is played both socially and competitively with over 400,000 players in Australia alone.

General tactics for touch

Touch is situated within the invasion or territorial game classification of the Teaching Games for Understanding (TGfU) model (Bunker & Thorpe, 1982); note, these terms are used interchangeably in the TGfU literature. Touch's simplicity makes it a useful game to develop tactical understanding and quality decision-making not only in touch, but territorial games more broadly.

Territory games involve teams invading the other team's territory and are games where scoring requires a game object to be sent into a goal (for example basketball, netball, hockey or football) or carried or passed across a line (for example rugby, rugby sevens and ultimate).

This chapter will use the conceptual model and vocabulary presented by Wilson (2002) as a framework for coaching touch. It will concentrate mainly on the four action principles of attack as identified by Wilson.

- Mobility: movement of the ball and all offensive team players to create and use space.
- Advancement: the use of forward space, the movement of players and ball towards the goal line.
- Width: the use of lateral space, the movement of players and ball towards the side line.
- Offensive depth: the movement of the ball away from the opposition goal line to generate time or space.

While the activities presented align with the attack principles, it is acknowledged that the nature of territory games means the action principles are interconnected. It is also acknowledged that in all game-like situations attack and defence occur simultaneously. For the purposes of simplicity the word "ball" will be used in this chapter as a generic term to describe the game object.

Driving forward is a fundamental tactic in touch with all teams trying to move the ball quickly to the opposition goal line using the least possible number of touches. Teams will often have specific driving patterns to be implemented in a game. While these patterns are structured, the combination of defensive pressure and unexpected opposition movements can offer opportunities to gain extra distance through quality decision-making. An on-ball attacker (the player who is carrying the ball) with the ability to identify gaps in the defence and to run through them, or to set up a supporting player to go through untouched is an asset to any team.

The challenge is to give players and teams the opportunity to develop quick thinking decision-making in game like situations. Players need to be able to evaluate quickly changing scenarios and make appropriate decisions.

In the following activities it is important to set the skill requirement at a level that allows the players to concentrate on good decision-making, without being restricted by their level of skill. This means the activities could involve a touch ball and normal passing and catching if the players have a good level of skill. Alternatively the equipment can be modified to allow ease of passing and catching. A bean bag or other easily caught ball could be substituted if required. The following activities are designed to develop decision-making and the specific skills associated with touch can be addressed in future sessions.

Activity one – mobility, width

Two teams (attack and defence) are in a marked out area. The objective is for the attacking team to successfully complete as many passes to each other without the defensive team intercepting the ball or knocking it to the ground. The ball can be passed in any direction for this activity.

- The attackers find their own space within the marked out area.
- The attacker with the ball is stationary.
- After each pass the passer must move to a new space.
- All off-ball attackers (supporting players) are encouraged to move into space so as to be available to receive a pass.

During the process of deciding where to throw the ball, the on-ball attacker should consider the position of the defenders and the off-ball attackers who can be passed to. They should also think about the position of off-ball attackers in relation to how far they can throw accurately before making the decision. Other factors to consider will be the speed of both defenders and off-ball attackers and the catching ability of the various off-ball attackers. The off-ball attackers also need to consider the position of the off-ball defenders and where they could move to receive the ball.

Modifications and extensions

- Start with half the amount of defenders to attackers (for example four attackers, two defenders), then slowly increase the amount of defenders (4 v 3, 4 v 4). The use of unbalanced teams is considered in greater detail in Chapter 13 on End Zone games.
- Start with a bean bag then use different game objects (such as a touch ball, basketball, netball, rugby ball).
- Add a timer and count how many successful passes and catches the attacking team makes in the allocated time. The count restarts if the bean bag is intercepted or knocked down.

Activity two – mobility, advancement, width

Extending on from activity one, the objective is for the attacking team to successfully get the ball across an end line without the defensive team intercepting the ball, knocking it to the ground or touching the attacking player with the ball in hand.

- Attackers and defenders start opposite each other in the playing area.
- Attacking players move from one end of the playing space to the other.
- The attacker in possession of the ball moves towards the end of the marked area (goal line).
- The ball can be passed to an off-ball attacker who is somewhere behind the on-ball attacker. No forward passes.
- Once the on-ball attacker goes over the end line (goal line) players rotate positions (including who is on attack and defence) and the new attacking team goes back the opposite way.

In addition to the considerations outlined in activity one, the off-ball attackers should also consider using the width of the playing area to draw defenders towards them to create space for the players with the ball.

The off-ball attackers should constantly monitor the position of the off-ball defenders and move to positions that require the defenders to adjust their position. It is also important that the off-ball attackers position themselves to be available to receive a pass if required.

Modifications and extensions

- Start with half the number of defenders to attackers (for example four attackers, two defenders), then slowly increase the amount of defenders (4 v 3, 4 v 4).
- Start with a bean bag then use different types of ball (such as a touch ball, basketball, volleyball, netball, rugby ball).
- Add a timer and count how many times the attacking team crosses the line in the allocated time as well as the amount of times the defence stops the attacking team from crossing the line. In this adaption, awarding two points for crossing the line and a point to the defence every time they successfully stop the attack will increase the defensive intensity.

Activity three – advancement, width, offensive depth

This activity introduces the dummy (or fake) pass. Start in a grid of 10 m by 5 m with two attackers and one defender (Figure 8.1). The objective is for the attackers to get past the defender and put the ball down over the line (this is a touch-specific skill). The defender attempts to intercept the ball, knock it to the ground or touch the attacking player with the ball in hand. The on-ball attacker chooses to draw the defender towards them and then pass the ball to the off-ball attacker or dummy the pass to the off-ball attacker and run through to the line. A dummy pass is pretending to pass the ball to an off-ball attacker. The dummy pass

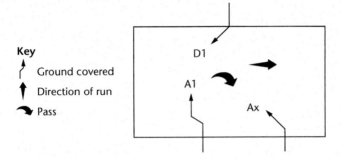

FIGURE 8.1 Grid for activity three

can be used by the on-ball attacker when wanting to keep the defender's attention on an off-ball attacker. The movement can prevent the defender from engaging the on-ball attacker, creating space for the on-ball attacker to run through.

- Attacking players begin with a ball at one end of a grid. Begin with walking only.
- One defender is in the middle of the grid.
- The on-ball attacker moves forward while the off-ball attacker provides width and depth.
- The on-ball attacker chooses to draw and pass or dummy the pass and run to the end of the grid and put the ball down over the line. No forward passes.
- Once an attacking player scores the players rotate position and the attack begins again in the reverse direction.

Players should be taught to hold the ball in two hands in front of them so the defender is aware that the player could pass at any time.

The decision whether to pass or not is made under some pressure and the player needs to take into account a variety of factors. These include the position of the defender, the defender's speed and skill level, the positioning of the off-ball defender and how much room there is available between the runner and the sideline.

The off-ball attacker should consider providing width and offensive depth to draw the defender towards them or creating distance from the defender. They could also think about having their hands ready to receive the ball, using their voice to draw the defender towards or away from them as well as the angle they run to draw the defender or prevent the defender from touching them.

Modifications and extensions

- Start with walking then move to jogging and running.
- Add a second grid directly after the first with another defender that the attackers have to move through (could also add a third grid).

- Slowly increase the amount of attackers and defenders (3 v 2) as well as the width of the grid.
- Add a timer and count how many times the attacking team crosses the line in the allocated time as well as the amount of times the defence stops the attacking team from crossing the line. In this adaption awarding two points for crossing the line and a point to the defence every time they successfully stop the attack will increase the defensive intensity.

Activity four – advancement, offensive depth

This activity extends activity three and introduces the wrap pass. Start in a grid of 10 m by 5 m with two attackers and one defender. In the wrap pass the on-ball attacker passes the ball to the off-ball attacker and then runs around that player, and receives the ball back again. The wrap pass can be used to create an overlap in most attacking plays.

- Attacking players begin with a ball at one end of a grid. Begin with walking only.
- One defender is in the middle of the grid. This defender lines up opposite the off-ball attacker.
- The off-ball attacker runs on an angle towards the on-ball attacker drawing the off-ball defender towards them.
- The on-ball attacker passes the ball to the off-ball attacker and then runs around that player and then receives the ball back.
- The player who wraps around receives the ball back and puts down over the end line (goal line).

Players should know to hold the ball in two hands so the defender is aware that the player could pass at any time. Players should also be taught to use the body, voice and ball to motion the pass (faking the pass) therefore keeping the defender guessing what is happening.

The decision to pass and wrap is made early to allow time to get around the off-ball attacker. A pass that is too late could prevent the attacker from getting around the off-ball attacker and being an option to pass to, and also give the defender time to advance closer and affect the touch. The decision whether to pass back to the attacker who is wrapping is made under some pressure and depends on a variety of factors. These include the position, speed and skill of the attacker who is wrapping, the position, speed and skill of the off-ball defender, how much room there is available between the runner and the sideline and how much distance there is between the defender and the on-ball attacker who could run through the gap themselves. The timing of both passes is important and will need practice. For example a pass that is too early could result in the defender adjusting their angle and affecting the touch on both players and a pass that is late could allow the defender to advance between both attackers and intercept the ball.

Modifications and extensions

- Start with walking then move to jogging and running.
- Add a second grid directly after the first with another defender that the attackers have to move through (could also add a third grid).
- Slowly increase the amount of attackers and defenders (3 v 2) as well as the width of the grid. Players wrapping would then need to take into consideration the extra defender and the distance and width which they can wrap before running into the off-ball defender.
- Add a timer and count how many times the attacking team gets past the defender within the allocated time as well as the amount of times the defence stops the attacking team getting past. This can be by either affecting the touch on an attacker with the ball, knocking the ball to the ground or intercepting the ball. The touch and pass rule could also be introduced which is when an on-ball attacker is touched by a defender and then proceeds to pass the ball. In a touch game a touch and pass will result in a turnover of possession. Awarding two points to the attacking team for getting past the defence and a point to the defence every time they successfully stop the attack will increase the defensive intensity.
- Add activities three and four together by allowing students to decide whether they run a dummy pass or wrap.
- Encourage the players to develop their own moves to beat the defenders.

Questioning

A focus on 'how to play' with quality questioning will support players to improve their understanding of skill development and tactics of game play (Harvey, Cope & Jones, 2016; Harvey & Light, 2015). Types of questions that teachers and coaches could use as a prompt for reflection include:

- How are you deciding …?
- How could you …?
- What is the most important thing and why …?
- If you … what might happen?
- That is just what we wanted to happen. What did you do to make it happen?

These questions are generic and could be adapted to a range of situations to generate answers and discussions.

Examples of the questions with a focus on touch could be:

- How are you deciding who to pass the game object to?
- How could you use your body to engage the off-ball defender in the draw and pass activity?
- What is the most important thing when acting as the off-ball attacker receiving the ball during the wrap pass, why is it important?

- If you change the angle you run as the off-ball attacker for the dummy pass what might happen?
- You scored easily by getting a player completely free of the defence. How did you do that?

Modifications and extensions have been provided as a guide for each of the activities outlined in this chapter. However, players could be given opportunities to share their perspective of the activities above with the teacher or coach acting as a facilitator, thus creating an environment for higher-order thinking. Players can then come up with the modifications and extensions for each of the activities. Coaches could offer various prompts to stimulate ideas, debate and discussion.

Examples include:

- How could we modify the activity to extend the tactics and skills being developed?
- What other tactics and strategies could we use to help us?
- How could this modification still be inclusive of a wide range of skills and knowledge?
- How do we feel about this modification/extension?

Players could then be asked to demonstrate the modification/extension, reflect on the activity and make changes accordingly.

Conclusion

This chapter gives coaches and teachers a number of ideas about how they can develop good decision-makers in the game of touch. While this offers a start it is important that as the players get more proficient at decision-making, and in the game itself they be given more and more opportunities to contribute to how the learning process occurs. This empowerment will help keep them engaged, encourage deeper levels of understanding and knowledge which in turn will help them reach their potential as players.

Discussion questions

As a coach, you need to know when to teach the specific skills that will allow the players to successfully enact the tactical decision-making within the game. How will you decide that they are ready to learn the skills?

You want players to make good tactical decisions within the game situation. To do this they need plenty of opportunities to practice. Even with this practice there is a strong likelihood that they will still make poor decisions within the pressure of a game. As the coach, it is important that your behaviour during and after games is congruent with what you do and say at practice. How will you respond to players making poor decisions during games? Do you need to think ahead and plan how you will respond?

Useful links

Touch New Zealand: www.touchnz.co.nz
Touch Football Australia: https://touchfootball.com.au

References

Bunker, D., & Thorpe, R. (1982). A model for the teaching of games in secondary schools. *Bulletin of Physical Education, 10*(1), 9–16.

Harvey, S., Cope, E., & Jones, R. (2016). Developing questioning in games-centered approaches. *Journal of Physical Education & Dance, 87*(3), 28–35.

Harvey, S., & Light, R. (2015). Questioning for learning in game-based approaches to teaching and coaching. *Asia-Pacific Journal of Health, Sport and Physical Education, 6*(2), 175–190.

Wilson, G.E. (2002). A framework for teaching tactical game knowledge. *Journal of Physical Education, Recreation & Dance, 73*, 20–26. 10.1080/07303084.2002.10605875.

9

ICE HOCKEY

Darren Lowe

Ice hockey is a fast-paced game that requires players to make split-second decisions. As the former Head Coach of the University of Toronto men's Varsity Blues hockey team, my philosophy is to provide an environment where players and teams can improve each and every day. I believe that this can be achieved in a setting where players are free to make decisions and try new things. The goal of my practices is to develop players in the areas of technical and tactical abilities, skill development, and conditioning. Given the nature of hockey, practices are dedicated to specific aspects of the game. For example, there are specific practices designed for breakouts, offensive attack and special teams, which include "power play" and "penalty kill".

For those readers who are not familiar with ice hockey vocabulary, a list of terms and meanings are found at the end of this chapter.

In practice, the "whole part whole" or "chaining" method is utilised to teach skills, team systems and tactics. The "whole, part, whole" method refers to a coaching approach where the coach sets up a practice where a specific skill or tactic is used. The coach then breaks the specific skill or tactic into smaller parts or chunks that are easier to learn. Then the coach puts the specific skill or tactic back together again in a game like practice. The "chaining" approach is an alternative method where the coach breaks the specific skill or tactic into a series of small parts or chunks and then works through these parts or chunks in a logical sequence from beginning to end. These practices are against live opposition, simulating game situations that require players to make split-second in-game tactical decisions.

In teaching offensive play, I use the breakout versus one, two or three forecheckers. This progresses to the addition of three backcheckers, which essentially becomes a 5 v 5 full-ice game practice. This game-centred approach requires both offensive and defensive tactical decision-making. For the offensive team, one

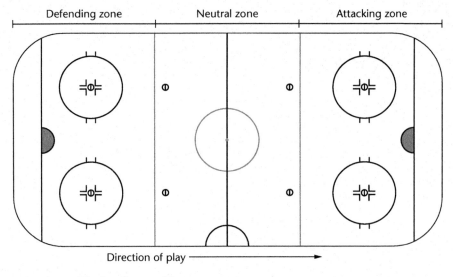

FIGURE 9.1 Hockey line markings

example of in-game tactical decision-making requires players to choose the most effective option for exiting the defensive zone and to decide what options are available when approaching the offensive zone.

In the fast-paced game of ice hockey, different offensive and defensive scenarios occur all the time. How players' process and react to so many rapidly changing situations is one of the biggest challenges that players and coaches face. In this chapter, I will examine some of these scenarios, which can change depending on the score, the time remaining in the game, the opponent's strengths and weaknesses, and his own team's strengths and weaknesses.

To fully understand my ideas, it will help those readers who are not familiar with the lines on the ice hockey rink, to refer to Figure 9.1.

The breakout

For the purpose of the rest of this chapter, the team with the puck will be called "the attacking team" and the team without the puck is "the defensive team". However, the speed of hockey, and the nature of the game, means that there are many turnovers and defence becomes offense very quickly.

Good defensive structure results in creating turnovers, which in turn allows quick transition to offense. When a team is in a good defensive position, both defencemen are back with a high forward (F3) supporting them. The remaining forwards F1 and F2 are backchecking hard through the middle of the ice. In this scenario, the attacking team may be outnumbered and forced to "dump" the puck into the defending team's zone. The defending team now has the opportunity to

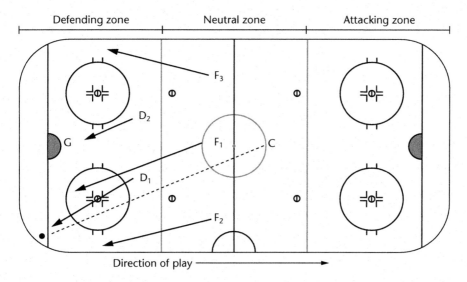

FIGURE 9.2 The breakout

retrieve the puck and transition to offence. There are several options presented to the transitioning team based on a number of factors. The puck can be handled by the goaltender or either of the two defencemen D1 and D2 to initiate most breakouts, there are several options presented below for the breakout.

Figure 9.2 shows the positioning of the six players G, D_1, D_2, F_1, F_2, F_3, and the Coach, C, to initiate a breakout. The coach dumps the puck into the corner and the five players skate to their positions to initiate one of the nine breakout options.

Option 1 – The goaltender (G) can play the puck to any of five teammates for a quick exit.

Option 2 – The goaltender can "set" the puck for one of the two defencemen D_1 and D_2 to initiate the breakout. If the goaltender cannot play or set the puck, one of the two defencemen will initiate the breakout. There are several options for the retrieving defenceman to initiate the breakout.

Option 3 – The defenceman can skate the puck out of their own zone, often referred to as "The wheel".

Option 4 – The defenceman can pass the puck to their defensive partner to initiate the breakout. The defence partner then could use any of options as well as passing back to their partner, D_1 to D_2.

Option 5 – The defenceman can make a quick up pass to any one of the three forwards, F_1, F_2 or F_3

Option 6 – The defenceman (D_1) can set the puck behind the net and wait to initiate the "set" or "controlled" breakout. Each of the four other players (D_2, F_1, F_2 and F_3) would go to predetermined positions in a set breakout and they would breakout as a group of five.

Option 7 – The defenceman can "rim" the puck behind the net around the boards to the opposite side winger.

Option 8 – The defenceman will flip the puck out of the zone and create a "foot race" in the neutral zone for the loose puck.

Option 9 – The defenceman could shoot the puck off the glass and again create a foot race in the neutral zone for the loose puck.

Note: Options 7, 8 and 9 have the least control and may result in turning over the puck.

The goaltender and the first defenceman (D_1) must quickly "read and react" to the opposition's forecheck and make a decision choosing the best option to remain in possession of the puck to initiate an offensive attack.

By practising the above options without any pressure (forecheckers) the players will become familiar with what their options are. Then by slowly taking away options (one, then two, then three forecheckers) players breaking out will read which options are taken away by the forecheckers and use one of the options that is available.

Although there are nine options listed each option may have several sub-options, hockey is a fluid game and thus teaching players decision-making is challenging.

Skills required

In order to execute the nine options, first with no pressure and then with increased pressure, players breaking out of their own zone must process and continuously hone several skills/abilities.

In practice, game-like situations for breakouts are created by the coach to challenge players to read and react quickly to a number of forecheck scenarios. Players require a variation of skating, puck handling, passing, receiving and communication skills in order to have success in breaking out of the defensive zone to create offence.

When teaching the skills required for a breakout, I use the "Whole – Part – Whole" method of skill teaching. The skills will be practised and then broken down into parts, this will allow for success in executing the necessary skills for a breakout.

At advanced levels, goaltenders must be able to skate well enough to leave their crease and play the puck. Specifically, the goaltender must be capable of setting the puck for the defence, passing on their forehand or backhand or shooting the puck out of the zone when there are no other options.

Defencemen are required to transition from backward to forward skating using elusive skating that includes pivots and turns. Defencemen must have the ability to make "tape to tape" passes. They must be in a support position for their defence partner after making a pass or when their partner is in possession of the puck, for a return pass.

Forwards must hustle to their defensive zone positions. Forwards are required to pivot while facing the puck, pass and receive. Centres (F_1) are primarily responsible for supporting the defence (D_1 and D_2) and wingers (F_2 and F_3) during breakouts. A common term used is "low and slow" implying that the Centre (F_1) is below the puck and is a quick and short option for either the defence of wingers. Wingers (F_2 and F_3) are generally closer to the boards or in the middle of the ice in the defensive zone and often have less time or space when receiving the puck on a breakout. The wingers (F_2 and F_3) because of their lack of space must be strong on the puck and quickly decide on making a direct pass, which may require a "one touch" pass or a chip out of the zone past a pinching defender to a teammate who skates on to the chipped puck. Communication is required for all players in the breakout as they often are the eyes and ears of the player processing the puck. The individual skills mentioned above must be, developed, improved and refined in the skills portion of practice.

There are a number of lead up drills for the breakout. These drills will provide players with an initial comfort level of being able to exit the defensive zone to create the offensive attack. The drills progress and create more split-second tactical decision-making. The drills increasingly take away more time and space from the players attempting to breakout, and create an offensive attack against pressure.

Note: F_1, F_2 and F_3 forwards can be interchangeable based on the first and last forward as they enter the defensive zone to initiate the breakout. The interchanging of position is more common at higher levels and is not necessarily suggested for less skilled players. With less skilled players the C (F_1) will always go to the middle of the ice and the right and left wingers (F_2 and F_3) will go to the right and left hash marks.

All five players on the attacking team will start in the neutral zone and retreat into the defensive zone to start all breakouts. Each breakout situation will be initiated by the puck being dumped in from centre ice by a coach (or opposing player). Once the attacking team breaks out of the defensive zone and are able to clear their own blueline, they will attack 5 on 0 (against no opposition) for a shot on the opposition's net in options 1–4.

The attacking team will breakout against no pressure. They will breakout using any of the nine options previously listed. These are:

- Goaltender (G) passes quickly to any teammate that is open.
- Goaltender (G) sets the puck for defenceman (D_1).
- Defenceman (D_1) carries the puck out on their own.
- Defenceman (D_1) pass to their defensive partner (D2)
- A controlled or set breakout, rim, flip and off the glass.

The coach will progress through these options with each forward line and defence pairing until all players are comfortable with the breakout options and have the ability to execute.

Note: Depending on the level of player, it may take multiple attempts to execute the breakouts. It may be necessary especially with less-skilled players to introduce only two or three of the above options at a time.

- The attacking team will breakout against one forechecker. The forechecker in this drill will be a coach can so that they can create a situation that he or she wants. By changing the area where the coach dumps the puck, the coach has taken away certain options and forces the players breaking out to choose the best option that is available to them.
- The attacking team will breakout against two forecheckers who are two forwards from another forward line (of the defending team) who are not breaking out.
- The coach can initially direct the two forecheckers to take away certain options. Eventually the forecheckers can choose to take away any options they would like.
- The attacking team will breakout against three forecheckers and follow the same practice as described in option 3.
- The attacking team will breakout against five checkers, which includes the addition of two opposing defencemen. The three forwards checking will drop out of the drill once the attacking team has exited their own zone by crossing their own blue line. The attacking team will attack five on two (two opposition defencemen) attempting to take a shot on the oppositions net.

These game-like situations can continue to progress by adding backcheckers 1, 2 and 3. The backcheckers are from the initial forechecking forwards or three new forwards. Eventually, the practice can be a continuous five-on-five game with forwards and defencemen rotating in and out. The rotation for the forwards is usually forecheck, backcheck, attack and drop out as there are three lines rotating in the game-like scenario. The coach can control the practice with their whistle, which can change the procession of the puck, or dumping a new puck in, which initiates a new breakout against new checkers. Depending on the level of the team, the practice can continue with little control by the coach.

The progression in game-like situations will depend on the level of players involved. Regardless of the level, the progressions can be made with the coach having lots of control by using their whistle to stop the play or very little use of the whistle and allowing the practice to have a continuous game-like play. These activities will present the opportunity for players to read and react to game-like situations in practice. Ultimately, through these game practice scenarios, players will be comfortable and capable of making split-second decisions in the fast-paced game of hockey.

Attacking the offensive zone

Once the attacking team has successfully exited their defensive zone, the puck carrier must read the situation. There are a number of scenarios that the puck carrier will face. If the attacking team outnumbers the defending team, which is referred to as an "odd man rush", typically a 3 on 2 or a 2 on 1, then puck procession is paramount.

3 on 2

A tactic often used in a 3 on 2 situation is that the player carries the puck in the middle of the ice to the offensive "blueline" (see Figure 9.1) and "kicks it out" wide to either winger. The player in the middle skates to the net creating a 2 on 1 against one of the two defencemen. The other winger trails the play in the "high slot" area that is above the faceoff circles in the attacking zone. This is referred to as *triangulation*; this is an offensive tactic that is used in most offensive attack situations. The other defending defenceman must decide between taking the forward driving to the net or the trailing forward in the "high slot". In either situation a forward will be open.

2 on 1

A 2 on 1 is the other common situation that often occurs where the defence is outnumbered. The key points in a 2 on 1 is for the puck carrier to always be a threat to shoot on their forehand. The second forward must drive to the net with their stick on the ice ready for a pass or rebound if there is a shot on goal. The forward carrying the puck in a 2 on 1 must continue to the net for any rebounds from their own shot or their teammate's shot.

In each of the above scenarios, the attacking team must keep their speed up, as the defending team will have backcheckers that can take away the outnumbered rush. If the attacking team has the same number of players as the defending team when approaching the attacking blue line, puck procession is still important. This can depend on the time of the game or score.

Tactics that can be used are "criss-crossing" in front of the defending players to create confusion or driving wide with the puck. The key is to remain in procession of the puck and not turning it over at the offensive blue line. A turnover at the offensive blue line can result in an outnumbered counter attack.

Even player attacks

On even player attacks, the offensive team enters the attacking zone carrying the puck wide. A number of options exist when entering the zone with even numbers.

1   Creating a 2 on 1 situation against one of the three defenders.
2   Continue to carry the puck wide and get to the offensive goal line or behind the net to set up in the attacking zone.
3   Delay by the puck carrier stopping or executing a tight turn to establish procession in the offensive zone.
4   Shoot on goal and drive to the net for a rebound.

Defending team outnumbers the attacking team

When the defending team outnumbers the attacking team, one option is to delay the play until teammates join attack, or a second option is to "dump the puck" to a place in the offensive zone to where the attacking team can establish a forecheck and regain procession of the puck. The attacking team must read and react to the situation presented to them and quickly select one of the options presented above. Drills can be built based on the initial breakout drills and manipulating how many defenders are present at the offensive blueline. Generally, the progression would be from little resistance 5 on 0 to full resistance 5 on 5 at the offensive "blueline".

The time left in the game and score will often dictate the decisions made when the attacking team is approaching the offensive "blueline". When leading in a game with limited time left on the game clock, a team would take less high-risk chances and ensure that the puck gets deep into the offensive zone. When trailing, the attacking team would take more risks on the attack. One example of a higher risk play is having a defenceman join the "rush" so it is a four-player attack. This option would increase the chance of outnumbering the opposition and thus have a greater chance of scoring. Conversely, if a goal is not scored, the possibility to be outnumbered in transition could result in a good scoring chance against the attacking team.

Conclusion

The use of chaining or the whole part whole method is crucial in teaching team play in the game of ice hockey. I use chaining and the whole part whole method to teach the skills that will allow a team to execute a breakout. I have my players practise each of the options that can be used to breakout of the defensive zone without pressure (no forecheckers). As the players demonstrate that they can execute the breakouts, forecheckers are introduced. Through repetition and practice players learn to read and react to the forechecking scenarios that they face and develop the ability to make split-second decisions.

Hockey terminology and vocabulary

Backchecking A player or players skating back to their defensive zone. They are pressuring the offensive team to regain possession of the puck to initiate a breakout or counter attack.

Chip Is a term used when the puck is shot off the boards to move the puck up ice. Chipping the puck can be used to exit the defensive zone on a breakout or to enter the offensive zone. A player can use a chip to themselves around a defender or as an indirect pass to a teammate.

Dump and chase A strategy to put the puck into the opponents' defensive zone and create a race to the loose puck in the attacking zone.

Forecheck   Applying pressure to the team that processes the puck in the offensive zone in order to stop their forward motion or create a turnover for a counter attack.

Foot race   A skating race with an opponent for a loose puck.

Hash marks   Hash marks are small lines, which are perpendicular to the edge of the face-off circles. Players cannot encroach on the hash mark areas during face-offs.

High forward   A forward who is positioned high in the offensive zone, usually above the top of the circle. The forward is in a good offensive position if the puck is turned over on the forecheck. The forward is in a good defensive position to retreat if the opposition is breaking out.

Kicking it out   When the puck is carried toward the offensive zone through the middle of the ice and is passed to either of the wingers. The puck will enter the offensive zone along the boards.

Forward line   The three forwards on the ice (centre and two wings)

Odd man rush   A situation where the offensive team outnumbers the defensive team during an offensive attack. An example is a 2-on-1 or 3-on-2.

Penalty kill   When a team is at a numerical disadvantage due to one of their players being sent to the penalty box.

Pinch   A pinch is when a defenceman tries to hold the offensive blueline by pressuring down the boards on an opposition forward who has received the puck or moved into the offensive zone from the blueline to play the puck.

Regroup   A regroup is the transition from defence to offence after recovering a turnover in the neutral zone.

Rim the puck   Shooting the puck around the boards

Rush   A rush is an offensive attack by any number of the five skaters on the offensive team when processing the puck.

Set the puck   The goalie stops the puck and places the puck in a position where the defenceman can start the breakout by either passing or skating with the puck.

Special team's power play   A numerical player advantage over the other team due to a player from the opposition being sent to the penalty box

Slot   A prime scoring position in between the circles in front of the oppositions net.

Strong side/Weak side   The strong side is the side of the ice where the puck is located. The weak side is the opposite side of the ice and there are usually fewer players on the weak side.

Tape to tape   A pass that is placed directly on to a teammates blade.

Triangulation   Three players are in the form of a triangle to create width and depth in an offensive attack. This usually creates at least three options for the puck carrier, shoot or pass to either of the two teammates.

Wheel   When a player is near their own net in the defensive zone other players will yell "wheel" which means they are clear to continue skating with the puck especially when that player has speed and there is little or no forechecking pressure.

Discussion questions

1   Can you think of additional skills/abilities that would be required to execute game-like situations?
2   How can the game-like situations used in practice be used in competitive games?
3   As a coach, how can you further develop your players' decision-making in practice?
4   How can players be more involved in creating game-like scenarios in practice?

Useful links

Lidstrom, N., & Nordstrom, G. (2019) *The Pursuit of Perfection*. Chicago, IL: Triumph Books.

Niklas Lidstrom spent 19 years playing for the Detroit Red Wings in the National Hockey League, winning four Stanley Cups, and is in the Hockey Hall of Fame. He talks about game intelligence in his book *The Pursuit of Perfection* (2019). Lidstrom talks about how he made in-game decisions by analysing on-ice situations ahead of time and then reduced the number of alternatives for him to choose from. This allowed him to make faster and better in-game decisions.

10

BASKETBALL

John Campbell

The recent adoption of FIBA rules in Canadian basketball, which reduces the number of game interventions a coach can make, has caused a significant shift in coaching philosophy and in methods of daily instruction. In addition to the number of intervention opportunities being reduced, the timing of coach interventions has been limited to dead ball situations during the game, forcing athletes to make their own tactical adjustments during live play.

This rule change is the impetus needed for coaches to begin the fundamental transition from teaching athletes "plays" to teaching athletes to play. Players must now have the autonomy on the court to make decisions in the flow of play without constant input by coaches. Athletes who can make the appropriate decisions in an open and fluid environment become more valuable, thus creating the opportunity to develop a more successful team. As the use of video in scouting and game preparation increases, it is essential that players can make innovative moves within the play to be less predictable and more effective.

Coaches must understand the challenges and benefits of coaching athletes in this manner. The athlete's ability to read scenarios and make the best decision for the team takes time to develop. Individual and team performance might initially suffer as athletes make mistakes, but this is an integral part of the athlete's learning process. As coaches we must take a leadership role in empowering athletes to be decision-makers on the floor rather than robots following instructions from the bench. It is essential to create a practice environment where mistakes are viewed as learning opportunities and are used as the basis for discovery and discussion, which form a vital part of the learning process.

In order for athletes to be taught in-game decision-making they must have mastered the requisite fundamental skills for the execution of the decision.

The number of options in any game scenario increases with the skill level of the player involved. Cues must be identified and athletes taught to recognise these cues in progressive scenarios within practice in preparation for the games.

As coaches, we must be prepared for the errors that are inevitable and necessary in the developmental process. We must create a supportive environment that not only allows for mistakes but also creates a learning process for the athlete. Athletes can discover on their own instead of relying solely on instructional learning through the coach. This philosophy is not limited to the practice environment but must also extend to game play, especially early in an athlete's development. Coaches must shift from a punitive reaction to a less than optimal decision, to one of instructional feedback both in the moment, as well as post-game during coaching and video sessions.

Teams that play with these guiding principles become very challenging opponents, as they are able to play in the moment. Each strategy employed by the opposition creates a counter response. Empowering athletes as decision-makers also increases confidence and resiliency, as the athletes understand that they control their play. Players become capable of having success in a variety of scenarios and ultimately are well suited for their next challenges within sport. The actual process of learning and playing is transferable from team to team, and in many ways, from sport to sport.

Throughout this chapter I will be using words and phrases that are common to the world of basketball. If there are some you do not understand, you can find a basketball vocabulary list at the end of the chapter.

Coaches can use progressive loading of the practice (sometimes called unbalanced games, where one team has more players than the other team) from 1–0, 1–1, 2–1, 2–2 all the way to 5 on 5 to build up decision-making practice scenarios. Progressive loading in the training environment initially limits the cues allowing athletes to easily identify the cue and the appropriate response. We can use coach-guided offensive and defensive plays to illustrate the possible reactions and cues as part of the progression to live play. As the coach progressively loads, the environment becomes more open, resulting in more feedback for the athlete to process, increasing the difficulty of decision-making. Coaches must appreciate that what is the correct decision for one player is situational and will change based on the athlete's skill set, experience and the state of the game. Athletes need to explore these scenarios in practice to gain the confidence and experience to be successful in games.

As coaches, how do we ensure that we are teaching our athletes to read the flow of play and make the appropriate decision, especially when each player is different and each situation within a game can be unique? We must empower the athletes to have both the confidence and the ability to be intelligent decision-makers in the dynamic environment of basketball game play.

Practical applications for coaches

Game-like practice – loading

As coaches we spend a great deal of time planning training sessions, asking ourselves what type of practice do we need to set up. Do we use blocked practice or variable practice during our sessions? Does this change depending on the type of skill we are teaching or the time of season? Regardless of your philosophy on the best practice to help create learning, we must decide how to progressively load game-like practices in order to create the optimal learning environment for our athletes, especially when this pertains to making good decisions in the flow of play.

Initially athletes must learn the necessary fundamental skills in order to complete the task. In offensive basketball, the ability to dribble, pass, complete lay-ups and shoot are essential at even the lowest levels of play. As these skills increase, the number of potential good decisions increases for a player in a particular game scenario. A lack of fundamental skill significantly limits the positive results in the decision-making process for athletes.

The initial phase of development involves the acquisition of fundamental skills. This will occur in an environment without defence (in an offensive scenario). The skill is practised without resistance in a progressive environment, increasing the degree of difficulty as proficiency increases. Once the basic skill is mastered at game pace, decision-making is added to the game-like practice in the form of guided defence, illustrating the cues and the corresponding responses. This is followed by live play in small-sided games (1 on 1, 2 on 2 …) limiting the cues for the athletes allowing them a more controlled environment to facilitate appropriate decisions. Game-like small-sided practices progress all the way to live play in 5 on 5 with controlled actions, open ended play and potentially overloaded situations for advanced players. Throughout the progression the focus is on making the right decision instead of being focussed solely on the result of the play.

Coaches must be willing to return to lower levels of game-like small-sided practices in order to consolidate simple fundamental skill work, reinforce good decisions and allow athletes to experience remedial learning. Feedback should be focused on the decision-making process and empowering athletes to feel confident in their ability to read the cues and make appropriate corresponding plays. If there is a breakdown in decision-making how do we aid the athlete in the error detection and correction process? Can we create a self-coaching mentality in our athletes?

Game play during training

Training situations should not be artificial in the nature of their design. Coaches need to spend time creating practices that not only mimic the environment of game situations but also create the competition and joy of game play. Athletes must be given the opportunity to develop their fundamental skills and decision-making abilities in a game-like environment, whether 1 v 1, 2 v 2 or in a true 5 on 5 scenarios. Game-like practice recreates the pace, pressure and randomness of a real game, which improves the transfer of skills from training to competition.

Coaches can implement a rule system that limits the options players will face by scripting the initial actions of a game-like practice and progress to a truly free game. A simple example is beginning a practice with a down screen, whether in a 3 on 3 small-sided game or in a 5 on 5 scenario. This forces players to begin play with the specific decision-making process involving a down screen. Players can be limited to scoring from this action or it can be simply the initiating phase of the game-like practice.

Scoring system

Once the basic fundamental skills have been developed and refined, every practice should have a competitive nature to it to encourage the development of both a competitive spirit in athletes but also to reward good decision-making. In the practice scenario, athletes and teams can be rewarded for making the appropriate decisions by receiving more points for scoring through that action. Simply stated if lay-ups and catch shots are the desired outcome of an offensive possession they are rewarded with more points than dribble jump shots. Correct reads that do not result in a scoring play can still be rewarded with partial points to reinforce the positives of making the right play. Coaches can use this scoring to accentuate "winning plays" while not punishing successful plays that were a result of inappropriate decisions. When encouraging players to make simple plays on offence, athletes can receive negative scores for turnovers or any out of bounds can be awarded to the defensive team, placing a high level of importance on ball possession. In a practice focusing on transition principles, teams can receive bonus points for scoring on a specific read in the transition, increasing the likelihood of athletes looking for that option. Coaches must be creative in using the competition and the scoring format of the drill to reinforce teaching points intended to improve team performance.

Individuality of decisions

There are numerous factors that determine what is a good decision in sport. In basketball, time and score have a significant influence on the decision-making process. What is a good decision early in a game might not be viewed the same way late in a game. Similarly, the score of a game can have an influence on the appropriate decision in a game scenario depending on the scoring gap and whether a team is leading or trailing in a game.

Perhaps more importantly, decision-making and the quality of a decision can depend on the individual skill of the players involved. A very skilled player not only has more options when it comes to decisions in a specific scenario, but they are also asked to be the decision-maker a greater percentage of the time. The best teams keep the ball in the hands of their best decision-makers a greater percentage of the time and certainly during key moments of a game. It is no surprise that the Toronto Raptors gave the ball to Kwahi Leonard in the last seconds of their 2019 National Basketball Association (NBA) Eastern Championship final play-off match against the Philadelphia 76s to shoot an unbelievable winning basket.

These scenarios must be discussed and practised in training. Players must fully understand the individual and situational differences in decision-making and also be trained in these situations. It is essential that players do not encounter novel situations in key moments of their season. A coach is responsible for preparing athletes for the pressure of big moments and to be capable of being a good decision-maker in those moments.

Tools for improving decision-making

Feedback

Athletes must be provided feedback throughout training and competition that most importantly is positive in nature and that reinforces their autonomy of play. The best feedback provides prescriptive information that not only corrects a mistake but provides instructive information regarding the next play. Coaches can also provide feedback that creates an opportunity for athlete self-discovery by asking open-ended questions that force the athlete to think about why they did what they did. Athletes can read cues incorrectly, read the cue correctly but choose the wrong response or choose an improper response based on the skill of the athlete or the situation within the game. It is essential that the athlete receives specific feedback regarding what caused the mistake and is encouraged to think of the correction. In an ideal situation we help the athlete through a process of self-reflection, which will promote better error detection and correction from the athlete themselves in the future.

If coaches are to empower athletes to make decisions on their own it is essential that they are not punished for mistakes in the process early in their learning. Athletes must feel comfortable to confidently read cues and react without the fear of lost playing time or significant physical or verbal punishment.

Video

The availability of video from both training and competition provides a tremendous opportunity for error detection and correction, especially concerning decisions. The ability to freeze video and isolate the cue, discuss and then illustrate the corresponding actions allows players and coaches to attribute poor reads to the correct factor, improving future decisions. The video allows us to determine if the players are able to recognise the cue, read it correctly and then determine the appropriate action. Each play can be read differently by different players and once again individual skill differences can be highlighted, allowing individualised and situational corrections. Video also provides the opportunity for group discussions regarding strategy and can provide the impetus for athletes to seek out opportunities to improve their basketball intelligence.

Game-like practice examples

In order to "paint a picture" of teaching decision-making basketball, I will use an offensive example to illustrate the progression involved in teaching penetration principles. Similar progressions can be applied to teaching all basketball fundamentals and team concepts. Coaches must strive to be innovative in the creation of training situations to teach and refine their key concepts.

Penetration, principles and progression

Attack the basket – players will attack the basket for a finish. The type of finish is varied depending on skill. Coaches can vary the starting point for the athlete and alter the practice to include a static start or progress to a dynamic start (off a pass). The coach can load the drill with guided defence – forcing the offence to read the appropriate finish at the rim based on the defensive response. This would progress to live 1 on 1.

Attack the basket to the kick – players will attack the basket but visualise a second defender coming to stop the drive. They will pass to the open player for a shot.

The coach can again load the practice with guided defence. This time forcing the original offensive player to determine whether to finish at the rim or if the defence stops them to pass to the open player. In scoring the practice, points can be awarded for the correct decision with bonus points given for the correct decision with a positive result. The practice would then progress to live 2 on 2. The start can be static or dynamic and the offense can be given an advantage to create the opportunity for penetration initially.

Attack the basket to the kick – players must now decide which player to kick the ball to on the penetration. As guided defence is introduced, players must read whether to finish, pass to player A or player B. As the practice progresses to live defence and ultimately 3 on 3, players are rewarded for correct decisions regardless of outcome and bonus points if the outcome is successful.

Final thoughts

Ultimately, the goal for coaches is to facilitate the transition from basketball decision-makers to athletes with true basketball intelligence. Athletes must be able to read a wide variety of situations in a dynamic environment and make the right play a high percentage of the time. As athletes continue to improve their decision-making ability, they will still make mistakes, but each mistake will provide a learning opportunity, which will ultimately lead to successful decisions in the immediate future.

Successful coaches will not only help athletes make better decisions but will have their teams play with the combination of skill and confidence that allows them to play creatively in the dynamic and open environment that is modern basketball. It is essential that we use a game-like training environment to create opportunities to empower an athlete's decision-making abilities, allowing athletes to play their best basketball under the lights of competition.

Basketball vocabulary

Loading – Changing the number of players on each side during a game-like practice. An example of this is playing three attackers versus one defender to increase the opportunities to score a basket.

Down screen – A player runs toward the baseline closest to their basketball goal to set a screen.

Transition principles – Principles of play transitioning from attack to defence. An example is delaying the team with the ball so that defensive players can reorganise.

Prescriptive feedback – Feedback that includes relevant information for the player. An example is "You need to get your hands up higher to block the shot".

Penetration – Driving or passing the ball past the defender.

Kick the ball – Pass the ball out quickly.

The rim – the metal rim of the basket.

Discussion questions

1   Can you think of any different game-like practices that will develop the decision-making abilities of your players?
2   How would you encourage a player to take chances in practice?
3   How would you encourage your players to transfer decision-making in game-like practice to a competitive game?

Useful weblinks

https://functionalbasketballcoaching.com/improve-teams-decision-making/
www.jrnba.ca/program-specs
https://basketball91.com/coaching/basketball-coaching-ideas/#.XZDVji3MwUQ

11

NETBALL

Nathalie Williams

Introduction

Netball is a fast-paced territorial game, played by teams of seven players. The game is traditionally played by women, although there are a small number of men in a select few countries who play the game. Netball is predominantly played in Commonwealth countries, and continues to grow in popularity. At present there are an estimated 20 million players playing the sport in over 80 countries.

The netball court is divided into three thirds (see Figure 11.1) and unlike other territory games, the players in netball are unable to run freely. Players are restricted as to which areas of the court they can move into depending on the position they are playing (see Table 11.1). Within each defensive third, there is a goal set on the back line within the shooting circle, similar to a basketball goal, but without a backboard. A team must pass the ball into the shooting circle for a goal attempt

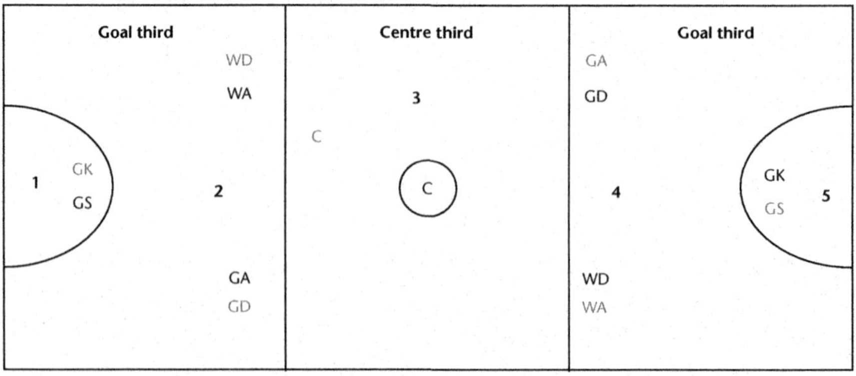

FIGURE 11.1 Netball court, player positions and responsibilities

TABLE 11.1 Netball player positions and responsibilities

Position	Zone	Responsibility
Goal Shooter (GS)	1, 2	Shoot and defend GK.
Goal Attack (GA)	1, 2, 3	Get ball into own circle, shoot and defend GD.
Wing Attack (WA)	2, 3	Get ball into own circle and defend WD.
Centre (C)	2, 3, 4	Link attacking play and defend opposing C.
Wing Defence (WD)	3, 4	Defend WA and prevent ball entering defensive circle.
Goal Defence (GD)	3, 4, 5	Defend GA and prevent a goal.
Goal Keeper (GK)	4, 5	Defend GS and prevent a goal.

to be made. Scoring can only occur if a shot is taken from within the shooting circle with only two players, the Goal Shooter (GS) and Goal Attack (GA) being allowed to shoot. This restriction on who can shoot is unusual in territorial games and places a great deal of pressure on the two shooters. For readers unfamiliar with netball there is further information on the game at the end of the chapter.

Tactical requirements in netball

In general terms, a team's ability to effectively control their attacking third of the court, will essentially determine their level of success. This chapter will explore attacking and defensive strategies based on the challenge's players face in making effective in-game decisions.

One important area of in-game decisions concerns the need to get the ball through the defence to either of the shooters, in good shooting positions. Defensive decision-making is driven by the need to ensure that this does not occur. Good in-game decision-making in and around the shooting circle is therefore vital for both attackers and defenders and for team success.

Decision-making is also impacted by a series of rules unique to the game. Players can only have possession of the ball for a maximum of three seconds at a time, and players must maintain a distance of 0.9 m when defending an opponent with the ball. Netball is a non-contact sport and re-gaining possession is therefore largely determined by effective timing to intercept passes.

Coaching philosophy

To get players thinking for themselves when under pressure, coaches need to provide a number of situational options from which to choose. This starts with deliberate, closed environment situations where they have time and no pressure from defenders, progressively leading up to game-like situations. Players need in-game intelligence where they are able to transfer decisions and skills to various contexts, leading to more consistent success.

I will focus on half court games that start with a centre pass, which in a real game, alternates between teams after each goal scored. Games are generally high scoring and therefore, the initial decision at the centre pass can make all the difference. Using the experience I have gained as a player, teacher and as a coach, I am hoping that this chapter will provide you with some ideas that you can adapt and apply to your own practice. There are no right or wrong decisions in a game; there are just more effective ones and the difficulty for coaches is getting players to make better decisions in the moment. To do this, more responsibility and freedom in training is needed, to allow for more opportunities for success. In-game intelligence comes with many hours of practice and experience, allowing players to retain the information on what works and what does not in various situations.

Coaching tactical decision-making in practice

I will now focus on a number of half-court scenarios, where you can use steps with your team to gradually increase pressure and difficulty. Players will become familiar with the various options and eventually be able to select the most appropriate one in the moment. A focus on attacking and defending decisions will be explored.

In all of the half-court scenarios, the C will be the first decision-maker and will dictate the subsequent stages. The shooters will need to be comfortable with one another and develop their communication skills, both verbal and non-verbal. The shooting circle is a small space and the more time the shooters (GS and GA) can spend with one another practising, the better they will be at predicting the other's next move.

Half-court games (see Figures 11.2 and 11.3)

The following layers are an example and can be adapted as needed depending on the level of your players and their understanding of the game.

Layer 1: For players to become familiar with each scenario (below), allow them to run through it a number of times without any pressure from defenders. This way they understand the order in which the ball must be passed in a relaxed state. You can choose at this point whether to use the three-second rule, depending on the level of your players. Even though there is an order behind each pass, the players still have freedom to create space and receive the ball wherever they feel comfortable and able to do so. It is important not to make the scenarios too rigid, as this is unrealistic when compared with the chaotic and unpredictable nature of the game.

Layer 2: At this point, players now understand the concept of the scenario(s) and you can begin to add defenders. I would make a suggestion to have players practise at least two different scenarios before adding in defenders so that they have options to choose from, otherwise they will be trying to force the one scenario they do know, and defenders will catch on to this. The shooting circle is where the ball must end up therefore, continuing to allow the shooters to have freedom without defenders may be a good option here. This means that the defensive centre and wing defence can now be brought in to increase the pressure. Remember, progressive overload here is key, not to overwhelm the players, and also to maintain confidence. To increase morale and cohesion with my teams, the attacking players used to come up with a "call" for each set play, so they can prepare in advance. This can be as simple as a number or can be more creative, for example a species of animal. Get players to stick to the plan rather than just 'looping' the ball over to the GS because at this time they are not being marked. This will help engrain the patterns of play.

Layer 3: You can now switch it so that the shooters, GA and GS, are marked by the GD and GK and the C and WA are free. The centre court players, C and WA, will now have to work harder to help the shooters get the ball. Another decision that the players must consider is the choice of pass into the circle depending on where the player is in relation to their defender, once again adding to the difficulties players face during a game.

The options are:

• A low bounce pass to either get around a player or to complete a short pass.
• A hard-fast chest pass to react quickly to an open player.
• A loopy overhead pass to get the ball over a defender.

The correct decisions; who to pass to and the type of pass, will ultimately determine success.

Layer 4: This is where the half-court game mimics a real-life game situation, as all players are marked, and a number of choices must be made for every pass. This increases the pressure, as players will now have an added distraction of every team member being marked by the opposing team who are trying to disrupt play to the shooting circle. To make it more enjoyable and realistic for the defenders, when they intercept the ball, their aim is to move the ball up past the halfway line and receive it under control to receive a "goal".

Defenders: If our focus is on maintaining possession and scoring a goal, we must also focus on the defence and what their decisions are as, in netball, possession can change very quickly. With regards to the GD and GK, their main responsibility is to keep the ball out of the net. Once again, their verbal and non-verbal communication is pivotal to their success. They must have a strategy in place and get to know how one another move. At times, man-to-man marking will work but other times will require zonal marking. As mentioned previously, the shooting circle is very small, and they must work together and trust one another to adjust depending on where the ball is. The ball moves very quickly around the edge of the circle between the C and WA and therefore, whoever is closest to the ball at the

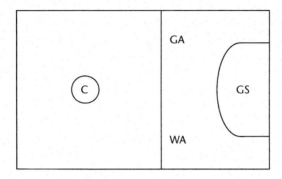

FIGURE 11.2 Half-court layout

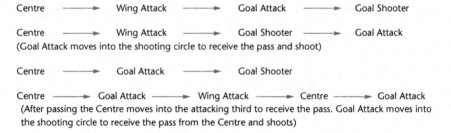

FIGURE 11.3 Half-court scenarios

time will take the lead. A clear strategy is needed here before you begin, otherwise you end up chasing the ball, making it very difficult to intercept the ball.

Netball is a fast-paced game where players have to make split-second decisions. Using the 'layer' approach players can be introduced to each scenario gradually. Choose one of the example scenarios or feel free to create your own and shape it for your athletes. An advantage of using the 'layer' approach is that you can start at any one of them, allowing it to be accessible to all abilities. When starting with a new team, keep it simple, allowing players to get comfortable and gain confidence. Once a strong foundation is built, start to add layers and more complicated scenarios, to improve their in-game decision-making. The overall objective is to keep the game flowing and make it difficult for the opposing team to intercept and figure out the play. By using this approach, I am hoping that you can discover what works for you and your team. Good luck and enjoy the process!

Discussion questions

1   If you have a group of players whose capabilities are lower or higher than the suggested scenarios, what could you do to make it easier or more challenging for them?

2   If your defenders are consistently intercepting the passes and the attackers'
     confidence is starting to drop, how could you adapt the activity?
3   Alternatively, if by the time you have got a real-life game scenario and the
     attackers are dominating play, what could you do to allow defenders a better
     chance and also to apply more pressure to the attackers?
4   Apart from the decision-making scenarios mentioned in this chapter, what
     other decisions do players face when playing netball?
5   Focus is key to making successful decisions during a game, therefore, how can
     we as coaches make scenario-based activities more engaging for players?

Useful links

https://netball.sport
https://netball.sport/game/netball-explained
www.bbc.co.uk/sport/netball

12

FOOTBALL (NFL/CFL)

John M. McCarthy and Dave Brunner

The game of American football has some distinguishing features that present teaching and learning challenges for coaches and players trying to make the best in-game decisions. Generally, football coaches must reduce the complexity and range of real-time options for players in order to facilitate the rapid recognition and adjustments to changing conditions that lead to good in-game choices. What distinguishes American football, henceforward referred to in this chapter as football, from most other sports is the unique feature of the game stopping after each play.

Indeed, the modern game of football is the only major territorial team sports in which a full stoppage of play followed by a resumption of play by all players is an integral part of the game. It is played with an ebb and flow consisting of roughly six to eight seconds of maximum effort, whereby each of 22 players (11 a side) executes a unique task, followed by 25 seconds of "rest". While intervals between active play allow players to recover, they also provide time for machinations intended to deceive and gain an advantage on the opposition. While intervals between plays allow room for more thoughtful scheming, such scheming introduces additional complexity to a very fast game. It is the combination of speed and complexity that is uniquely challenging for coaches and players charged with making optimal real-time decisions.

In the highest levels of competition, where the financial stakes are quite high, such as the National Football League (NFL) and Canadian Football League (CFL), success is often determined by relatively small marginal advantages. The quest for every legal advantage, strategic and tactical, requires enormous commitments of time and energy. For example, Nick Saban, the highly successful head coach of the University of Alabama, indicates that the optimal number of work hours per coach per week is 100. This massive effort to gather and process information involves specialised staff, coaches, and players. One of several challenges is the distillation of all of this intelligence to the point that players can not only learn what is necessary, but also reflexively and intuitively execute it at the speed that the game demands.

The play selection of the coach is based on several factors, most often characterised by the location of the ball on the field, the down, the distance to earn a first down or score, and the anticipated defensive alignment from the opponent. In essence, each coach may realign any of his 11 players in order to gain the optimal advantage. This kind of tactical manoeuvring by coaches also takes place in other sports during set plays. Unlike flow games such as soccer (corner kicks), lacrosse/ ice-hockey (face-offs), and basketball (in-bounds plays) that occasionally utilise set plays, the game of football is unique in the sense that almost every action is normally heavily influenced by the play call/scheme of the coach.

As it pertains to decision-making, the objective of this realignment is to gain a tactical advantage by creating some doubt or confusion in the defensive team, while accounting for the fact that the defensive coach is attempting to do the same to you. For the purposes of simplicity, in this chapter we will discuss decision-making from the standpoint of an offensive coach who teaches their offensive players how to make better and quicker decisions. We will examine a situation faced by ball carriers, and how a coach might prepare ball carriers, to both improve the technical and decision-making skills required in this situation. Other players that are likely to become ball carriers such as receivers, quarterbacks, and other running positions can also participate in a game-like drill that we call "Beat 'em or Split 'em" that will be explained later in the chapter.

For those unfamiliar with the sport of football, following a given play, the offensive team is allowed only 25 seconds to initiate the next play. Within those 25 seconds:

- Coaches must spot/locate the position of the ball on the field.
- In less than 10 seconds, the coach must call a play and indicate if there is a change in the personnel on the field.
- The play call must be communicated to the Quarterback (QB).
- The QB must call the play, get the team to the line of scrimmage, and initiate the next play.

Despite the time constraints on calling the right play and extraordinary efforts made by coaches to set up their teams for success in the moments before the snap of the ball, the real work of the football coach is to prepare players for successful in-game decision-making. This work centres on helping their players do the following better:

- Understand their scheme – knowing what they are supposed to do;
- Recognise the opponent's scheme – seeing the shape of the defence and anticipating what the defence plans to do;
- Make in-play adjustments – when the ball is snapped, and play is initiated the player must be able to react to what happens as the play unfolds.

There are many ways of thinking about how players learn to make decisions. The three timeframes described above are very similar at all levels of play in the sport be it at youth, high school, college, or professional. At the higher levels of play, the defensive units are sometimes able to disguise their intentions by showing a decoy defensive alignment before jumping into a different alignment at the snap of the ball. In the highest level of play in the NFL, players rapidly make adjustments to the changing defensive alignments. What separates them from players at lower levels of play is their ability to cope with the speed of play. There are two elements of this speed; the speed at which players can physically move to execute a play; and the speed at which they process cognitively to recognise, respond, and react during the milliseconds within the brief seconds of play. In the next section we will discuss three in-game time frames within which coaches teach players to make better decisions: the pre-snap, the post-snap, and the in-play-adjustment.

Pre-snap

Football plays are really a series of actions taken by players requiring just a few seconds to complete. Everything that is consequential in most plays happens in the first two to three seconds. Long runs or pass plays are usually only a few of the total number of plays throughout the game. As a result, a lot of the teaching of decision-making for offensive coaches centres on how well they can get their players to learn to read and anticipate the intentions of the defensive unit right before the play is initiated. This timeframe is referred to as the pre-snap. Except for kick-offs almost every other play is started with the snap of the ball, which normally is directly to the quarterback. Very often the defensive unit will try to disguise their defensive scheme in order to obscure a clear pre-snap read for the offensive players. At the same time, coaches can show their players there is ample opportunity for alert offensive players of every position to learn to pick up clues about the intentions of the defensive players.

Post-snap

Once the ball is snapped, everyone moves at full force to gain an advantage to dominate their opponent, position themselves to make a play, make fakes, misdirect or out-manoeuvre pursuing defenders. The post-snap is when the two teams fully show their cards and reveal the strategy they have planned.

In-play adjustments

During the post snap-instants, when the defensive play unfolds and becomes more apparent to the offensive team, there are usually one or two key decision points for a player. In these key moments, players must make in-play adjustments according to what the defence presents. These adjustments represent the response aimed to overcome the defence's technique and plan. These are the crucial moments in which players must make decisions that maximise the territory or yards gained on any play. During the unfolding chaos, even the most well-designed offensive play rarely unfolds exactly as planned. A large part of the decision-making skill depends on the players learning to make in-play-adjustments that maximise gains but also ensure the play does not go horribly wrong. Coaches with novice decision-makers, must focus on minimising the downside of negative plays, as much as promoting decisions that result in positive ones.

Observe-Orient-Decide-Act (OODA) Loop – a framework for understanding decision-making

The study of developing expertise in tactical decision-making has been applied in various domains such as the military, chess, firefighting, etc. In the military, where making sound and timely tactical decisions can be a matter of life and death, famous World War II US Air Force pilot Colonel John Boyd, developed the model of the OODA Loop to explain the elements of the decision-making process. Boyd described how making tactical decisions involves a continuous cycle in which one must continually:

- Observe the unfolding environment.
- Orient to the expected and unexpected manoeuvres of their opponent or targets.
- Decide what to do based on recognition of what is unfolding in the operating environment, and then,
- Act – execute intended tactical manoeuvre.

Boyd's OODA loop describes the decision-making process but not how one develops such decision-making expertise broadly. Below we will consider how decision-makers are developed.

Developing expertise

Coaches must understand how novice decision-makers differ from more expert decision-makers when attempting to orient themselves to solving the in-game problems they face. In the learning continuum presented in Figure 12.1, it can be seen that novice performers deal with the cognitive and physical challenges of execution, while more expert decision-makers, with less cognitive effort, tend to rely on patterns, strategies, and cues to orient themselves to respond.

Cognitive Enhancement for Performance Programme (CEPP) model

Analytical versus intuitive thinking

Figure 12.1 illustrates some of the factors for the development of expertise and the relationship to cognitive enhancement skills. Coaches prepare players to become more intuitive decision-makers who recognise key stimuli and respond appropriately. The challenge for novice performers is to advance beyond the limitations of the purely analytical decision-maker. Let's illustrate with a football passing play in which the quarterback (QB) advances the ball by throwing it to a receiver downfield. As the QB approaches the line of scrimmage to execute a play chosen based on an anticipated pattern of defensive response, he has only a few seconds to observe the field and assess the defensive alignment before the ball is snapped. Once the ball is snapped, the QB drops behind blockers to orient rapidly by scanning the field in search of an open or weakly defended receiver.

Frequently within this brief and chaotic moment, the QB might suddenly face a hard-charging opponent who has broken through the blockers, which represents a distortion of the anticipated pattern. Instantly, the QB's options reduce to throwing the ball away (guaranteeing no loss of yardage) or evading the defender to prolong the play (risking a large loss of yardage). The purely analytical decision-maker has yet to develop the expertise and intuition required for the kind of accurate post-snap pattern recognition that makes evading the defender to prolong the play a viable option. The highly skilled intuitive decision-maker not only could evade the rusher but also buy themselves time to be able to still complete a pass downfield to their receiver.

In OODA-Loop terms, observation dominates during pre-snap, while further observation and very dynamic orientation dominate during post-snap. The ability

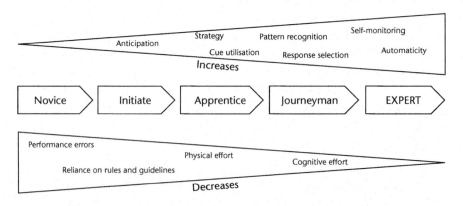

FIGURE 12.1 The expertise continuum

Source: Brunner, D., Harada, C., Ray. A., Hazelwood, D., Inbody, A., Brookhouse, E., Ko, C.

to make sense of the distorted post-snap pattern (one different than anticipated) through the fluid creation of knowledge from the use of existing knowledge/skill is what separates the expert (intuitive) decision-maker from the less accomplished (purely analytical) decision-maker.

In sport, coaches must assist novices by narrowing the possible courses of action because having too many options to choose from slows down decision-making. In tactical terms, if decision-making is too slow then the advantage will go to the opponent. As a result, coaches will often try to impart basic rules to simplify the environment and reduce the complexity of the decision-making process to create for the learner an either/or decision. That is to say, narrowing choices between two clear options.

In the following example we will take the perspective of one player, the Running Back (RB) on an outside running play. Rule: try to "beat" or run outside in a footrace to the sideline/pylon, if you cannot outrun all of them, then cut behind the first tackler and splitting between that first defender and the second one. This binary or two-way decision is based on one condition: either outrun them or cut behind the first defender. This clear rule represents an analytical approach to guiding the player to Decide and Act. If the player is an expert decision-maker, they might be able to engage in a second decision-making process. For example, could they make a second-order decision that ensues after the first decision.

John Boyd's OODA loop framework shows the difficulty for novice performers to orient and recognise patterns in a complex unfolding environment.

Situation – Intention – Execution (SIE)

- Situation – Where are we on the field, in relation to the ball, the goal, and other people?
- Intention – What is my intention? Understand that not deciding is making a decision, too!
- Execution – How do I do this?

Learning and pedagogy of enhancing decision-making

Since the journey from novice to expert decision-maker is long, the coach has to structure the practice environment for players to develop both the physical competence to perform skills while also gaining valuable experience in making decisions. Taken together, developing all these skills is particularly challenging for football coaches as each positional role requires different physical skills, as well as skills in making position-specific decisions. As one might imagine, the types of decisions pass throwers make are different than those made by blockers, ball carriers, and pass receivers. Additionally, the coach must be able to accelerate the learning of backup players who are afforded fewer in-game learning experiences.

Given these demands, we would suggest a sound teaching approach using a questioning approach designed to keep players continually engaged.

Preparing players to make decisions involves engaging players in the process of thinking and eventually trusting what they see, continually considering possible options and weighing different courses of action. Learners can profit from an interactive and questioning approach whereby coaches routinely ask players questions about what they see, prodding them to consider different situations, and encouraging them to respond. This might also involve asking all players from rookie to established players to weigh the merits of teammates' responses to coaches' questions. A second part of this coaching method emphasises the need for balancing understanding with repetition. Some football coaches prioritise getting lots of repetitions on the practice field. They value keeping a fast-paced practice above all else and address misunderstandings or confusion in after-practice meetings or video sessions.

While it is important to build player experience through repetition, we have seen too many coaches power through entire practice segments, despite the fact that players do not understand what they are doing. Instead, when new plays or defensive schemes are being introduced, it is vital that coaches plan on slowing the learning pace of the practice down to allow players to grasp new patterns and new information. To create a learning environment that takes into account the challenges that exist for learners of different levels of expertise, the coach must design the practice session with varied learning tempos progressing at slow, half-speed or full speed. For example, one method to facilitate the reading of in-play adjustments is to engage players in super slow-motion rehearsals that quickly lead to quicker recognition. Then smooth movement patterns are eventually applied at full speed. Taken together, a questioning approach, balancing understanding with repetition and varied learning tempos, and adjusting coaching methods to the level of the learner will all aid in the development of in-game decision-makers.

Training decision-making for ball carriers

The objective of the Beat 'em or Split 'em game is for the ball carrier or RB to attempt to cross the goal line by running away from the defenders (labelled as X in Figure 12.2) towards the sideline to the goal line marker (pylon). The RB receives the ball at the five-yard line, behind the line of scrimmage, in a pitch from the quarterback. The RB aims to outflank all the defenders and score. But if they cannot, they will stretch the defenders so they can cut back between the closest pursuing defender and the next defender to score. A tactical understanding a coach must get their ball carriers to appreciate is to try to gain as much yardage as possible while attempting to try to cross the goal line. The intention of the RB must be to use all of their speed to drive to the sideline while gaining as much territory as possible. The secondary intention of the ball carrier is to advance the ball as close to the goal line as possible. Two pursuing defenders are set up in a

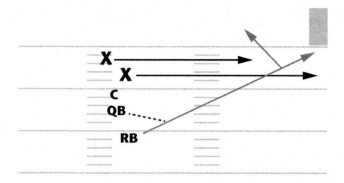

FIGURE 12.2   Beat 'em or split 'em game

staggered fashion to pursue the ball carrier and prevent the RB from crossing the goal line by tackling them. Usually the first key skill the decision the RB must make is being able to gauge whether they can outrun the first pursuing defender to the outside or to cut back. If the first defender's speed forces a cutback, the runner must try to split between the first defender and the next pursuing defender. Next, they must learn to judge when the ideal timing is to change course and to split between the two defenders. Embedded in this drill are so many other important skills such as:

- Judging the proper angles of the cut based on the speed of the defenders
- Making quick cuts
- Lowering one's centre of gravity before contact
- Ball security
- Driving your legs on contact
- Scoring

Since many players are right-handed, running this same drill to the left is a valuable way for developing the comfort and expertise to execute under pressure.

Conclusion

The Beat 'em or Split 'em game shows one example of how coaches can put players in a position to develop important technical and decision-making skills. Often coaches rely simply on trying to get players to do as many repetitions in as many situations as possible. While repetition is important, more important is that their players gain tactical understanding, which eventually leads to making better in-game decisions. To accelerate athlete learning coaches can first consider where their players are along the spectrum from analytical or intuitive in their decision-makers. Coaches can also incorporate other teaching approaches such as questioning what players see and how they would react by getting them to think about the elements of situation-intention-execution. In addition, coaches might consider slowing the pace of practice to assist players in learning to be able to recognise and absorb important cues and respond appropriately. Finally, coaches can even have players practice in slow motion to support their learning.

Football vocabulary

Quarterback (QB) – in most teams this is the offensive teams' key decision-maker, who will be tasked with making major play changes and must react to defensive changes with in-game decisions.

Running back (RB) – the ball carrier who is trying to advance the ball down the field on the ground with the aim of advancing all the way to the goal line with the aim of scoring a touchdown (six points).

Snap – In most offensive plays, action is initiated by the most central offensive player on the line of scrimmage, the player in Centre position will pass the ball through their legs to the QB, this action is called "the snap". So, the period before the snap is referred to as "pre-snap" and just afterwards as "post-snap."

Down and distance – The offensive team has possession of the ball and they must advance the ball 10 yards in four or fewer attempts or they will give up possession to the opposing team. Each of those four attempts is called a down. If successful, another new set of downs is awarded.

Discussion questions

1   What makes the coaching of novice decision-makers different from that of expert players?
2   What are some ways that coaches can assist in players in their development as better decision-makers?
3   Thinking of the Situation, Intention and Execution (SIE) approach to decision-making, what are some of the specific situations in which you need to players coach your players on?

Reference

Brunner, D., Harada, C., Ray. A., Haselwood, D., Inbody, A., Brookhouse, E., & Ko, C. (2018). *Mapping expertise progression through cognitive skills.* Unpublished white paper. Washington, DC: Science Applications International Corporation.

Useful weblink

www.viqtorysports.com/

13

STRATEGIES FOR TEACHING AND COACHING TERRITORY GAMES – "THE END ZONE GAME"

David Cooper

As a practical assignment in my third year KPE (Kinesiology and Physical Education) "The Pedagogy of Playing Games" academic course that I teach at the University of Toronto, my students are introduced to the lead-up game called "End Zone". Launder and Piltz (2013) introduced this game as an excellent learning tool for teaching GCA (Game-Centred Approach). Based on my current teaching experiences, I explore the multiple small-sided games that can be created using the "End Zone Game". Each version can be designed to bring about a different response for attackers and defenders. In this chapter, I will describe various ways this game can be adapted.

A benefit of using small-sided games is that it is very easy to play what I call "unbalanced teams". This means that one team, usually the attacking team, or the team with the ball, has more players than the defending team, or the team without the ball. Creating "unbalanced teams" such as 4 v 2 gives the team with more players a greater chance to be successful in achieving their desired outcome. It also introduces the concept of "delay" for the defending team who find themselves outnumbered. The goal of "unbalanced teams" is to create learning situations for both attacking and defending teams. It will eventually become a game with an equal number of players on each team.

The basic End Zone playing area is shown in Figure 13.1. The actual playing area is shown as a rectangular area (A, B, C, D). The length (A, G) and width (A, B) can be determined based on whatever space is available. The areas (A, B, C, D) and (E, F, G, H) are the End Zones. Team o is trying to move the ball, disc etc. into area (E, F, G, H) while team x is trying to stop them. Team X is trying to move the ball, disc etc. into area (A, B, C, D) while team O is trying to stop them.

Figure 13.1 is set up as a 5 v 5 game in a space that it is approximately 30 m by 20 m. Players are allowed to move anywhere in the space (C, D, E, F). When the

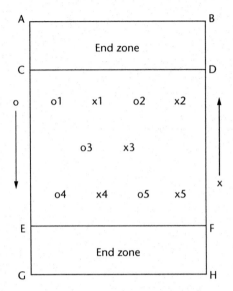

FIGURE 13.1 Basic "End Zone Game"

ball goes outside the area, the team not responsible gets to put the ball back into play. This game can be adapted for all levels of ability by increasing or decreasing the dimensions of the space. The game is usually played as a passing, possession and movement game with the objective of "scoring a goal".

Turnover rules

These rules are used for each of the four variations described below. If the ball is dropped, it is a "turnover" and the other team gains possession. The same occurs if the defending team intercepts a throw and makes a successful catch, they become the attacking team and move towards their End Zone.

The game can be played initially with or without dribbling or tackling. The game encourages deliberate practice by

- Maintaining possession by throwing and catching the ball and moving towards the goal.
- Tactical concepts such as creating space to receive the ball.
- Moving the ball into attacking areas to create a goal-scoring opportunity. The teams can be evenly balanced, such as 5 v 5 but could start at 6 v 4 (or even 8 v 2). By overloading one team it gives the "loaded" team a better chance of being successful. In a 6 v 4 game once the loaded team has scored, then two players switch to the other team so that the "4" are not always playing against "6".

All End Zones games can be adapted to use with Territory or Invasion Games such as soccer, basketball, netball, all forms of hockey (ice, field and ball), football, rugby and ultimate.

In the End Zone Game called "Catcher" (Figure 13.2), One player from both the O and X team is designated as the "Catcher" and has to remain on the line (C, D) or (E, F). The "Catcher" for team O can move along lines (C, D) and the "Catcher" for team X can move along lines (E, F). To score a goal the 'Catcher" has to catch the ball while staying on the line. By moving along the line, the "Catcher" can create scoring opportunities.

Catching the ball on the End Zone line is an excellent lead-up game for basketball, netball and ultimate. However, the same format can be used for soccer and all the forms of hockey. In soccer, the "Catcher" has to stop the ball on the line with their foot. In all forms of hockey, the "Catcher" has to control the ball with their stick.

Once the "Catcher" makes a successful catch they can be rotated back into the game and another player becomes the "Catcher". Once every member of the team has successfully caught the ball on the line, then the game is over.

A simple progression from "Catcher" is the End Zone game called "Runner Catcher" (Figure 13.3). In this variation of the End Zone Game, there is no designated "Catcher", but any player can run into the End Zone and score a goal by making a successful catch. This way of scoring resembles the way that touchdowns are scored in football and goals are scored in ultimate.

Once again, the attacker in possession of the ball cannot move and must rely on their teammates to maintain possession by moving about the field until a

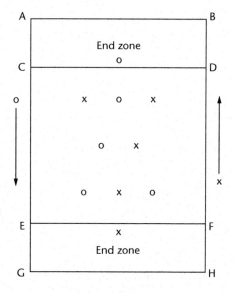

FIGURE 13.2   End Zone Game 1 – catcher

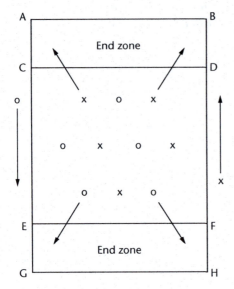

FIGURE 13.3 End Zone Game 2 – runner catcher

scoring pass is open. Other teammates must run into the End Zone, get free from a defender and find space to make a successful catch. Defenders can guard and block attackers without touching them. Defenders can intercept throws by catching a pass and then start an attack of their own. Once every member of the team has successfully caught the ball in the End Zone, then the game is over.

Another version of the End Zone Game combines the two objectives of the previous games (Figure 13.4). To score a goal an attacker must run and find space on the End Zone line (C, D) or (E, F). A goal only counts if the attacker keeping both feet on the line makes a successful catch. In the case of soccer and hockey, the ball must be controlled exactly on the line.

Again, this game encourages the attacking players to move continually and then at the correct moment run to the End Zone Line to make a successful catch. Attackers are not allowed to stand still on the line but must time their run exactly to score a goal. Often attackers running from deep positions will lose their markers and find themselves in a good scoring position. Defenders must learn to track the attackers so that the attacker does not get free to make a catch. More complex defensive strategies such as "person-to-person marking" or "zonal marking" tactics can be introduced at this point. Once every member of the team has successfully caught or controlled the ball on the End Zone line, then the game is over.

Yet another version of the game is an example of deliberate practice where both teams must place one player on the line, as shown in Figure 13.5. Either team must pass the ball to one of the players who is designated to stay on the sideline

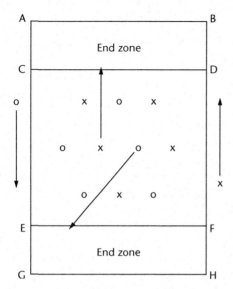

FIGURE 13.4   End Zone Game 3 – catch the ball on the line

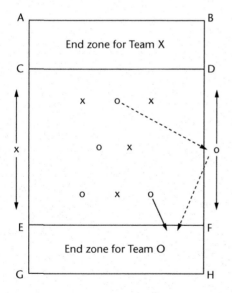

FIGURE 13.5   End Zone Game 4 – play the ball wide

(C, E) and (D, F) before the team can make an attempt to score a goal. The player on the line is free to move up and down the line to receive the pass.

This is an excellent game to introduce the concept of playing the ball wide to create open space for attacking players to run into to score. Defenders must pay close attention to the runs made by attacking players to get into the End Zone and score. This can be done by as "person-to-person marking" or "zonal marking" as was done in the previous game. Once every member of the team has success-fully caught or controlled the ball on the End Zone line, then the game is over.

End Zone Game progressions

The use of End Zone Games can progress the game from easy to difficult so that players can develop both technical and tactical skills at the same time. As such it meets the criteria of the GCA to teaching and coaching games. Many Territory-Games-like scenarios can be re-created in small-sided games in restricted space. Once coaches and players become familiar with the format of the End Zone Game, then the only thing limiting their use of this approach is their imagination.

In the four games described, beginners through to advanced players can benefit from playing these games or variations of them. The individual technical and tactical skills that can be developed through playing most or some of these games are:

- Attacking – passing (throwing), receiving (catching), ball control/moving into space, keeping possession, advancing the ball into attacking positions, seeing attacking space, running into space, timing running into space and losing your marker.
- Defending – person-to-person marking, zonal marking, delaying the attacker, tracking runners, interceptions, covering, guarding, denying attacking players' space, keeping a defensive shape and transitions from defence into attack.

The four versions described above do not include other skills that are important, such as dribbling and tackling. By imaginative use of the End Zone Game format these skills can be introduced by combining them with possession skills. Including dribbling and tackling skills and tactics might lead to more turnovers and more unstructured play, which is very similar to the real game. In this case it might be a good idea to increase the size of the End Zone playing area. An alternative to the End Zone game that many coaches use is some form of "keep ball" in a grid; however, by maintaining the End Zones it gives the attacking teams the oppor-tunity to score a goal or the defending teams to stop a goal being scored and so keep a competitive game-like environment.

Progressions

End Zone Games allow coaches to change the ratio of attackers to defenders by overloading one team. The four versions of End Zone Games that have been described are based on having ten players divided equally to make 5 v 5 small-sided games. I would suggest that this 5 v 5 format is the final version, as it most closely resembles a real game scenario. However, in the beginning, it will be easier to teach/coach both technical and tactical skills together if "unbalanced teams" play each other. These could be combinations such as 8 v 2, 7 v 3, 6 v 4, which lead up to 5 v 5.

An example of how a 8 v 2 or 7 v 3 soccer game might be used with beginners could focus on attacking by keeping possession, providing different angles for passing and moving into dangerous attacking positions. For defenders it could focus on delaying tactics, playing offside, attacking the ball and providing cover. The numerical imbalance of the teams makes it easier for the overloaded attacking team to be successful, which will please both the players and the coach.

In playing unbalanced teams, once the defending team gains possession, it will be difficult for them to play as they have fewer players than the attacking team. The coach can then decide to give the attacking team five attacks to score a goal before switching players or, once the defending team gains possession, players from the attacking team join the defending team. For example, in a 7 v 3 small-sided game, four attacking players join the defending team so that the play can move back and forth in the playing area without having to restart attacks at one end.

Modified Game Play (see Figure 13.6)

Object of the game

Focus – On technical and tactical skill development. High physical intensity. Attack against defence game play. Decision-making.

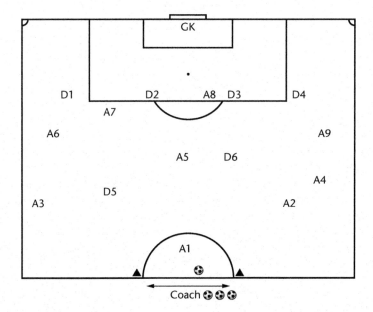

FIGURE 13.6   Attack v defence. Attentional focus shifts. Attacking and defensive principles

Structure – Played on half the pitch (goal line to halfway line). Attacking team has nine players. Defending team has seven players (six plus the GK). Two pylons are placed on the intersection of the centre circle line and the halfway line. For the defending team to "score a goal" they have to pass the ball to the coach who must control the ball on the halfway line. The coach stands on this line with numerous soccer balls. Play starts when the coach passes the ball out to the attacking team. The game is played just like a real game with throw ins, corners, goal kicks and fouls, etc. Play continues until either a goal is scored, the defending team passes the ball to the coach or the coach decides to change the point of attack and introduce a new ball.

For the attacking team – Create and score as many goal-scoring opportunities as possible. The attacking team has an overload of 9 v 6 players. They use various principles of play such as width in attack to draw defenders away from the goal, playing "give and goes" around the box, keeping meaningful possession and trying to draw defenders out of position. Pressing the defenders when losing possession. Making good offensive tactical decisions and choices.

For the defending team – Making good defensive tactical decisions and choices. Not allowing the attacking team to score despite their numerical advantage. Maintaining their defensive shape despite being outnumbered. Clearing the ball away from the danger area. Trying to keep possession safely and move the ball forward as quickly as possible to the coach situated between the pylons on the halfway line to "score a goal".

Decision-making strategies – These are so numerous it is impossible to list them all here. Certain basic principles can be continually practised and reinforced. Basic attacking situations can be set up in different parts of the half. For example, a sequence of passing and moving to create the opportunity for the wide attacker to get behind the defence and cross the ball. The following are attacking plays that can be rehearsed using this approach so that when players find themselves in the same position or situation, they know how to create the best attacking option.

Attacking team principles of play

- Width in attack
- Getting behind the defensive line
- Creating overload situations
- Maintaining meaningful possession
- Playing the ball forward when the opportunity is there
- Shooting when the opportunity presents itself
- Playing "give and goes" to pass the ball between the last line of defenders
- High pressing when losing the ball
- Broad attentional focus if the coach changes the play

Just as the attacking team can rehearse attacking opportunities as described above, so the defensive team can practice how to contain and delay the attacking team. For example, despite being outnumbered, they can organise their back defensive line to not drop any deeper than the penalty area. The two midfielders can protect the area in front of the back four, choosing when to confront the attackers and when to push them into areas that are less dangerous, i.e. away from the goal. The following are defensive plays that can be rehearsed using this approach so that when players find themselves in the same position or situation, they know how to create the best defending option.

Defending team principles of play

- Maintaining defensive shape
- Not getting drawn out of position
- Defending the important areas close to the goal
- Setting up the defensive line on the edge of the penalty area
- Not being pushed closer to the goal
- Clearing the ball deep where and when appropriate
- Keeping possession despite being outnumbered
- Trying to "score a goal" by getting the ball to the coach
- Broad attentional focus if the coach changes the play

Related to game play

Playing with goals and goalkeepers involves technical, tactical and physical abilities. The coach periodically puts a new ball into play to create a new game moment; players must focus on the new ball and ignore the previous one (this trains quick attentional shifts and quickly re-establishing a disciplined team shape under the new circumstances).

Occupying and controlling the central playing area is key to having a team that is sound defensively (difficult to penetrate) and potent in attack (having many options going forward), e.g. central midfielders and centre backs stay central; holding midfielders and centre backs stay connected; centre backs prioritise defending. The defensive concept of "ball oriented" marking can be introduced and discussed. In this model, the defence uses neither zonal nor person marking. The players must learn to orient their defensive positioning and movements in accordance with both the current location of the ball and its next likely destination or recipient.

Conclusion

I was first introduced to the concept of End Zone Games while I was training to be a physical education teacher in the 1970s (see Chapter 21 for a more detailed description). It was part of the Football Association Preliminary Coaching badge and I have used these games ever since. From teaching football and basketball as part of our high school curriculum, to coaching representative county (provincial) football teams in London, UK, to training future PE teachers and coaches at the University of Toronto, the End Zone Game has been a constant in my collection of small-sided games.

The format of the End Zone Game is so flexible that it can be adapted to a variety of Territory games and used with different levels of ability. It can be used in developing technical skills while still reproducing game-like playing scenarios a well as developing tactical awareness and decision-making. It can be progressed from its simplest form, such as described in End Zone Game 1 – The Catcher where the object of the game is to get the ball to your catcher positioned in the End Zone to a much more complicated version, as described in in End Zone Game 4 – Play the ball wide. This game introduces the principle of width in attack, which so important in the majority of Territory games.

From playing End Zone Games it is a very short step to playing half field or half court games of attack against defence where some of the principles of play practised in small-sided games can be transferred to the full field and a full game.

If you are a coach or teacher of soccer, field hockey, basketball, rugby, football, ultimate or lacrosse, I would challenge and encourage you to use End Zone Games in your coaching or teaching. Your students will enjoy the opportunity to develop their technical, tactical and decision-making skills while playing a game that closely resembles the real game.

Discussion questions

1   How does changing the game subtly change the nature of the various End Zone Games?
2   What changes to the rules are necessary for each type of Territory game played?
3   Can you think of any further progressions you could design to help players understand different tactical principles?

Useful weblinks

https://ca.video.search.yahoo.com/search/video?fr=yfp-t&p=you+tube+end+zone+games#id=1&vid=398e4fc8958019896228bdf07506c2c3&action=click

www.soccerxpert.com/printdrill.aspx?id=73

References

Almond, L. (Ed.) (2012). *Physical Education in Schools*. London: Routledge.
Launder, A.G., & Piltz, W. (2013). *Play Practice: Engaging and Developing Skilled Players from Beginners to Elite*. Champaign, IL: Human Kinetics.

Light, R. (2013). *Game Sense: Pedagogy for Performance, Participation and Enjoyment*. New York: Routledge.

Mitchell, S.A., Oslin, J.L., & Griffin, L.L. (2013). *Teaching Sport Concepts and Skills: A Tactical Games Approach for Ages 7 to 18*. Champaign, IL: Human Kinetics.

Pill, S. (Ed.) (2017). *Perspectives on Athlete-centred Coaching*. New York: Routledge.

14

VOLLEYBALL

John Barrett

This chapter will focus on the training of tactical decision-making processes, specifically developing outside hitters in the sport of volleyball. Outside hitters can attack the ball from the left side or right side of the court. The basic fundamentals of attacking the volleyball with the maximum number of options available depends on the individual development and skill level of the volleyball attacker and how often they have used different skills under the duress of competition. The decision-making processes of the outside hitter in volleyball starts with developing the basic fundamentals of the hitting range.

Experienced volleyball coaches introduce a variety of drills and practices that encourage the athlete to experiment in order to broaden their own personal hitting range. I will take you through this process, beginning with my definition of hitting range.

The gradual progression of technical skills is purposefully integrated into situation simulations and helps outside hitters develop their own "arsenal of shots". The goal of the coach, in facilitating the growth of the individual athlete, is to empower the athlete to tactically know when to employ the "which one [choice] when?" strategy within their decision-making process. I will return to this thought process later in the chapter.

I define hitting range as the height, pace, places, mode and tempo, as described in Table 14.1.

An attacker's hitting range can take years and years to develop. International volleyball players now can play well into their 30s, and they often continue to develop different aspects of their own personal hitting range. It is very common for volleyball players that have a long career, and to continue to improve their hitting range in order to remain successful. There are a number of different factors

TABLE 14.1 Hitting range in volleyball

Hitting range in volleyball can be described as mode, tempo, height, paces, places, and deception.

Mode refers to the type of attack the outside hitter uses. For example, using a high hard topspin followed by secondary shots such as off-speed placement with normal hand contact or tips using different hand and finger placement on the ball. Using power tips, which are an advanced form of attaching the ball aggressively with the wrist and fingers and which can be referred to as throwing or pushing the ball. Hitting the ball flat with a solid straight hand which simulates flat contact. This is intended to touch the block before rebounding off in a positive manner for the attacker.

Tempo refers to the timing of the outside hitter when attacking the ball. Such as on the way up, or at the maximum top point of the jump, or on the way down, or delaying the play by holding the attacking position or during the spike jump to change the options presented to the hitter.

Height refers to how high an attacker can attack the ball over the top of the net.

Paces refers to the different types of velocities the attacker can use from his personal power range such as using maximum power hard driven, or any other velocity other than 100 per cent maximum power that is used to place the ball in a location on the volleyball court.

Places refers to the number of different spots or areas on the court that the attacker is capable of placing the ball as well as the number of different contact points the hitter can contact the ball within their own personal arm swing hitting window, for example the maximum reach at the top of the arm extension and jump, or out to the side of the body to hit the ball cross court inside the block, or over the shoulder to pull the ball back across the body, down the line.

Deception Refers to how well the attacker can disguise the intended shot or choice that they have chosen from their hitting range.

involved in continuing to improve and refine the hitting range to remain successful at a certain level of play.

The physical capabilities of jumping height and hitting power are the two most common aspects a volleyball attacker encounters, and necessitate the attacker to continue to hone their own personal hitting range. The ability to continue to develop the required skills to remain at a certain level of play necessitates the layering of an attacker's game. By layering I mean the added shots and options added to an expanded hitting range, which assists in finding the right tactical solution.

Volleyball is a situational game. By this I mean the same situation presents itself over and over again in rallies. For example, a high ball set to position 4 is the most common set in the game of volleyball. This particular scenario, although repeated hundreds of times in a volleyball match, is never exactly the same. The height of the set to the attacker, the distance of the ball from the net, the attacker's timing to the ball, the defensive set up of and timing of the block, the defensive setup behind the block, are all situationally different every single time.

Even if the situation appears to be very similar, there are micro differences that make every attacking scenario different and unique. I describe this as "Every ball has its own story". The greater the hitting range of the attacker, the more likely a successful execution of a tactical decision can be made. Although quite simple in appearance, tactical decision-making in volleyball is a complex process that takes place very quickly and depends largely on the situational experience of the attacker. The ability of the attacker to recognise micro cues and to employ the best tactical decision in that particular situation is what I call "Which one when."

"Which one when" refers to which shot to use in what situation and when to use it. The greater the hitting range of the attacker, and the more often the attacker can use the information gained from their situational experience, the more likely they are to be successful. The powerful attacker that can hit the ball consistently at a very high height, and at a very hard velocity, has a much higher likelihood of a positive outcome than a player who does not have the same physical characteristics, or situational experience.

However, if the very athletic attacker who jumps high and hits hard has also developed an expanded hitting range, then it becomes much more difficult for the defending team to deal with the attacker and their options. A very athletically gifted attacker, when in possession of an expanded hitting range, and the ability to recognise and evaluate micro cues from his or her situational experience, has increased their odds of making the correct tactical decision.

I define micro cues as the culmination of "many moving parts in a developing situation with every volleyball set". The reading and deciphering of micro cues to execute the best tactical decision is the goal of the coach when developing the hitting range of the individual attacker. I call the situational experience of the attacker as "information banking". To be able to access the "banked information", to read and evaluate the micro cues, and make a good tactical decision is the ultimate goal of developing the hitting range of the athlete.

This leads us to the questions of how to develop the hitting range, and the situational experience of an attacker in volleyball. How to best assist the individual to make the best tactical decision at the most crucial time in competition? How do we teach outside attackers in volleyball to be able to recognise micro cues in situational experiences to help them make the correct tactical decision consistently?

There is no substitute for competition in improving the outside attacker. Athletes and coaches have learned not to change what has been successful. However, what happens when what has worked before, stops working? The higher that an athlete rises in their sphere of competition, the more likely it is that they will need to develop increased skill execution to continue to be successful.

This is a very common occurrence in the skill development of an outside attacker in volleyball. Exposure to failure is often the experience that is needed for the athlete to change. For an athlete to adapt and continue to develop their own personal skills, experiencing failure is often what is needed to raise their level of competitive play.

So, how do we prepare our younger volleyball players to develop an expanded hitting range when they may be having success at their current level of play? Often our coaching provides the athlete with the skills and knowledge that they require to be successful at their current level. But we know that to make the progress we need to challenge the athlete and encourage them to experiment and create to develop new options of attack. For me, this is a fundamental question that we must face and embrace.

I believe this is where coaches need to create a supportive training environment that encourages athletes to experiment, and if necessary, to fail. When trying a new skill of attacking variations, failure will absolutely be a part of the initial process. This is exactly what we are looking for. Acquisition of a new skill is always a challenge to any athlete often resulting in failure. This is part of the learning process. Too high a failure rate may cause the athlete to shut down, and not pursue the new skill acquisition while too low a failure rate may mean that the athlete is not being sufficiently challenged.

In practice, through the use of modified games and practice, we want to help the athlete access the parts of the brain where skill acquisition takes place. What this means, is the athlete needs not only to "act" but also to "think" in order to facilitate the learning of a new skill, which does not come automatically. The goal is to empower the athlete and to present the athlete with a range of drills and practice games to create a training environment that rewards experimentation and creativity.

I will outline a three-phase drill that we use to encourage athletes to experiment, create and enjoy the acquisition of new attacking variables for their hitting range. I call this practice Risk and Reward.

Phase 1: experimental phase with secondary shots

In phase 1 of the drill, the outside hitters are not allowed to hit the ball hard or use their normal variations within their hitting range. They can only use what we term secondary shots, to keep the rally going and to try to execute a good tactical decision and score a point. The coach will have profiled the athletes and know what particular shots they have within their own personal hitting range. They must function outside of this normal hitting range. What we are attempting to do here, is reinforce experimentation over outcome of performance. We are trying to add to their "information bank", or "hardwiring", of what they can execute in competition under duress. The athlete will not be able to access a new secondary shot under duress without having experienced some sort of success using this shot during training or competitive game-play practice.

I often play mini games to seven, and the attacker can only score a point, if they have employed a new secondary shot. The attacker cannot use the hard-driven ball. This creates a training environment where the ball is in the air more often than normal, and creates the opportunity to touch and experiment with the ball more often than normal.

Phase 2: power phase

In phase 2 of the drill, the attacker is only allowed to hit the ball as hard as they can, regardless of the quality of the set. This creates an opportunity for the pendulum of the drill to swing in the complete opposite direction, as well as rewarding the hitter for scoring a point with the hard-driven ball off a bad set. I call this particular skill "bad ball hitting", and it is fundamental in becoming a successful outside attacker. Aggressively attacking the volleyball is often how rallies are ended, but the shot must be done with precision and intent. The higher and harder the ball is hit off the hands of the block, the more likely the outcome of a positive tactical point being scored. However, if this is the only variable of the attack the hitter uses, eventually it will become less effective. In this particular phase of the drill, the hard-driven ball is the only option the attacker is allowed to use. Once again, mini games to seven are used, and feedback in winning or losing the game is immediate.

Phase 3: risk and reward scoring

In this phase of the game-play practice, all the shots in the hitting range of the attacker can be used. However, the coach can reward two points for a new attack variable that is tactically executed correctly by the attacker. The coach, having profiled his attackers, is the point judge on the execution of the attack variable. In playing mini games to seven, there is an opportunity to score two points with one well-executed shot. This creates the motivation to use and master a new attacking variable to add to the hitting range, while also competing to win the drill.

"Redemption Ball" or "The Redeemer"

I use many variations of this risk and reward system in practice, however, there is one that the athletes seem to particularly enjoy. I call this the "Redemption Ball" or "The Redeemer". This is how it works. Side A wins the mini game by a score of 7–3. Side B will have one ball introduced to the attacker; this ball is called the "Redeemer". If the attacker scores a point on this one attack, outside of their current hitting range, the game will be tied at 7–7. Thereafter normal risk and reward scoring, will continue, with each side having the opportunity at one

"Redemption Ball". This creates the necessity for attackers to develop new shot variables for their hitting range to compete in the mini games and perform new tactical decision-making.

Mini games played to seven are really good because they offer quick feedback on the execution. I can flip back and forth between different phases of the game play practice depending on the desired outcome.

Summary

The content of this chapter has not only been volleyball specific but also position specific. It has focused on developing the tactical decision-making process of the outside hitter (attacker). The sport of volleyball is a repeating situational game, i.e. the same game situations repeat themselves, with minor variations, over and over again. The outside hitter is faced with resolving a tactical situation, repeatedly throughout the course of a match. The outside hitter's proficiency at tactical decision-making, through the use of their own personal arsenal of shots will determine their success in positive "finishes" and ultimately in winning or losing. The layering of an individual attacker's hitting range can be increased throughout the course of their career, through specific targeted practices and mini games.

These mini-games and practices are designed to force the hitter to learn what works and does not work in different game situations and results in encouraging the player to expand their personal arsenal of shots. The expanded hitting range of an attacker will lead to more tactical options, thus enhancing the possibility of the player choosing the best tactical decision at the appropriate time.

The term "The art of which one when?" encapsulates this whole process by simply stating what is the best shot choice in this particular situation. Through repeated game practice, where failure is encouraged, we can expand the athlete's options, by enhancing their "information bank" to help them choose the most appropriate tactical solution. I believe this can be done through a fun, competitive environment where getting a player out of their comfort zone becomes rewarding. Ultimately this can lead to the athletes improving their ability to resolve different game situations with better in-game tactical decision-making.

Discussion questions

1   When should we start developing an athlete's hitting range in order to offer them more options in making the best tactical decision?
2   How do we encourage athletes to get out of their comfort zone and enhance their hitting range if they are already having repeated success at their current level of development?
3   How do we encourage an athlete to explore new technical solutions when the athlete is not seeing any positive feedback through their repeated practising of new skill development?

Weblinks

www.theartofcoachingvolleyball.com
www.bestvolleyballdrills.com
www.volleyballadvice.com

15

SOFTBALL/BASEBALL

Barrie Gordon

In the Developing Thinking Players (DTP™) coaching approach, which is discussed in Chapter 2, there is a strong emphasis on developing tactical understanding and good decision-making. These two areas are the framework from which players develop a mature sense of the game and become "thinking players". In this chapter, we look at using DTP™ with game scenarios that mimic real-life game situations, for coaching softball and baseball. For simplicity, the scenarios will be explained as if run with normal equipment and a pitched ball. Depending on the experience and skill levels of the players, however, as is explained later in this chapter, the coach can adjust this in a variety of ways.

The use of scenarios gives players an insight into the level of tactical understanding that can be required in sports and games. This complexity can be demonstrated in softball and baseball in the common situation of having a runner on third base. The decision-making for a fielder in this situation will be influenced by numerous external factors that need to be considered:

- How many outs?
- The score
- The innings
- Who are the next batters?
- How fast is the runner?
- What are the ground and environment conditions?
- Where is the ball hit?
- Was it fielded cleanly?

If the runner on third base occurred in a tied game at the bottom of the final innings, the only option for the fielding team is to try to stop the runner from scoring. What, however, is the smart play if the fielding team is up by three runs in the bottom of the final innings, there is one out and the ninth batter is on deck? How does this context alter the decisions made? What if it is the top of the final inning rather than the bottom? Does this situation result in a different decision being made?

In the same situation, what will the batting team be hoping to achieve? Where is the best place to hit the ball and how does this change with different game contexts?

In this scenario (Figure 15.1) the fielding team is faced with a situation where there is a runner on second base, there is one out at the top of the sixth (of seven) innings, and they hold a one-run lead.

The runner is in scoring position on two and the batting team has a chance a chance to tie the game. With one out the batting team must balance the advancing of the runner with the risk of a second out. The same tension occurs for the fielding team. Is it better to hold the runner at two, without getting an out, or get the second out and have a runner on three? What importance should be placed on having a potential force play at first, second and third if the play ends with runners on first and second with one out?

In a coaching session, the scenario is set up on the diamond, as described, and then it is played out by the teams. The players are all aware of the score, the innings and the number of outs. As explained in Chapter 2, the way that it is played will

	Score			
Outs	Fielding 4	Innings	Runner	Scenario
1	Batting 3	Top of six	Two	**1**

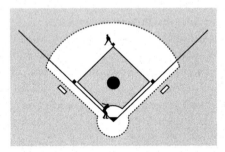

Batting Team	Scoring		Fielding Team	Scoring
Score the runner from second Batter is safe (1 out)	3 points (Best scenario)		Keep the runner at second Batter is out (2 outs)	3 points (Best scenario)
Runner is safe at 3 Batter is safe (1 out)	2 points		Keep the runner at second Batter is safe (1 out)	2 points
Runner is safe at 3 Batter is out (2 outs)	1 point		Runner is safe at 3 Batter is out (2 outs)	1 point

FIGURE 15.1 Softball scenario 1

Source: Reproduced with permission from: *Developing Thinking Players. Baseball/Softball Edition* (Gordon, 2015).

depend on the skill levels of the players. At all times, the intention is to set the skill required at a level that allows players to concentrate on tactics and to physically enact their decisions. If the players are highly skilled, the coach may decide to play the scenario as in a normal game, with a pitcher pitching a regulation ball to a batter and fielders using gloves. With less skilled players, the coach may decide that it is best to have the batting team bat off a tee, with a softer ball, to a fielding team not using gloves. With introductory level players, the size of the diamond may be reduced, and the "batter" may be asked to throw a softer ball to the fielders. While modifications like these may seem to limit the development of sport-specific skills, it should be remembered that the focus in these activities is on developing tactical understanding and decision-making not these skills. Skill development will be discussed later in this chapter.

There are a variety of outcomes that can result from playing out this scenario. Depending on the outcome, after the play has run its course, the batting and fielding teams are awarded three, two, one or zero points. In scenario 1, if a run is scored and there remains only one out, the batting team receives three points and the fielding team zero. If, however, the play ended with two outs and the runner is still on second base then the fielding team would receive three points and the batting team zero (see Figure 15.1).

There are different ways in which the scenarios can be enacted but a common one is to have the two teams competing to be the first to reach a predetermined number of points. The fielding team can either remain fielding while the scenario is repeated several times, or the fielding and batting teams can alternate. Infield only games are also a useful option, any ball hit through the infield is a two-base hit and if a ball is hit into the outfield the batter is out.

The scenario-based activities place the players in situations which have the potential to develop their tactical knowledge and to give them experience in tactical decision-making. To achieve this potential, it is crucial that both the fielding and batting teams are given adequate time to discuss the best ways for them to maximise their points, while minimising the points awarded to the opposition. Encouraging tactical thinking by the batting team is important, because decision-making by the batting team can sometimes be reduced to a level of "hit the ball or bunt". In the scenarios, especially where the batters are batting off a tee and have full control over where they place the ball, decision-making can become far more sophisticated. Every time a ball is put into play, there should be consideration given to where it should be placed and why.

Team discussions should occur after each play is completed, the coach should listen but not interfere unless the players are not engaged at a suitable level or they ask for comment. If the coach contributes it should be in the form of open questions rather than supplying answers.

• What are the advantages and disadvantages of holding the runner rather than trying for the out?

- You have decided that it is better to get an out and let a run score, what is the thinking behind that decision?
- Given the context you know what the fielding team will want to do. Where is the best place to hit the ball to reduce the chance they can do so?

Skill development

Coaches have traditionally taught skills in isolation first and then provided opportunities for players to practice these skills in small or full game contexts (Bunker & Thorpe, 1982). A number of games-centred approaches have challenged this, asking the fundamental question. Why should we teach players skills before they understand where and how they would use them in a game?

The scenario-based activities place the players in situations whereby they gain a sense of the game's tactics and gain experience in making tactical decisions. It is during this process that they also learn what skills are needed to implement these decisions in practice and whether they have those skills. If they lack the necessary skills, then their failure to be successful in a 'real sense' is a powerful motivator to learn and practice them. When players can clearly see the reasons for a specific skill (and that not having it has real consequences), they become highly motivated to improve.

A player in the shortstop position, in scenario 1, knows that they should field the ball cleanly, hold the runner at second base and then throw accurately to first base to get the batter out to score the maximum three points. If they field and/or throw poorly and the runner advanced and the batter is safe, then they clearly understand that in future they will have to develop a skill set that allows them to field cleanly and throw accurately. As a coach, you may identify that the problem is the player's body position during the fielding phase. You now have a specific context to frame your feedback and teaching of this skill along with a player who is highly motivated to learn.

Coaches developing their own scenarios

To generate deeper levels of understanding from players, coaches can use the 30 scenarios presented in the *Developing Thinking Players: Baseball/Softball Edition* (2015) or develop their own scenarios using a similar template. The coach can set up a scenario and then ask the players to identify and prioritise the three best outcomes for both the fielding and the batting team. Players can be asked to do this individually and then to discuss their rankings in groups of three or four with the requirement that the group reaches a consensus. I have found that this process has been very successful in generating in-depth discussion and engagement from the players. As a coach, you should remain open to alternative ideas and conclusions and not squash their ideas and enthusiasm by telling them what is right or wrong. In this case, it is the process of thinking and discussing that is important rather than any specific outcome.

Conclusion

During game play, a player's decision-making is influenced by many factors. The number of different combinations of these factors that can occur is astronomical, and it is therefore vital that players learn to analyse situations as they arise and develop the ability to make good decisions based on the situations they face. The DTP™ scenario-based approach gives players this opportunity, as they get to decide what they want and then try to achieve the outcome in real-life situations. After the action has finished, they get a chance to think about what happened, what was effective and what was not. It is this process that generates a feel for the game and deeper learning. The depth of understanding that players develop will be influenced by the degree to which they are engaged with the learning process. In simple terms, if the coach tells players what to do, they will learn at a surface level to react in certain ways. This may not serve them well when the pressure goes on in a game, or a new situation arises that they have not been prepared for. If, however, players are encouraged to engage in thinking and contemplating this will lead to them being better able to think through problems and having a greater understanding of the game. These attributes will make them be better equipped to handle real game situations in the future.

This chapter considers a scenario-based approach for developing players who are tactically aware and who can make good decisions under pressure in game situations. While the context here is baseball and softball, the principle of using scenarios, with points awarded for various outcomes, can be implemented with a range of sports and games. Crucial to this approach is encouraging players to engage in the process cognitively, to have them actively engaged in analysing the changing situations and empower them to offer their thoughts and opinions. Facilitating this to happen offers coaches the opportunity to develop players who are knowledgeable, good decision-makers under pressure and who have a good 'feel' for the game.

Questions

1   In this chapter, three alternative outcomes ranked by priority are listed for both the batting and the fielding team. Would one or two outcomes work as well?
2   In what other sports would this approach to developing tactical decision-making work?
3   How useful would it be to get the players to design the scenarios?

References

Bunker, D., & Thorpe, R. (1982). A model for the teaching of games in secondary schools. *Bulletin of Physical Education, 10*(1), 9–16.

Gordon, B. (2015). *Developing Thinking Players: Baseball/Softball Edition*. Wellington, New Zealand: ETNZ Ltd.

16
CRICKET

David Cooper

This chapter will focus on the decision-making that all cricketers are called upon to make at different times as they develop as cricketers. While a cricketer may be considered primarily as a batter, a bowler, or both, all players also have to be fielders. The skills of batting, bowling or fielding are performed at various times in the game and decision-making related to each skill set often determines if the performance of those skills is effective. Basically, each skill set has their own particular decision-making mechanism.

For example, if we consider just the skill and performance of batting, then batting can be broken into two processes:

The first process is based on the preparation that each batter makes prior to facing a delivery. This might include:

- Self-knowledge and understanding of his strengths and weaknesses.
- Knowledge of the skills of the opposition's bowlers and fielders.
- The state and situation of the game.
- The overall batting strategy of the team.

The second process is related to what the batter does when the bowler releases the ball. This includes:

- Seeing the ball.
- Processing the information that the batter gains from seeing the ball.
- Decision-making about what shot to play. Either playing an attacking shot, playing a defensive shot or leaving the ball.
- Executing the decision and either attempting to hit the ball or leave it alone.

Depending on the type of the bowler, the batter has a limited amount of time to do all these things.

An alternative to the above process is pre-determining the shot before the bowler releases the ball.

Similar decision-making processes can take place for both the bowler and fielder. Rather than focus solely on the decision-making processes that face the batter, bowler and fielder at the actual moment when the play happens, this chapter will focus on how the coach can help a cricketer make better in-game decisions. This will include actual practice plans and suggestions. These are designed so that the coach can help batters, bowlers, and fielders face game-like decision-making situations.

As in the previous chapter on softball and baseball, every ball or pitch can be seen as an *event* that has a beginning and an end. The outcome can depend on many factors and can influence the game positively or negatively for either batting or fielding teams. For example, in cricket, it only takes one ball to change the game if the bowler dismisses a batsman or the batsman hits the ball for a six.

For the purposes of this chapter, I will focus on two decision-making scenarios as they relate to all of the forms of cricket, which include limited over cricket (20 and 50 over matches) and longer form cricket matches (three, four or five day Test matches. A description of the practice facilities that are available to most cricket coaches and how best to use them is included at the end of the chapter.

First decision-making scenario – related to bowling

The first decision-making scenario was highlighted in an international test match between Sri Lanka and England in 2018. It involves the bowling of a no ball by the bowler overstepping the popping crease. The popping crease is the line on which the bowler must have part of their front foot on or behind when delivering the ball (see Figure 16.1).

The Creases

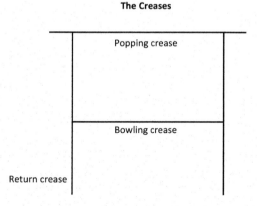

FIGURE 16.1   Cricket crease terminology

The scenario, which prompted this discussion and explanation, happened in the third international match between Sri Lanka and England in Sri Lanka in November 2018. England were batting in their second innings needing to make a good score to give them a lead over Sri Lanka, who were last to bat. England was struggling at 32–4 with just over a 100 run lead. Ben Stokes and Jos Buttler were fighting hard to increase their lead, facing good quality spin bowling on a turning pitch. During this important partnership, the young Sri Lankan bowler Sandakan dismissed Stokes twice, only for Stokes to be recalled on both occasions because Sandakan had bowled a no ball for overstepping the popping crease on each occasion that he had got Stokes out.

It was the use of technology by the umpire that showed that Sandakan had overstepped the front foot crease line, known officially as the popping crease, each time by nothing more than a centimetre. Watching the video of Sandakan bowling showed that he was very close to overstepping the front foot crease line and occasionally bowled no balls that the umpires did not spot. The use of technology is only used in determining the legality of a dismissal and not to determine if a no ball has been bowled in regular play. The outcome of Stokes twice escaping from being given *out* meant that he scored an extra 42 very valuable runs and combined with Buttler in scoring 90 runs. This partnership extended England's lead to almost 200 runs and eventually was a deciding factor in England winning the 3rd Test and creating history with a three test clean sweep against Sri Lanka in Sri Lanka. A more detailed explanation of what law Sandakan violated and its consequences are discussed at the end of the chapter.

This passage of play highlights, and is a very clear example of, poor decision-making by Sandakan (the Sri Lankan young bowler). How could a cricket coach use this scenario to help bowlers, young and old, recreational and professional, not make the same mistake as Sandakan? There are a few questions I would like to ask Sandakan to see what his thought process was during this passage of play and what was his decision-making process as he ran up to bowl in the match.

These are:

- Did you know that your front foot was very close to overstepping front foot crease line (popping crease)?
- Did you know that on many occasions you bowled a front foot no ball? If his answer was "Yes", I would ask him "Why did you not pull your foot back a few centimetres to ensure this did not happen?" It is this dialogue between the player and coach that will help get to the root of the problem and hopefully find an answer.
- What was your thought process after the first time you got Stokes out, only to find that you had bowled a no ball?
- Having been called for a no ball the first time Stokes was given out, but then recalled, why did you not pull your front foot back a few centimetres to make sure you did not bowl another no ball.

Whatever his thought processes were, it did not change Sandakan's approach to bowling. Every time a bowler runs up and delivers a ball, he or she is making a decision or several decisions about what type of delivery to bowl. Usually these decisions relate to the type of delivery – grip of the ball, direction of the ball and speed of the ball and have to be processed before letting go of the ball. Also, the bowler is watching the batter for as long as possible.

There are many decisions that the bowler makes every time they bowl a ball. Not having to worry about where their feet are going to be placed helps the bowler to focus on these decisions. The exception happens when the bowler makes a decision to change the position of their feet in the delivery stride to alter their angle of delivery to create a new problem for the batter.

Sandakan is a spin bowler who only takes a few steps before getting into his delivery action and traditionally spin bowlers of all abilities rarely ever bowl a no ball. If Sandakan had been a medium or fast bowler running 20 metres to deliver the ball, there is always the possibility that such a bowler might bowl a no ball. This may happen due to tiredness or if a bowler is trying to bowl a fast, short pitched ball and lengthens his delivery stride to achieve this. However, I have yet to hear an acceptable reason from any bowler why they regularly need to get so close to the popping crease.

As a coach, or bowling coach of Sandakan, what intervention could the coach make to ensure that a young bowler did not make the same mistakes Sandakan did? I would suggest there are positive ways that all bowlers can be coached technically not to bowl no balls as well helping the bowler make better in-game tactical decisions. The bowling of a no ball can have a significant outcome in all forms of cricket. Where this is applicable, I will comment as to the significance of bowling a no ball. However, as a coach or bowling coach, I would make it one of my seasonal goals, to reduce the number of no balls my bowlers bowl throughout the cricket season. In my opinion this is an achievable goal and would reduce the number of no ball extras (or free hits in 50 or 20-over games) that my team gives away.

Decision-making suggestions

The first suggestion will involve both the bowler(s) and the coach. In pre-season training, the coach should explain the rationale for reducing the number of no balls in all forms of the game. The coach should not assume that the bowlers are already aware of penalties that can be awarded by the umpire for the bowling of a no ball. An explanation of the penalties for bowing a no ball can be found at the end of the chapter.

So it makes sense for the coach to try to reduce the number of no balls the team bowls. It would be unreasonable to expect to eradicate every no ball but it is possible to reduce the number bowled if the bowler and coach work together.

Technical intervention by the coach

The organization of meaningful net game play

Net practice is the most used form of bowling and batting practice. It has been used for as long as teams have had practice facilities. Traditionally it has been a place for practising and honing the technical skills of batting and bowling. With creative thinking, as described below, a cricket coach could develop net practice to extend to *net games*, *net scenarios* and *net play* which would bring other cognitive dimensions to the practice.

Many bowlers may not like bowling in the nets, as they believe it is more of a batting than bowling practice. Often they will run in at less than full pace and usually deliver the ball from somewhere near the popping crease (often overstepping the popping crease) without any comment from the coach.

This is the first challenge that the coach has to overcome. The coach must instil in his bowlers that this practice is important for both batters and bowlers and should be taken seriously. This would include using a full run up when and where possible and being mindful of *not* overstepping the popping crease and bowling a no ball. Coaching practice has accepted the mantra of *Practice like you Play* and *Perfect Practice makes Perfect*. Having convinced the bowlers of this approach, then where the bowlers are putting their front foot has to be monitored in the same way that an umpire does in the game. An assistant coach or a bowler who is waiting to bowl or even an umpire who wants to practise could undertake this task. If the bowler oversteps the popping crease, then a call of no ball should be heard.

One way that I used to adapt *net practice* to *net play* was to try to create a more holistic and realistic in-game situation. Instead of having the traditional one batter in the net, I would add in a second batter. Two batters have the objective of scoring 50 runs in 10 overs (60 balls.) This is different from traditional net practice where there is only one batter who receives every delivery. In this adaptation, batters have to actually run the number of runs called by the umpire. The coach and bowler set an imaginary field. The umpire determines if any runs are scored from the delivery and shouts loudly how many and the batters run. This gives the batters a more meaningful batting practice. To maintain the in-game situation, instead of having several bowlers bowling after each other, I would just use one bowler.

The bowler has to bowl six balls plus any extra deliveries for wides and no balls, which is what the bowler has to do in a game, and then becomes the resting bowler. The other resting bowler now bowls his or her over (six balls). The bowlers alternate like they would in a game, bowling five overs each. If the batter is given out by the umpire, that batter remains in the net but does not bat, but runs with the second batter until the 50 runs are scored, the 10 overs are completed or the second batter is out. This type of practice involves four players so with a maximum of five nets, 20 players could be involved in meaningful practice. This would include both bowlers and batters making in-game tactical decisions, which can be transferred into the real game. This type of *net game practice* would also increase the fitness of both batters and bowlers.

Having set this structure up, the focus returns to the bowlers who are trying to develop a real run up and legal delivery. As in many skill-learning situations, repetitive practice is one way to groove the technique of the run up and delivery into the muscle memory. Once the bowler believes he or she has found a rhythmical run up and delivery action without overstepping or even getting so close to overstepping, then this needs to be analysed using video. Traditionally, the length of the run up was determined (and still is in non-professional club cricket) by the bowler pacing out their run up and then using a marker to show the starting position. Now bowlers are seen before the start of a game with a long tape measure carefully measuring out their run up and then using some lime based marking (similar to that used to mark the batting crease) to show their starting place. The effectiveness of measuring out run ups is debatable as bowlers sometimes only use this as a reference point and often subtly change their approach depending on the state of the game or what type of delivery they intend to bowl.

Once this pattern of practice has been established, individual bowlers can be videoed to check their run up, delivery stride and delivery action. Bowlers who continue to bowl no balls could find themselves doing extra bowling practice until they learn to make better in-game practice decisions to not overstep the popping crease. This extra practice needs to closely monitored with young age-group cricketers where there are restrictions placed on the game and practice bowling quotas.

Bowlers with short run ups, like Sandakan, would practice with the same adaptations. I would encourage Sandakan to bring his front foot back so that the front foot clearly cuts the popping crease and there is no danger of bowling wasteful no balls. However, if Sandakan were to bowl a no ball, I hope he would have developed the decision-making process to realise that he must bring his front foot back until some part of his front foot is behind the popping crease.

Second decision-making scenario – related to batting

This decision-making scenario focuses on the batter whose batting partner has just been dismissed and is now joined by the next batter. This situation occurs every time the batting team loses a wicket in every version of the game. The new batter is faced with the challenge of quickly becoming ready to play, which is often complicated by the state of the game. In longer versions of the game and even 50 over games, the new batter can usually take their time and build their innings without taking any risks, but often in a 20/20 game, the batter has to start scoring runs immediately.

The new batter has little or no time to play themselves in and is immediately faced with keeping the score moving. The established batter is now faced with making one of two choices as to how to carry on batting. Does the established batter continue to play aggressively and risk losing a second wicket? Does this batter play conservatively until the new batter is feeling more confident? Again, an appreciation of the state of the game will influence the thought processes of the established batter and determine their batting strategy.

Working with the coach in game-like practice, the established batter must decide what approach he or she should make in shot selection. The fielding side would be delighted to get another out almost immediately, as this would change the game situation. So the coach could ask their players to follow the batting game plan below and make good in-game decisions.

- Set a team goal of *not* losing two wickets quickly.
- The established batter must not make rash or risky batting decisions that would increase the chances of getting out but *must* continue to keep the strike to keep the score moving until at least 10 runs (coach could ask for more) are added to the score.
- The incoming batter must rotate the strike and make every effort to give as much of the bowling to the established batter.
- Keeping the score moving by safely hitting the ball into spaces and then running singles or more is the best way to achieve this. The fielding team will be making every effort to stop this from happening in the hope of creating pressure on the batters so that they play a risky shot or make a poor decision. If both batters follow these decision-making processes, then the likelihood of losing another wicket can be minimised. However, coaches who wish to develop decision-making batting techniques should suggest a variety of ways to rotate the strike but rely on each batter's strengths to choose the most effective method.

In a meaningful game-like practice, it would be very possible to practise these decision-making scenarios for batters, bowlers, and fielders.

This also applies to all types of cricket, from international Test matches to junior club matches. Often it is said by cricket commentators and watchers "The score is 100 for 0 but it would very quickly change if it became 100 for 2". The losing of two quick wickets in all forms of the game changes the game position considerably.

It is apparent from observing England play international 50-over matches in the 2019 Cricket World Cup that it is the job of Joe Root, coming into bat after either Jason Roy and Jonny Bairstow being out, to bat conservatively and give the strike to the established batter. He does this by effectively rotating the strike by placing the ball into gaps in the field and running a single to get off strike.

A new partnership is built, maintaining the tempo of the innings without losing a second wicket.

Game-play training suggestion

Organisation

For the purposes of this practice, the coach tries to recreate the playing conditions that are found in a 20/20 match. But it could also be used in longer form matches depending on how much practice time the coach has. Between 15 or 16 players is the minimum number to make this practice work.

The first batting team are numbered batters 1, 2, 3, etc. to 11. However only batters 1 to 4 are padded up ready to bat. The other 11 fielders take their places and bowling line up as if for a real game. In this way all 15 players are actively involved. The coach will act as umpire and scorer. The batting team tries to score as many runs as they can off 20 six ball overs. The bowlers rotate as they would in a real match only being allowed four overs each. The fielding team has a designated captain to make the bowling and fielding changes just as they would in a game.

Batters, bowlers, and fielders play as they would in a real 20/20 game. The coach could set them a target of scoring 180 runs off 20 overs. Once a batter is out, the next batter comes in and continues to play. The "out" batter switches with one of the fielders, who then becomes batter 5. The "out" batter joins the fielding team. This continues for 20 overs or until 10 batters are out. One artificial rule that might be included is that when a batter reaches 30 runs, they are retired, to allow other batters the chance to bat. The score is recorded and now becomes the target for the second batting team. The second batting team now includes the four players who did not bat in the first innings. The second batting team attempts to score more runs that the first batting team and win the match.

Playing conditions used for 20/20 include cut-off times before which teams must bowl their 20 overs. It would make sense to include this playing condition to replicate real 20/20 conditions as well as keep the practice moving. If organised well this practice could be completed in three hours.

By re-creating game-like 20/20 playing conditions, the coach is able to see up close, as the umpire, how each player is performing in game-like scenarios. The coach is able to focus on many different game-like situations at the same time. For example, working with the batters to take quick singles to rotate the strike and keep the score moving in the early overs. Or, with the bowlers, bowling to a plan that they have discussed, such as focusing their deliveries either outside off stump, on the stumps or specifically on the leg stump with fielders spread according to the bowling plan. Also with the fielders, trying to stop the batters taking quick singles. A well-organised coach may decide to hold several such practice sessions where specific decision-making situations are discussed and practised.

The ability of the cricket coach to create meaningful practices is key for players to develop their in-game tactical (and technical) decision-making. For far too long cricket net practice has been a place where bowling and batting technical skills are honed but rarely do they require the players to think beyond the technical. By re-creating game-like scenarios in practice, the thinking coach can develop in-game cricket thinking players.

Cricket terminology

Practice sites

The traditional site for both indoor winter and outdoor summer practice is in a facility that cricketers know as the "nets", which are very similar to the batting cages that are used in baseball and softball. The way in which batting and bowling practice goes on in nets has very slowly evolved over the past 100 years. If the club, where the practice takes place, has a sympathetic and understanding groundsman or curator, the nets might be placed on the edge of the square (which is where match wicket is prepared). Failing that, the groundsman or curator may have time and space to create a net practice area in the outfield or in a location close to the ground. However, this practice area will need considerable time and effort to create a good net practice surface.

Practice in the middle

As an alternative to net practice, practice can take place in the middle, especially if there is an artificial practice pitch on the edge. In this practice scenario, a more game-like practice can take place with bowlers, batters, and fielders.

No ball – explanation

At this point it should be clear to the player, umpire and coach as to what the Laws of Cricket say about the bowling of a no ball. In all the different forms of cricket, the bowling of a no ball is a bowling error and against the Laws of the Game. The most common way that a no ball occurs is when the bowler places his or her foot (or feet) outside the designated crease lines as stated in the Laws of the Game (Figure 16.1).

Law 21.5.2 Fair Delivery covers the bowling of what has become known as a "front foot no ball". The actual wording is "the bowler's front foot must land with some part of the foot, whether grounded or raised on or behind the popping crease." If the bowler goes over the popping crease, then the umpire should call no ball. (Taken from *The Laws of Cricket 2017 Code* (2nd Edition, 2019.)

However, it has become a current trend in cricket for umpires to miss this type of no ball and in international cricket, it is left to the off-field third umpire, with the use of frame by frame video playback technology, to check the legality of a delivery. This does not happen with every ball that is bowled but only after a batter has been dismissed. The third umpire then checks to ensure that the delivery is not a no ball. If the video playback inspection shows that the bowler has bowled a no ball, the umpire informs the on field umpire and the batter is given "not out" and continues their innings.

A no ball is an illegal delivery and it means that the batter cannot be out from that delivery except by being run out. It is up to the umpire at the bowler's end to see where the bowler places their foot or feet in relation to the popping crease and then shouts, "no ball" and extends their arm sideways. This is to let the players, scorers, and spectators know that the bowler has bowled a no ball. Figure 16.1 shows the crease lines of what is called in cricket terms as the "popping crease".

No ball – penalties and consequences

Depending on the length of the game, these penalties are as follows.

Professional cricket (including internationals)

The long form of the game, mostly three- or four-day county, state or regional matches, as well as most one-day non-professional club games. International matches between countries are called Test matches, which can last up to five days.

• Penalty – one extra run to the batting team. The batter cannot be out except by being run out. The batter scores all the runs hit off that no ball. So if the batter hits the no ball for a four, the batting team score a total of five runs. The bowler still has to bowl an extra ball.
  The shorter version of the game (20/20 or 50 over matches played by all).
• Penalty – one extra run to the batting team, the batter scores all the runs hit off that no ball. The batter cannot be out except run out and the bowler has to bowl an extra ball. This extra ball is a free hit to the batter who cannot be out except run out from this hit.
• The penalty in the short version of the game is more severe than in the long version, as it is possible for the following to happen
• The batter hits the no ball for a boundary (four runs).
• The team score increases automatically by one run, which is recorded as an "extra".
• The bowler has to bowl another ball, which is a free hit to the batter who could, without the fear of being out, swing away and hit the ball over the boundary scoring six runs.
• So in total that is an extra 11 runs to the batting side, which is a considerable addition to the team score from just one illegal delivery.

Cricket vocabulary

Padded up – batters in cricket wear protective padding on their legs so when the ball hits the leg it does not hurt. Padded up has come to mean the next batter to go in.

Popping crease – the line which the bowler must either cut with their front foot or have their front foot behind the line. Overstepping this line is a no ball.

Over – six legal balls or deliveries. When an over is completed, the play switches to the other end of the cricket pitch, unlike in baseball or softball where the play never changes.

Cricket net – the same concept as a batting cage in baseball and softball.

Practice in the middle – the middle is where the cricket pitch is located. It is located in the middle of the cricket field.

Test cricket – another name for international cricket between two countries.

Discussion questions

1   How can the coach (and players) create a cricket training culture that reflects the real game?
2   How can the coach create other meaningful training games that players are engaged in?
3   Apart from the decision-making scenarios discussed in this chapter, what other decision-making scenarios relevant to batters, bowlers and fielders are faced in playing cricket.
4   How can a coach encourage a cricketer to correct technical weaknesses using decision-making techniques?

Useful links

www.icc-cricket.com/news
www.lords.org/mcc/all-laws
www.bbc.co.uk/sport/cricket

Reference

The Laws of Cricket 2017 Code (2nd Edition, 2019). MCC.

Appendix

Examples from the 2019 England v Australia Ashes series

On Sunday August 25 2019 in a Test match between England and Australia at Headingley, Leeds, we witnessed a sustained period of play where English cricketers

Ben Stokes and Jack Leach scored an amazing 73 runs for the 9th wicket to give England victory over Australia and win the 3rd Test, so levelling the Ashes series 1–1 with two matches to play.

When Leach joined Stokes, England were 286–9 chasing a record 359 runs and an Australia victory was almost assured. But from that moment, Stokes and Leach won the game by hitting the runs off just 11 overs, of which Leach only scored one run. Stokes hit the rest going on to score 135. The win was achieved by Stokes and Leach playing exceptional shots and making outstanding batting decisions while Australia, feeling the pressure, as the winning total got closer, made several poor decisions. Stokes managed to score nearly all the required runs by manipulating the strike so that in nearly every over Leach only faced one or two deliveries. When Stokes had the strike, he hit the ball to all parts of the ground, off an Australian bowling attack that had previously dominated the match. Stokes' decisions to either hit the ball for a four or six and then leave Leach to bat out the rest of the over were impeccable and worked for the 11 overs it took to win the match. Leach's decision-making and ability to just defend during this period until he scored the run that brought the scores level were just as impeccable. This was a classic example of both batters making many correct decisions to win the match.

At the same time, the Australians made several bad decisions and managed to lose the match. Poor fielding, poor captaincy so that Stokes was able to manage the 11 overs and win the match, and finally a poor decision by Australian captain, Tim Paine, to use his last umpire's review on questioning a review that was clearly "not out". Two overs later, Stokes was given "not out" by the umpire only for the television replay to show he was clearly "out". If Paine had not wasted his last umpire's review, he could have used it to review that decision and Stokes would have been given out and Australia would have won the match.

In the 4th Test, played at Old Trafford, Manchester, England's slow left arm spinner, Jack Leach made the same mistake as Sandakan. Australia's Steve Smith was at 118 when he edged a ball from Leach and was caught by Ben Stokes at slip. When the position of Leach's front foot was checked by video, it showed that he had overstepped the popping crease and bowled a no ball. Smith survived and went onto score 211 out of Australia's first innings score of 478–9 declared. Australia went onto win the 4th Test and keep the Ashes.

The issue of bowlers overstepping the popping crease continues to be a problem that bowlers and coaches face in the modern game. It is the advent of technology, where so many crucial decisions are now reviewed by video replay and the off-field umpire, that bowling no balls in all forms of the game is proving to have serious repercussions and often influences the result of the game.

17

COACHING TACTICS AND DECISION-MAKING IN TARGET GAMES

Barrie Gordon

Target games are one of the four categories of games that are commonly identified within the Teaching Games for Understanding and Games Sense frameworks (Bunker & Thorpe, 1982). They include games such as golf, archery, ten pin bowling, bowls, shooting, curling, bocce and darts. Target games are defined as games where players try to get their object ball, dart, rock or arrow closest to an agreed target.

Over recent years there has been a rapid growth in athlete-centred coaching and teaching in sports within the territory classification, with an emphasis on developing game understanding, tactical awareness and good decision-making (Griffin, Butler & Sheppard, 2018). There has, however, been less interest and progress in the other categories, including target games (Light 2018).

Tactically there are similarities between target games and this chapter will look at ways in which a simple generic game can be used to teach tactical decision-making that is applicable across different games. This is done with the understanding that different target games will have different physical demands and skills specific to that sport. In regards to tactical decision-making, while there are some tactics specific to each sport there are many others that are common across the classification.

As in all games, players in target games need to have the ability to make clear and correct tactical decisions, often under pressure. For a coach it is therefore important to ensure that players develop an understanding of the relevant tactics, and that they be given ample opportunities to practice making good tactical decisions. Crucial components of making good decisions is being aware of important contextual factors and having the flexibility to react appropriately to changes as they occur. Factors to consider include the score, how far through the game it is, the skill level of the opponent, how they respond to pressure, what are their, and your, strengths and weaknesses and what has happened in similar situations previously. When consideration is given to these factors, what initially appears to be a relatively simple decision can become complicated very quickly. For many, although not all, target games the decision-making is not impacted by physical fatigue and exertion and therefore it is not necessary to practise under fatigue conditions.

Scenario

Imagine a situation where a golfer has to decide how to hit their second shot on a par four hole with a stream crossing the fairway just short of the green. The decision is whether to use a short iron to 'lay-up' short of a stream or use a long iron and attempt to hit over the stream and land close to or on the green.

Some of the factors to consider in this decision are:

- The skill level of the player and where their ball lies in relation to the stream and the green.
- Score of the game.
- Where the opposition player's ball lies and how many shots they have already taken. If they have laid up short of the stream this may lead to a different decision than if they had cleared the stream already and are close to the green.
- Whose turn it is to play first?
- The type of competition. A match play where each hole is counted as a win, loss or drawn may lead to a different decision to a game where the total score over 18 holes decides the winner.
- Are you part of a team event? If so, the team standing may impact on the decision. If for instance your team had already won three of four games you may well decide to go for the long iron over the stream.
- The level of confidence of the player, are there self-doubts about their ability to play the long iron successfully.
- What has happened in the past in similar situations?

In the case above, the player is deciding what are the risks and rewards of choosing either action: what happens in each case if the chosen shot is successful or unsuccessful? They must then balance out these two factors before making the decision. In deciding to take the long iron, for example, the risk is landing in the stream and losing a stroke. This means the fourth shot will be over the stream. The risk of laying up is that this may take an extra stroke compared with a successful long shot, but the reward is a relatively easy third shot to the green.

Along with the factors previously mentioned, the decision may be affected by such things as the belief that a successful shot over the stream will put extra pressure on the opponent to also hit a long shot. The risk, of course, is that a bad shot takes pressure off the opponent. If the opponent has previously had a problem with a long iron this may increase the temptation to hit the long iron. This is only a sample of the many factors that can influence this particular decision. Decisions are made in a constantly changing environment and players must be equipped with the flexibility to adjust as required. The complexity means that it is not possible to teach players that when A happens you should do B. What is needed is for players to experience the complexity, under pressure, learn to read the situation and make clear reasoned decisions.

In line with the Developing Thinking Players (DTP™) philosophy opportunities to practise decision-making will occur in a modified game. The game will be designed to remove the need for high levels of skill and will allow players to concentrate on the changing context being presented and the tactical decisions to be made.

Description of game setup

This simple game is designed to develop tactical decision-making related to risk and reward. The decisions made are, in a tactical sense, identical to the scenario above where the player is deciding whether to lay up or try to hit over the stream.

The game involves teams competing to hit a variety of targets which are of varying distances and point value (see Figure 17.1). The closest target is the easiest to hit and worth the lowest number of points (cone – 1 point), further away is a second target (cone – 3 points) and the furthest away is the most difficult to hit and worth the greatest number of points (cone – 5 points). While in this example cones are used, any combination of targets can be presented as long as they are increasingly difficult to hit. Before throwing, the player announces which of the three targets they will be aiming at. If they miss this target and hit a different one no points are scored.

There are multiple ways in which this game can be played, but the most common is to have teams of two or three players each having two throws. After tossing to decide who starts, the lead off player of the team selected to throw first has their initial throw. This is followed by the opposition team's lead player. This sequence is then repeated. After the lead players have had their two throws the remaining

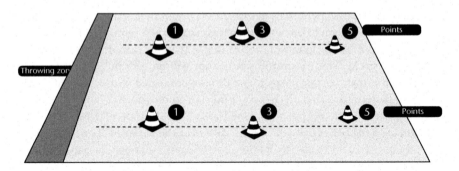

FIGURE 17.1   Generic target game

players in the team take their turns following the same pattern. Scores are updated after each throw and accumulated for each team.

All decisions become tactical ones. Even making what seems a relatively simple decision on the order of throwing within the team, requires a variety of factors to be considered. Does the team select their best player to lead off in order to put on initial pressure? If so should they be encouraged to try for the high stakes targets because, if successful, the reward will be to immediately place pressure on the opposition. The risk, of course, is they may miss and this will reduce the pressure on their opponents. Would it therefore be better to place a less skilled player to lead off and 'bank' points through hitting lower scoring targets?

As each game progresses it requires constant decision-making as to which target to aim for. A missed throw by either team can change the context quickly and players need to remain flexible in their thinking. There can be a surprising amount of pressure on players and this can lead to them becoming flustered and being influenced by others. A player with the last throw of the game for their team, with an opposition player to follow, for example, may find their team up by two points. A one point score will require the opposition to at least score three to draw. Would it be better to risk a three pointer which, if successful would require the opposition to score a five pointer just to stay in the game. What is the best decision? What are the risks and the potential rewards of the different options?

One interesting dynamic is that with pressure decisions, the dominant personality in the team can often drive the decision-making. In many cases, these players are not the most tactically able and this dynamic can lead players to take poor options. When this situation occurs there are numerous opportunities for a coach to lead discussions on the roles and responsibilities of all players. Were they persuaded to change their mind about a decision they initially were confident in, why did they change, would they in the future? This can be challenging. A player can take what they know is a poor decision because they are comfortable that they can blame someone else if it goes wrong. Addressing this reality can be confronting and while it needs to be addressed, it should be done in a supportive manner. Coaches want players to be thoughtful and courageous in their decision-making. There is little benefit in a player making great decisions at a cognitive level if they do not enact them in the game situation.

This scenario gives the player an opportunity to examine their own confidence levels within a relatively low-skill game. Hopefully, when the same scenario arises in a high-stakes situation in the future, they will be better equipped to make good decisions and have the confidence to trust their judgement.

As a coach there are numerous variations to this game that you can introduce to set up specific scenarios requiring different types of decision-making. The distance the targets are set from the throwing line and the distance between targets can be adjusted to the skill level of the players. It should be challenging but within their skill capabilities. A simple change of point value can influence the decision-making. If the targets are set at one point, two points and five with the five pointer moved further away, for example, this alters the game dynamics substantially. The actual targets can be made bigger or easier to hit. This helps players achieve success and increases their engagement with the game.

One variation that I have used successfully is to introduce a double point card. Each team has a card which they can use on one turn only. The card is played by the team before the throw is taken and can be used at any time in the game by any player. The player still has to identify which target they are aiming for before throwing. Questions for the team to decide on include:

- Which player will use the card?
- When in the game should it be used. Early or later. Should it be held to the last throw or used earlier to put pressure on the other teams?
- Tactically specific questions during the game, such as 'Is an attempt at the 5 pointer the best when a double three pointer will gain 6, more points than the maximum available without the double card?'

Again players' confidence levels in their skills and their ability to handle pressure comes into play.

Tiebreakers

Many games, including target games, have some variation of a tiebreaker system if the game is tied at the end of play. The tiebreaker brings with it increased pressure and different tactical decision-making. This game sets up easily for tiebreakers, and all the pressures and tactical decision-making associated with tiebreakers can easily be replicated in a variety of ways. How the coach chooses to run the tiebreaker should mirror the process used in the particular sport they are coaching.

One option is to run a straight-off sudden death scenario. One player from each team has one throw each. Toss a coin for the choice of going first or second. This in itself is a tactical decision. Do we want to lead off, get a good score and put pressure on the opposition or wait and respond to their score? What is your reading of the other team's handling of pressure, is this a factor to consider? Does the player leading off try for a single pointer? If the lead off player is successful, what does the next player go for? Does the lead off player take the risk and try for a three or five pointer, which, if successful, will have the reward of forcing the opposition to try for a three as well. The risk is, if missed, this will leave a relatively easy one point shot for the win.

If the teams are still tied then another shoot-out occurs with two different players. This continues until one team wins. Usually the more confident players go first, so as the shootout continues the less confident players are required to throw. This is always interesting, as in many cases, players who are generally able to avoid pressure situations are required to step up. Every throw changes the scenario and resultant decision-making. The personalities of the players become a factor with the more aggressive players often being more tempted by the high-risk high-reward options. Other players may gravitate to the low-risk low-reward options. Both have strengths and weaknesses depending on the game situation.

Questioning

When using the DTP™ approach, questioning is central to establishing a good depth of understanding by players. Simply asking why they reached a particular decision can be illuminating as to the lack of thought that has occurred. This again can be exposing and challenging for players and needs to be handled carefully. I have successfully used simple questions such as:

• What are the risks and rewards of choosing to go for the three-point target at this point of the game? What will happen if you miss?
• If you hit it, what will the opposition need to do?
• Who is their next player and are they a confident skilled player?
• Do you think they will try for a big score?
• Can they handle pressure?

This is a simple game that can be played anywhere, players can throw or roll a variety of implements including bean bags, tennis balls or even pencil cases. On one occasion it was played by a group of elderly adults waiting in the middle of New Zealand bush to be picked up by a bus after finishing a short tramp. In this case, the targets involved were ice block sticks, pine cones and rocks, with stones for throwing. Apart from the arguments around non-standard rock sizes, it was a great success and became highly competitive to the degree that when the bus arrived, a bus load of passengers were kept waiting while the deciding four throws were completed.

The basic design of the game as outlined can be used in a variety of ways by coaches who know their own sport and the personalities of the players. By analysing the tactical requirements of their own sport, coaches can establish a variation of the game that meets these requirements. When first introduced to this game there may be some reluctance from players who do not immediately understand the relevance to their own sport. Introducing immediate rewards for winning and a fun forfeit for losing will soon get their attention and full engagement.

Conclusion

This chapter looks at using a simple modified game to help players develop tactical understanding and to help them develop their decision-making skills in target games. It follows the principles of the DTP™ approach, as previously described in Chapter 2, including simplifying the activity to the degree that allows players to concentrate on their decision-making without being distracted by the need for high levels of skill. While the decision-making strategies described in this chapter are particularly relevant to target games, many are also applicable to games in other classifications. The concept of risk and reward, for example, is central to many games, while tiebreakers of various formats are ubiquitous throughout the sporting domain. For this reason, the activities described in this chapter could be useful for coaches in a range of non-target games sports and games.

Questions

1   What other target-game-related tactical principles could be developed through this game?
2   How could the principles of risk and reward, as developed in these activities, be transferred to other non-target games and sports?

References

Bunker, D., & Thorpe, R. (1982). A model for the teaching of games in secondary schools. *Bulletin of Physical Education, 10*(1), 9–16.

Griffin, L., Butler, J., & Sheppard, J. (2018). Athlete-centred coaching. In S. Pill (Ed.), *Perspectives on Athlete-Centred Coaching* (pp. 9–23). New York: Routledge.

Light, R. (2018). Athlete-centred coaching for individual sports. In S. Pill (Ed.), *Perspectives on Athlete-Centred Coaching* (pp. 139–149). New York: Routledge.

18

SQUASH

Mike Way

Learning to make good decisions under stress is a life-long process for athletes, and I hope this chapter contributes to the discussion on how to best facilitate this growth. I have outlined 11 areas for consideration. The first three deal with changing bad habits and adding a new shot, at an intermediate level, within the game of squash. The remainder are aimed at advanced to elite level squash players but are transferable to other sports.

Introduction to the game of squash

The game of squash is played on a court about half the size of a tennis court contained by four walls. Only a small percentage of attacking shots are outright winners because of the confined space. This results in long rallies and high levels of physical and mental stress. Squash is a game of time and space, patience and endurance. If my opponent hits hard or volleys, I have less time. If I keep the ball tight to the side walls and into the back corners, I reduce their options as they have less space. These two aspects – time and space – determine attacking or defensive positions.

Finding the back corners makes life very difficult for the opposition to apply pressure. Nearly all attacking positions are built from the back corners, as they are in baseline tennis. We rally patiently into the back corners until an attacking position presents itself in the mid or front court. Figure 18.1 shows areas of the squash court floor for attacking or defensive strategies.

In the early years of playing competitive squash, winning or losing is about who is fastest, who hits the ball the hardest, who has great hands and who is more determined.

At the higher levels, players have technical proficiency in all the shots as well as fitness, speed and agility. The rallies are much longer and it is having consecutive long

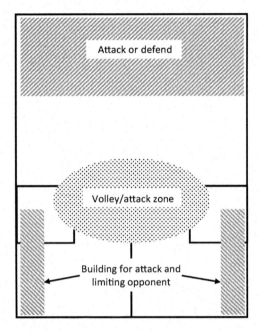

FIGURE 18.1 Squash court zones

rallies that makes the difference. This aspect is one of the signatures of elite squash, with points often being decided on unforced errors as physical and mental fatigue sets in.

As you will see in this chapter, the mental aspects of the game take on more significance as the player moves up the ladder.

The 11 topics covered in this chapter are:

- Black and White decisions
- Adding a new shot
- Deception
- Different phases of a match
- Counter strategy
- Individual style
- Elite tactics
- Broader mental considerations
- Mindset
- The ladder of expectations
- Maturity and character

Black and White decisions

'Black and White' usually means there is only one correct choice, but even those situations can be problematic if players are not properly trained.

Here are four basic squash examples of Black/White, and a conditioned game to train the athlete to make the correct choice. This is for intermediate and higher level players.

1   The lob

The lob is a high soft shot which arcs above the mid-court and lands in a back corner. By intermediate level, squash players have learned to defend by lobbing the ball cross court to get out of trouble.

Lobbing = Time. Time that is used to recover to a central position (called the T) and to prevent further attack.

Lifting the ball is used anywhere on the court but the classic lob is mostly played from the front. Lifting can also be part of a counter strategy against fast or hard hitting players, good volleyers or when fatigue sets in.

2   The counter drop

If the pressure is extreme when retrieving from the front, experienced players will play a 'counter drop' to the nearest corner. This is mostly played if the player feels a lob would not clear the mid-court where their opponent is looking to volley the ball to the back. A quick counter drop is also played when a player feels their opponent is slow to the front or hanging back.

> If you are under pressure the Black/White decision is to lob cross- court.

> If you are under extreme pressure in the front court, the Black/White decision is to play a straight counter drop.

In squash, many players mistakenly hit crosscourt drives under pressure. This becomes very readable and their opponent will look to volley, creating even more pressure or winning the point outright.

Our other two Black and White examples are from balls hit down the middle of the court – an attacking position.

3   If player 'A' miss-hits their drive from a back corner and the ball shoots down the middle, player 'B' should hit the ball to the front; usually a drop shot to the opposite corner. A difficult shot to execute but the correct choice.

4   If player 'A' has miss-hit down the middle of the court when they are in the front, the Black and White decision dictates 'B' hit the ball to the back; again, to the opposite corner: a straight drive or volley deep.

These are part of the non-negotiable squash tactics, but they need to be trained into a habit. Again, like the first two examples, it is the crosscourt volley drive that is hit out of habit.

One training exercise to help build good habits is called 'Wrong shot not'. We will use this drill/game for our four shots listed above. These are when to attack from the mid court, when to lob or counter drop out of trouble and recognising when to simply rally patiently for position. The player must be clear of what to hit in these Black and White situations.

'Wrong shot not!' is practised in conditioned games and can also be used in practice matches.

Here is an example of deliberate practice or a conditioned game.

Length games (any shot to the back) are a very common conditioned game in squash and similar to baseline tennis drills.

Unlike tennis, however, we don't want our intermediate players hitting the ball back to their opponent when the shot comes down the middle of the court. We therefore add a drop or volley drop to the game so they can practise making the correct choice as it presents. After a drop is played, the opposing player, now under pressure in the front, can either lob out of trouble or counter drop to the same front corner.

In a 'wrong shot not!' game, the rally is interrupted by the coach immediately a B/W (Black/White) 'wrong shot' has been hit. An explanation is rarely required (level appropriate) and the rally is re-played. If the player repeats the mistake, the rally may be awarded to their opponent. If the player 'catches' their own mistake by stopping before the coach interrupts, the rally is re-played.

(NB: The volley drop is a difficult shot to master. A drop programme might precede this conditioned game.)

Such interruptions sound annoying. They are!

Correct decision-making, however, improves very quickly until interruptions become unnecessary.

This approach takes much of the thinking out of 'how to think'.

The player starts to execute the black/white on autopilot.

A note here: basic tactics such as these, are more commonly discussed after practice games or matches. The *lesson moment* is lost as the coach refers back to situations from earlier. Interrupting the rally brings immediate awareness. It reduces habitual tactical mistakes and forces the player to make adjustments; to take the correct shot when it presents.

Adding a new shot

As mentioned above, the most commonly played shot in squash is the cross-court drive; often hit randomly from habit. When under stress, the untrained player will select the easiest shot to hit which is the one that's hit most. It's an automatic thing; in squash it's the cross-court drive. For another shot to have any chance of being selected under stress, the shot must be added to the mental 'shot file' in the player's subconscious.

In other words, new shots are not only practised for technical proficiency and confidence but also to ensure they are added to the subconscious autopilot file for quick and automatic selection.

It is in this area that many athletes falter in their tactical development. They learn a new shot technically but fail to put it in the subconscious shot file.

The first four attacking shots we teach in squash are: attacking straight and cross-court drives, the straight drop, and the attacking boast (a shot hit off the side wall).

These four – forehand and backhand – are also the first four attacking shots learned on the volley, giving a player eight weapons to use on both sides.

The straight drop, is the *least* chosen for three reasons:

- It is the most difficult to play with any consistency.
- It results in more unforced errors than any other shot.
- If poorly played, it sets up your opponent for a counterattack.

These reasons make the straight drop more nerve-wracking to attempt in the heat of battle. It takes a certain 'feel' to place a bouncy ball delicately in a front corner, a lot of confidence and a clear mind to make the selection.

I will use this shot as an example to show the training regime to add a new shot. As you will see, the pressure increases through each section; mentally as well as technically.

- The student must hit a few hundred drops each week in a controlled coach feed/drop practice. Fairly static; just small feet adjustments to keep flow and rhythm in the drill, but no real stress.

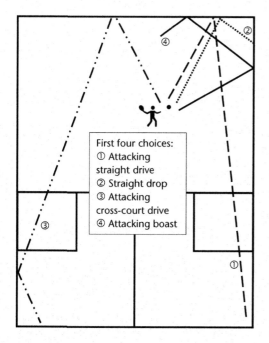

First four choices:
① Attacking straight drive
② Straight drop
③ Attacking cross-court drive
④ Attacking boast

FIGURE 18.2 Attacking shot target areas

Like all technical teaching, the shot may be mechanical in its look, but the required number takes 'mechanics' to 'feel' (to the hand) and to greater understanding and confidence.

Confidence underlies everything; confidence and good habits add to our sub-conscious file.

- From here, simple drills are introduced with movement and conditioned games for Black and White scenarios to take the drop option.
- The coach will introduce the drop to practice games, where stress is a little higher but there is freedom to take any drop opportunity; freedom to make a mistake.
- Stress is further increased through practice matches (best 3/5) and various condition games. The number of drops practised are now in the thousands to put the shot in the bank.
- Same level, same age (for juniors) practice matches increase mental pressure and the shot selection is tested more fully with 'wrong shot not' guidance to help. Both technical and tactical video feedback is very beneficial and over the course of a season we can see real improvement in the players' attacking play.

Deception: a choice of shots

The attacking straight or cross-court drives and the attacking boast from the front are easier shots to hit and all juniors are quite proficient by the intermediate level. After adding the straight drop, we can now work on deception using these four options.

A focus with a 'same feel/same position' is introduced to basic feeding drills as the athlete learns to not 'show' their intent. There needs to be a threat of two or more possibilities that an opponent has to cover. We start, for example, alternating straight and cross-court drives when attacking from the front and then our (new) drop shot is practised alternating with straight drives.

From there we move from *alternating* the shots to an *either/or* approach; i.e. there is a decision to make: straight drop *or* straight drive. (These two options – straight drop or straight drive – ensure a rhythmic practice. The drop or crosscourt drive option, a good combination for sure, has too many interruptions. They are added to 'coach + 2 player' drills.)

Deception drills are fun. Everyone likes to fool their opponent.

The athlete begins to understand many aspects of subtlety in technique and their own creativity.

Condition games with frequent opportunities for deception are introduced and, of course, the choices expand: straight or crosscourt drive, straight or cross-court drop, attacking boast.

All of that said, there is an important truth that top players understand: as pressure goes up, shot discipline becomes more important. More pressure = fewer opportunities and less time on the ball to be deceptive.

We are now going to consider more advanced aspects that play a role in decision-making under pressure. Some of these can be introduced at the intermediate level depending on the athlete.

If decision-making is too complicated or has been introduced too soon, then the athlete may switch off.

As is often the case, these aspects are level and maturity based.

Different phases of a match

As young players progress with their basic tactics and execute them on a regular basis, we can expand tactical 'discipline' to understand the tactical 'phases' in a match. A 'this is what I need to do now' mentality.

The basic phases of a match to learn are:

*   Early rallies
*   Critical score
*   Resetting
*   Back-up plan
*   Fatigue

The difference between these five may be small in the specifics.

It is the instructions in the head that make the difference

Experienced athletes have a constant self-dialogue between rallies:

*   What is working? What is not? Maintain or adjust.
*   A recognition of the phase of the game and 'What I need to do now.'

Let's take a look.

Early rallies

In squash, early rallies are longish. The mindset is one of 'playing to settle', 'playing into confidence'. This begins with hitting consistently to the back to negate volley opportunities while looking to take one's own. Also, finding the length: keeping the ball deep and tight.

Consecutive long rallies in the early stages can be a shock to the body. Athletes can go into early oxygen deficit as the body catches up with the workload. This can be very unsettling for ill-prepared players. Being mentally ready means no surprises.

In early rallies, attacking short opportunities are taken, but only when they are Black and White.

Critical score phase

Staying positive with strong self-talk is essential toward the end of the game when the score is close. There is an ongoing assessment with regard to tactics, momentum and fatigue factors.

What has worked? What has not?

Who has momentum? Do I maintain tactics or change tactics?

A player will assess his opponent physically, mentally as well as the tactically.

Is the opponent handling the workload or stalling between rallies to get a breather?

There should be less attacking from the back. Black and White opportunities are taken but the rallies are often longer.

Patience and discipline are required.

Resetting phase

A recognition after two to three unforced errors in close succession that the player must adjust mentally in order to adjust tactically.

'Re-group' rallies are required. The focus is on tighter, deeper, and of course awareness of where the mistakes came from.

The player may not hit a certain shot for a while, especially if the shot was from a 'half opportunity' position; i.e. too much risk.

Black/white attacks are taken except for any shot that resulted in repeated errors.

Resetting rallies are often longer, similar to 'early rallies' but now with a 're-setting' mindset.

Again, the self-talk makes the difference.

Back-up plan

Players develop their own style: how they like to play and how they like to think. What they want to happen and what they want to prevent. But on tough days, when things are not clicking, the drops are not tight, the legs are tired … the player should have a 'B' game. 'B' as in Back Up or Basic.

The 'B' game is much the same as resetting but with a broader assessment. The player can't drift to a completely different style (it's the same athlete) but again, strong self-talk will guide them through.

The tight, straight length in squash is now even more important, and fewer cross-court shots. When cross-court shots are used, they must be wide; although they are often *high* and wide.

There may be more lifting in a 'B' game to either slow the game down and/ or to frustrate the opponent. The player is trying to 'contain', to reduce their opponent's attack.

There is more running/scrambling to stay in the match and, as always, fewer attacks from the back.

The 'B' game might be necessary for the rest of the match but once a player settles and confidence builds, they may return to their normal game plan. Perhaps it is their opponent who now has to adjust with fewer attacking positions presented.

All players have such days and professionals know intuitively what to do. They don't prevail every time, but they warrior through the encounter, adding to their understanding about a particular opponent and, importantly, always displaying a survival mentality when the going is tough.

How one handles those 'B' game days is an indicator of mental maturity. It separates the pros from the rest of us.

Fatigue

This is an awareness of a player's own physical state *before* it reaches emergency levels. This comes from experience through tournament play. It is an evaluation beyond just knowing their own reserves. Apart from the mileage in the match they have also assessed the cumulative mileage from previous matches in the tournament; of themselves and their opponent.

Deeper considerations around fatigue include how determined their opponent is by reputation/history.

The ranking may be a factor here, especially for less experienced players. Does their opponent have the belief they can win? (See more of this under "Ladder of Expectations", see Figure 18.3.)

There may be an adjustment before they start the match as part of a counter strategy.

Awareness of an opponent's fatigue sometimes results in less experienced players attacking too soon from half positions. They try to finish rallies quickly and often from the back.

If a B/W opportunity presents, great. Take it … but recognise it is the tired opponent who has to 'make' something happen when energy reserves are seriously depleted. Tired players make more mistakes through going for half opportunities. If you are in the driver's seat … stay there. Don't 'gift' a tired opponent free points.

The general rule when fatigue builds is to slow the pace through lifting and to reduce volley opportunities by focusing on a tight length. There are fewer cross courts; when they are hit, it is usually high and wide.

A final note: the five phases need to be understood and then rehearsed (see page **000** for a list of the five phases).

This is not complicated, but all too often only spoken about, not rehearsed on court. The athlete needs to be reminded as situations arise in their weekly games and matches. Self-discipline builds over time through repetition.

Counter strategy

Counter strategy is an awareness of a player's own strengths and weaknesses versus their opponents' strengths and weaknesses. *Their* style versus their opponent's.

This is discussed before the match and may also help with regrouping if a player has gone off track tactically or another consideration arises: not feeling strong, or opponent is 'on' today.

Counter strategy is the art, the challenge, of turning the tables in your favour by negating a strength and/or giving yourself more opportunities. It often takes very little to turn a game around and all top players are masters at it.

As said at the beginning of this section, the tactical variations of the five phases discussed are often minimal. In some small way, they are a part of a counter strategy. Whether it is dealing with a phase of a game, or our opponent's strengths, it is all about dealing with something; countering it.

All possible scenarios must be discussed, scripted, visualised and rehearsed for clarity of thought.

This is the stuff of champions!

Individual style

The type of game a player likes, their style, affects everything. Their style is a factor for the mindset that guides the tactics.

A players' strengths from junior days will often determine this.

- Are they physical beasts?
- Do they love the power side of the game?
- Do they have natural hands?
- Are they a shot maker?

What does the player naturally draw towards tactically?

- A shot maker or an attritional player?
- The latter must still have weapons but are not as creative.
- The former has better hands but needs to be patient.

Who are their favourite professional players that their style is similar to?

- "Play like" a certain professional is a good visualisation tool.
- Having young players experiment with what it might *feel* like to be an Ali Farag versus Nick Matthew (world champions) may open doors or confirm they're on track.

Elite/professional tactics

This final aspect of tactical development is not easy to describe but I will do my best in the next few paragraphs.

At the professional level all attacking shots are firmly deposited in the subconscious shot file that I covered earlier. The elite player trusts that all shots will be executed as expected. The technical is operating as it should, on autopilot, and the athlete is free to 'feel' their way through the match.

The player 'feels' what their opponent's next shot will be (anticipation) and also 'feels' what their opponent is expecting from them. The player 'feels' their opponent's position.

We may see slight 'holding', a pause before the swing, a body position that shows a straight shot only to go cross-court, and vice versa. This is not just in classic attacking positions where we talked about deception – this 'feel' is to delay the opponent's response time by a fraction; to interrupt the flow of movement and the rhythm all athletes love to perform with, to feel *what* the opponent is expecting and keep them off balance both physically and mentally.

This does not happen for each and every shot and very rarely when defending. Not every shot can be a 'wrong-footer'.

Top players will rally predictably at times, but this awareness is always there; they are setting things up.

Coaches teach all players to get their opponent *off* the T (tactical centre) to create an opening. Top players often try to keep their opponent *on* the T until the last split second. Stopping and starting is much more difficult and interrupts the natural flow of movement.

Correct selection is confirmed or not through the 'outcome' of each shot: outcome positive = pressure for the opponent; outcome negative = counterattack. Very often the outcome may be seen as neutral, but the player is always building his or her next attacking opportunity. They adjust accordingly the next time they are in the same position. This type of attacking squash, as in tennis, has great subtlety. The difference in mileage is small, the difference in change of direction not always obvious to the layman.

Everything counts; all mileage is accumulative and change of direction more taxing.

Good players are deceptive from a front court attacking position, but this is at another level. It is a subtle process of wearing down an opponent through tactical dominance.

Professionals must be free and clear of all technical instructions and outside distractions. They are tactically focused; the mental strain is real and adds to the overall competitive stress.

It is beyond frustrating when your opponent is in command like this. It can be embarrassing for a pro player to flounder tactically in such a way.

Less experienced players execute a basic plan that is simple to coach and implement. They have awareness if an attacking shot was effective or not (i.e. wins the rally) but for the elite player tactical considerations are more like chess; it is not always black and white. Because of speed, fitness, and excellent defensive skills, top players manoeuvre and out-manoeuvre each other in subtle ways to gain the smallest advantage. Rallies are much longer. Accumulative mileage takes its toll and the constant twisting and turning through this subtle tactical awareness makes the difference.

This aspect can be layered and for the true masters – it is a gift.

Our current and recent stars of this are Ali Farag, Nour El Tayeb, James Wilstrop, Amr Shabana and the Canadian world champion, Jonathon Power.

Broader mental considerations

Defensive shots in the heat of battle are not difficult for an experienced player. It is the attacking shots, the volleys and the higher risk short shots, that bring stress. It can hinder a player from effectively executing these two shots even from the most basic position.

Having a plan *does* help an athlete focus, but comprehensive mental training makes the difference.

A level of calmness is essential to execute delicate shots when the pressure in high. Mental or tactical awareness improves through experience but is accelerated through a systematic approach.

A well thought out mental programme sees results quickly at the beginning. This builds confidence; confidence in their game but also to keep doing the work in the head. Confidence brings more clarity and frees the athlete to play the right shot.

A comprehensive mental approach involves scripting, visualising, finding their mindset and using the best words and phrases to steady the ship. Like any training, it takes a *lot* of repetition.

Mental components should be evident in most training sessions to build awareness. It's an *incremental* process.

The repetitive cycles and tests (matches) allow for adjustments, and eventually understanding becomes 'knowing'.

Mindset

Your mindset is how you think and feel about the upcoming contest. It is an attitude, a summary of your approach to bring out the best of everything. Mindsets can have varying vocabularies for different matches, but whatever is chosen on the day fits with a required competitive state.

Finding the right mindset helps with focus and instructions to self.

The words, phrases and tone that keep an athlete on track and help them re-set after an error.

It keeps things simple.

Imagine the mindset, the self-talk, of:

- Lebron James v Steph Curry
- Roger Federer v Rafael Nadal

- Serena Williams v Naomi Osaka
- Ali Farag v Mohamed El Shorbagy.

They are likely very different from one another in tone and vocabulary, but they get the job done!

Strong mindsets include most of these characteristics:

- Focused, strong face, eye control
- Confident/belief
- Calm/clear
- Determined/purposeful
- Resilient

Ladder of expectations

The higher ranked player is expected to win and so they have more to lose. If the gap is big they are usually relaxed, but in a match against someone close to their level expectation will play a role.

Coaches refer to this as *Playing to win* versus *Playing to not lose.*

'Playing to win' = mental freedom; to play with purpose.

In squash terms: move up on the T (tactical centre), take the volleys and execute those drops.

---

1. Stress of Competition and the Untrained Mind   11

Ladder of Expectations

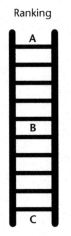

Ranking

- **C vs. A**
  - *"He's too good"*
  - No expectation. Free to play as long as …

- **A vs. C**
  - *"I'm very strong"*
  - (versus *"I'm too good"*)

- **B vs. A or C vs. B**
  - *"She's ranked higher, but I have a good chance of winning"*
  - Free to play. Best performances

- **A vs. B or B vs. C**
  - *"I should win, but this would be a bad loss. I need to be careful".* Weakest performances

FIGURE 18.3 Ladder of expectations

Hands feel good when the mind does.

Playing to not lose in squash means the player sits deep in the court (nearer the back wall). The player is nervous about any volley and going short. They play with no clear plan as the mind races to find a foothold.

The 'playing to win' athlete moves better and lasts longer.

They relish the encounter; they enjoy the battle.

Here is our goal: to "play to win" irrespective of the ranking

The lower ranked player is 'free' to compete (as long as there is no fear of being embarrassed).

If they win: Wow! Fantastic! Headline news!

When they lose they take comfort in: "You fought well; you looked great out there!" The other guy was ranked higher: shrug and move on.

I refer to these scenarios as *Arrow Up* or *Arrow Down* syndrome, i.e. playing a higher or lower ranked player.

Arrow Up matches are the ones parents and inexperienced coaches use to gauge their players' level and development. But this is not their true level. It may be a glimpse of potential but not their true level. Why? Lower expectations = less stress.

Want to play your best? Play for fun.

Competitive sport is like taking an exam. There is a result, and it will be posted.

The higher ranked player carries the burden.

Yes, the goal is to be 'free to play', like the lower ranked opponent, but that takes training. Until that has happened they are acutely aware of the rankings, the outcome if they lose and perhaps broader ramifications or judgments from others.

Arrow up

- Energised/excited/focused
- Feeling good/feeling fast
- Relaxed/ready
- Arrows for the target

Arrow down

- SOS!
- Worried/nervous/fearful
- Irritable/anxious
- Arrows of doubt

Our goal: play with arrow up ... at the target

A note here to parents

Parents can fall into the trap of obsessing about training partners and coaching programmes, having their children always train 'up' with older and better players. 'Playing up' certainly has a place in development, but avoiding same level practices avoids mental stress and delays building resiliency. It also inhibits the development of attacking shots in game situations because the athletes are in a defensive posture too often against their stronger practice partners.

This is an important issue and not for this chapter beyond raising awareness of it. Suffice to say: it should not be ignored. It must be addressed in their training and through character building and mental programmes.

Maturity and character

This last sub-heading may sound odd with regard to "tactical choices under pressure" but character determines the athlete's attitude. The right attitude get the right things done.

Good mental programmes include character development.

Character development is a prerequisite for many who struggle emotionally or are closed-minded.

Athletes who have the most to gain from a mental programme are often the ones least likely to engage or consider they could help. They very likely got away with negative behaviour when they were younger. Perhaps they were not taught how to control their emotions. They may be stuck mentally, they may have a block to learning; a block to growth and maturity.

This is where character 'training' makes the difference. Athletes are more coachable when character runs the show. They may have to go way outside their comfort zone but the pay-off is well worth it. Bjorn Borg went through this (his parents took his racquets away for 6 months). Federer too. And who knows how good Nick Kyrgios will be when he grows up.

It is through mentors, role models and character conversations that we see humility peek through.

Humility opens that mind, brings respect and allows for growth. It takes the coach/athlete relationship to another level.

A mental programme without a character component is like fitness training without flexibility – something will break.

Character 'chatting' is not enough. Words such as *discipline, determination, perseverance* are common in sport. *Forgiveness, enthusiasm, respect, humility*, not so much.

The words must have actions. These words need to be lifted off the paper to make a difference.

Making character a part of a programme broadens perspectives. That in turn will help deal with 'silly stress' and the athletes will enjoy the process more. They will enjoy their sport more.

I will close with two of my favourite quotes:

From sports psychologist Jim Loehr: 'Who you become as a result of the chase is the most important thing.'

Or, as Virgil wrote: 'As the twig is bent, so shall it grow'

Vocabulary of squash

Lobbing – lifting the ball high over your opponent into the back court.
The T – where the short line meets the half court line. Generally considered as the optimum court position.
Drop shot – a low, controlled shot that dies in either of the front corners.
Attacking boast – hitting the ball to the front wall via the side wall.
Counter drop shot – returning any short shot with your own drop shot.
Conditioned game/deliberate practice – a game or practice that is designed to bring about a desired outcome. For example, a point can only be won if it bounces in the back court

Discussion questions

1   Design a deliberate practice that will help your player make better in-game decisions when the ball is bouncing freely in the front forehand corner.
2   How would you advise your player who is losing a match they should be winning?
3   You are the coach of a talented junior player. Are you helping or hindering by telling them how to win the match?
4   How can you make *deliberate practice* more enjoyable?

Useful weblinks

https://psaworldtour.com
https://squashskills.com
www.serioussquash.com/2018/11/squash–decision–making–training.html

19

KARATE

Gerard Lauziere

When a fighter is involved in sparring there are many opportunities to make good decisions. These decisions range from simple to complex. Sometimes they need to be taken in a split second and other times they can be prepared well in advance. In some situations your athlete will have to think fast, and in others they will have time to set up their opponent, two or three moves ahead, as in a chess match.

Scouting and having an opportunity to analyse an opponent's style of fighting before a match will help in establishing appropriate tactics. Before a match, it is helpful to know if the opponent is more offensive or defensive, what their scoring techniques are, how they tend to get scored on and whether they are linear or multidirectional fighters. Antonio Oliva Seba's categorisation of fighters as physical, emotional or intellectual can also be a useful framework to analyse an opponent. When there is no opportunity to analyse the opponent before a match, this will have to happen during the first part of the match, which will serve as a discovery phase.

The ability to perceive relevant cues during a match are crucial to your athlete's success. Cues can be obvious, such as an opponent that is constantly escaping. They can also be discreet, such as noticing if the opponent is surprised when you bridge the distance to initiate an attack.

Training to make the right decisions can be introduced as soon as each individual skill involved in a tactic has been perfected. These decisions can be trained just as easily, and you would develop a given skill. Well-planned tactical decision-making practices will help your athletes apply their techniques in the right circumstances.

Here are some practices (Figures 19.1, 19.2 and 19.3) that can be used to train the decision-making process in sparring.

Hitting a moving target

It can be hitting a moving punching bag or a sparring partner moving randomly around without avoiding the attacks.

Choosing the most appropriate target

The sparring partner will move around and stop in a position offering certain openings. The athlete must react as quickly as possible with a well-executed scoring technique.

Modifying the attack or counterattack

Attacks need to be lightning fast; however, there is a critical point or point of no return in each attack or counterattack. Before reaching that point, it is possible to modify the attack to suit the situation. The beginning of an attack or combination attack can have one, two or three alternative endings.

Changing an attack mid-way to adjust to a different opening

Single attack: A sparring partner stands in fighting stance with both hands up on each side of their head. The point of no return for this skill is about 10 to 20 centimetres before the knee reaches its highest position (see Figure 19.1).

The attacker will aim to do a front leg roundhouse to the head (see Figure 19.2).

The alternative ending in this exercise, is a hook kick to the head (see Figure 19.3).

It is important that the athlete train the front leg roundhouse kick to the head as well as the front leg hook kick to the head separately and is able to apply them with a good success rate, before adding the following decision-making training.

FIGURE 19.1 The point of no return

Source: Jean–Noel Blanchette.

FIGURE 19.2   Front leg roundhouse kick

Source: Jean-Noel Blanchette.

FIGURE 19.3   Hook kick to the head

Source: Jean-Noel Blanchette.

Decision-making training

As the attacker kicks, the sparring partner will put one hand down creating an opening on one side of the face. Just before the point of no return, the target opening will determine if the attacker must continue with the roundhouse kick or do a hook kick to the other side of the face.

Fake and attack: The attacker wants to score by doing a fake reverse punch to the body and follow up by shifting to the side and executing a front leg roundhouse kick to the body. The point of no return in this attack is just before the shift to the side. The alternative ending in this case would be a front leg hook kick to the head. You could also add a level of difficulty to this exercise by adding a second decision to be taken. The defender would either be surprised and let the roundhouse kick go in to the body or protect the mid-section to force the attacker to change to a hook kick to the head, or when he or she sees the attacker start the hook kick, protect the head so the attacker would once again stop mid-attack and bring the leg down for a takedown and punch.

The first decision is to do a roundhouse kick to the body or the hook kick to the head. The second, would be to continue with the hook kick to the head or bring the leg down for a takedown and punch. The skills to master before practising this drill are:

- Make a reverse punch and front leg roundhouse kick to the body.
- Fake a reverse punch and front leg hook kick to the head.
- Fake a reverse punch and start hook kick to switch into a sweep with punch.

Decision-making training

Once the attacker is in the right distance, he or she will initiate the fake reverse punch to the body. Randomly, the defender will either act surprised and not react, protect their midsection before the point of no return or protect their head from the hook kick. If the defender is surprised and leaves an opening to the body, the attacker continues with the front leg roundhouse kick to the body. If the defender moves their arms to protect their body, the attacker will change their attack to do a hook kick to the head. If the sparring partner decides to also protect their head, the attacker will stop the hook kick to bring the leg back down to do a takedown and punch.

Multiple attack: In this case, the attacker wants to score with a combination Blitz reverse punch and jab. The Blitz is like a sprint start, diving towards the opponent. The alternative attack is a Blitz reverse punch, jab and add a third punch to the head. The point of no return is as the jab is initiated. At this time the attacker must decide if they will be able to hit the target with the jab or if they will fall short. As soon as they see that they will not make it to the target, the third punch is initiated.

Decision-making training

Start by having your athlete train the Blitz–jab and the Blitz–jab–punch combinations separately with a partner. The training partner will either step back normally and let the jab reach the target with the jab or they will move farther back to get the attacker to do the third punch. The attacker will start the Blitz–jab combination and as soon as they see that the target is too far, they immediately add the third punch.

Action – reaction

Getting your opponent to move so you can attack them when they are not ready

Decision-making training

In this type of decision-making training, the attacker gets the defender to react to an action. The action is designed to get the defender to react in a predictable way. The main goal is to create a situation where you can attack your opponent with the most effective attack when they are not ready. The attacker will have practised optimal answers for each of their opponent's probable reactions.

In this example, both fighters are in a fighting stance left leg in front. The attacker switches legs, simultaneously moving 45 degrees to the left. The opponent will usually, either pivot on the front leg and turn towards the attacker or will also switch legs simultaneously turning towards the attacker. The two combinations needed for this next practice are the reverse punch–jab blitz and jab and step in punch.

Decision-making training

After the attacker shifts to the left, the sparring partner will randomly either pivot or switch legs. If the defender just pivots, the attacker will do a reverse punch–jab blitz and finish on the outside of the opponent's stance. If the opponent switches legs, the attacker will execute a jab and step in punch to the head to also end up on the outside of the opponent's stance.

Armouring your attacks

Continue an attack or stop to protect yourself when needed

Often, fighters are vulnerable to a counterattack when they attack. The following type of drill will help avoid this vulnerability.

Training: Have your athletes practise their attack combinations with a sparring partner. The sparring partner will react naturally and most of the time let the attacker complete their combination successfully. However, about three times out of ten, the partner will test the attacker by attacking or countering them immediately before, during or after the combination.

Your athlete will learn to be ready and be able to abort an attack safely. It will also give them the confidence to initiate attacks without being afraid of getting hit. It will also minimise the risk of them getting injured.

Reading your opponent

Choice of tactics according to cues from your opponent

Learning to read cues will help your athlete choose the adequate tactics and strategies.

If the opponent always escapes backward in a straight line, it could be the time to set up a double or multiple attack combination.

If your athlete has an opponent whose fighting style is to circle your athlete, it could be a good tactic to cut them off when they try to go around. Your athlete can then pressure them into the corner. Once the opponent is cornered, your athlete can purposefully leave them an opening to escape the corner. As the opponent escapes, your athlete can take advantage of the situation by executing an appropriate attack.

Decision-making training

Do small bouts in which a training partner will be given a specific role, such as being very defensive, very offensive, always escaping back in a straight line, circling their opponent to attack, counterattack every time, etc. Your athlete must adapt and choose the appropriate tactics for that style of fighter.

Reading the situation

Choice of attacks according to the score and time left in the match

The first person to score has an advantage in the case of a tie. Tactics may vary depending on the time (beginning, middle or end of a match) and the score at a given time. The last 15 seconds of a match are critical. An athlete could lose the advantage gained by the first score by receiving a penalty in those last 15 seconds of the match. If the match is tight, it will be critical to avoid getting a penalty during those last 15 seconds. When your athlete has a good lead, it can be advantageous to take a penalty to prevent them from scoring. A punch to the body or head scores 1 point, a kick to the body is 2 points and a kick to the head or a takedown with attack are worth 3 points.

Decision-making training

Set up scenario cards such as:

- You are ahead by one point, there is 10 seconds left to the match.
- You are behind by three points with only 5 seconds left.
- You are tied, you have the advantage and there is 15 seconds left.

Have the athletes read the scenario and give them 30 seconds to prepare mentally for the match situation.

Decision-making training to make the right tactical decisions is usually done considering your opponent's normal reactions. Practices are developed to capitalise on your opponents most probable reactions.

How can you discover your opponent's most probable reactions to a fake or set-up?

Analyse videos of your opponent, see how they react in different situations. Practice your fake and set-ups on many different training partners. Without telling them what attack you will do, ask them to react as they would naturally.

As you practise a fake, throw in the real attack once in a while to make sure your fake is realistic. The beginning should be exactly the same. Ask your sparring partners to block if they think it is a real attack and to do nothing if it is a fake. If they react to the fake, you can rest assured that the fake has a good chance of working.

In combat sports, technique needs to be supported by effective decision-making. Make sure to incorporate decision-making training in your yearly training plan, particularly in the specific preparation and competition phases of the plan

Discussion questions

1 How can the coach find out what probable reactions athletes will have to a fake?
2 During a match, what are the decision-making situations that come up frequently?
3 How can a coach apply similar scenarios as the ones presented here in their combat sport?
4 How can the coach create a good progression of drills to address complicated decision-making situations?

Karate vocabulary

Fighting stance – the fighter focuses on being light on the front foot while having their weight on the back foot

The point of no return – the point at which an attack or defence cannot be changed

Roundhouse kick – the fighter lifts their knee while turning the supporting foot and body in a semi-circular movement, extending the leg and striking the opponent with the lower part of the leg or foot

Hook kick – the kick appears to miss the target before snapping back and making contact with the heel of the foot. Sometimes combined with a spinning movement to increase power.

Reverse punch – rotate at the hips using the front hip as a hinge while the back foot creates torsion to drive the punch into your opponent.

Useful resource

Vickers, J.N. (2007). *Perception Cognition and Decision Training, the Quiet Eye in Action.* Champaign, IL: Human Kinetics.

PART IV

Through the lens
of a coach

20

A COACH'S JOURNEY

Greg Gary

I grew up in Southern California and I vividly remember watching UCLA (University of California, Los Angeles) basketball and USC (University of Southern California) football when I was eight- or nine-years old and thinking how great it would be to play "like that." That is really how it started, I just wanted to be really good, I had no idea how I would get there, but it did not matter at the time. The seed was planted, and I started on my journey into high performance sport. I have been on that journey for 48 years and have learned incredible lessons from the coaches I have played for and the players I have coached. These lessons define my coaching philosophy.

My first memory of sport "getting real" and performance mattering was in my 10th grade of high school. I tried out for and made the football team as a back-up quarterback and starting free safety. The dominant memory I have of that season is my head coach telling me during warm-ups that I would be starting the game at quarterback against our cross-town rival, Damien High School. I wish I could say I went out there and played an amazing game. I did not, I actually flopped. I was overwhelmed by the moment but I was taught a valuable lesson by an inexperienced coach. I am grateful for having that experience, it taught me to always be prepared to perform and to expect the unexpected. This was a lesson that I would encourage coaches to intentionally teach young athletes. It is the foundation of developing thinking players.

Basketball season followed football season in high school. Again, I tried out for the team and made it. We had a new coach who today would be considered an athlete-centred coach. He focused on developing the fundamentals needed to play basketball at a high level. He also taught us to think about the game by teaching us options to counter the opponent's attacks.

Over the next three high school basketball seasons, I experienced the importance of having a base set of fundamental skills. Developing the fundamental skills and abilities of a player has become the core to my coaching and player development philosophy. Players are better able to make in-game decisions when they have a sound base of fundamentals. I focused on developing as a basketball player during my remaining three years of high school. Focused coaching on skill development was key to me earning a scholarship to a National Collegiate Athletic Association (NCAA) Division 1 university.

Things did not quite work out how I hoped at university, and I transferred universities a couple of times before deciding to return to football and enrolling at California State University Fullerton (CSUF). At CSUF I was coached by, and worked with, the best people in sport. Our head coach was an athlete-centred coach. He expected high performance and when you underperformed, he would let you know. Sometimes I think athletes confuse athlete-centred coaching with "athlete-coddling coaching". Trust me, there is a significant difference between the two approaches.

Effective coaches understand that to be successful, they will need to build authentic relationships with the individuals they coach. My head coach at CSUF understood this and he expected the athletes he coached to accept and trust his feedback and direction. I have tried to bring this philosophy to my work with athletes.

My defensive back coach at CSUF taught me how to play football. Strangely, we spent a lot of time on the basketball court working on football movements. Coach and I had a lot of early morning sessions together. My nickname at CSUF was the Milkman because I had so many mandatory dawn patrol sessions. We primarily focused on my efficiency of movement in our morning sessions. He would bark "no wasted movement." His technique for teaching movement was to divide the overall movement into small movement chunks. Then he would have me combine all the smaller movements to execute the larger, overall movement. Once you have demonstrated the ability to execute the movement, he would have you repeat the movement over and over, saying "Do it again, do it again …" until you demonstrated the competency to execute movement in competition. Coach's refrain of "Finish Strong" as I completed each repetition has remained with me to this day whenever I am struggling to complete a task.

The core lessons I learned from my university defensive back coach was the effectiveness of using building blocks when teaching movement skills. He also taught me the value of the player–coach relationship. I have learned this lesson from many successful high performance coaches I have played for, worked with, and spoken to.

During my senior year at CSUF I worked with a sport psychologist and performance coach. This was a life changing experience that took my mental preparation for performance to another level. The mental preparation skills I developed were: goal setting, rehearsal, visualisation, performing in the zone/flow, breathing techniques, focused and soft vision. The additional benefit of working with a sport psychologist and performance coach was an early introduction to the concept of transitioning to becoming a high performance athlete.

What I learned from working with a sport psychologist and performance coach was the importance of adding mental preparation techniques and practices to the out-of-competition training phase. When mental preparation techniques and practices are introduced during the out-of-competition training phase, it becomes part of the routine and increases confidence as athletes enter the competitive phase of the training cycle.

At the completion of my university football career, I had become a thinking athlete. The next step in my journey would be to professional football and my introduction to the National Football League (NFL). Professional sport is business; you are rewarded for the present and future performances. I really value the lessons I learned as a professional athlete.

I was an undrafted free agent when I signed a contract with my first professional NFL team, the Los Angeles Rams. I knew it would be a challenge to make the team. I applied the lessons I learned in university to navigate the professional football world. I would need to learn the fundamentals and techniques in the NFL that I had not learned in university, and I needed to learn a new system fast. The relationships I had with the coaching staff in university were very different from what I encountered in the NFL as a first-year free agent.

Developing a relationship with the head coach was not an option but I was able to develop a relationship with my positional coach, although he did keep a professional distance, knowing I likely would not be part of the team after training camp. The mental preparation remained the same as university but it was up to each individual to get themselves mentally prepared to play the game. There was not a lot of "rah, rah" in the locker room. These were professional athletes and we were playing pre-season games. It was all business. After the pre-season I was released from the team. I had not been cut from a team since I tried out for basketball in grade 9. I wish I could say the transitional skills I developed while working with the sport psychologist helped me work through the challenges of being released from team. They did not. I instead drifted into a dark three-month period of drinking and sleeping. I thought I had failed, and I had lost a part of my high-performance athlete identity. But slowly the transitional work I had done with the sport psychologist began to break through my uncertainty and I began to focus on what I could control, which was getting a job and training for my next opportunity.

It took me a while, but I eventually realised that being released from the team taught me so much about who I was as a high-performance athlete and how important it would be for me to prepare myself for life after sport. I believe this is a gift that every coach can give the players they coach. Challenge them to see themselves as more than a high-performance athlete. Only a small percentage of high-performance university athletes become professional athletes. The reality is that athletes are in high-performance sport for a small compressed period of their lives. A coach can teach athletes how the skills they have developed as elite athletes are the same skills that will help them to be successful outside of sport. This is all part of developing thinking athletes.

Eventually I was signed by the Hamilton Tiger Cats, a professional Canadian Football League (CFL) team, in 1982. I played for the Hamilton Tiger Cats for four years, winning a Grey Cup championship in 1986 in my final season. I played with an incredible group of men. It was a great experience but the team released me after my fourth season.

I spent 10 years out of sport before returning to coach my son's pee wee football team. Coaching pee wee football is where I learned to be an athlete-centred coach. Teaching fundamentals, building relations, teaching players to think about the game is core to working with 8–10 year olds. I continued to coach my son as he moved into club and representative football. I coach the same way at every level: teaching fundamentals, building trusting relationships with the players, and teaching players to become thinking athletes.

Teaching the thinking part of the game increases as a coach moves up the age group ladder. In pee wee football you are basically teaching players the rules, positions, and what each position can do. At club, representative, and university level you are teaching players to recognise offensive, defensive and special team's formations and what tendencies teams have when they are in specific formations. Players are taught pre-snap reads that cue players to make adjustments or to change the play depending on formation. Even though football is a "start–stop game" there is a lot going on during the stoppages that players have to process and adjust to before play re-starts.

From 2011 to 2017 I was the University of Toronto Varsity Blues Football Head Coach. We game-planned for offensive, defensive and special team's formations that we identified through scouting and film study of our opponents. University coaches and players spend hours' game planning for an opponent. And the game planning multiplies as players and coaches move up levels. By the time you get to the NFL or CFL, players are in meetings for three to five hours and practising two hours daily in preparation for an opponent. Preparation for a football game is extensive, time consuming, and demanding.

When I was coaching the Varsity Blues, because the players were students first and football players second, I had to balance the amount of football practice and planning against their academic studies. This is a challenge every university coach faces. Just like I want my players to be decision-making players on the field, I want them to transfer this skill to their everyday school lives.

I am fortunate to have played basketball and football at a high level. I compare basketball to jazz and football to a symphony. And even though each game is played at a different pace and rhythm, both games require players to be thinking athletes.

21

REFLECTION ON A LIFETIME OF COACHING

David Cooper

My journey as a teacher, coach and educator has had many unexpected twists and turns. Starting my teaching career in an inner-city London secondary school and ending it at the University of Toronto, Canada, has been a marvellous experience. This journey has lasted nearly 45 years and is now focused on athlete-centred coaching, game-centred approaches and developing thinking players.

This chapter is written from an autoethnographic perspective, which focuses on many of my playing, teaching and coaching experiences and how these experiences have influenced my teaching and coaching philosophy. As a qualitative research method, autoethnography focuses on the lived experiences of individuals (Dench, 2003). This method has been used by numerous researchers (Holt, 2003; Sparkes, 2000; Headley-Cooper 2018) to recount their own journeys from a sociological analysis point of view as an acceptable academic method of writing and research.

I have been coaching since 1976, when I started my first teaching job as a physical education teacher at a football mad (or soccer mad) school called Burlington Danes in Shepherd's Bush, West London. We were a good stone's throw away from Queens's Park Rangers football club. It was said that our students used to dribble footballs around the corridors on their way to classes! This was an exaggeration, but the school had a fine soccer tradition in London. It was only natural that I should start coaching the U12 soccer team, using many of the methods that I had learned from playing football at the county or provincial level for Middlesex Schools 1st XI and from four years at St. Paul's College of Education, Cheltenham. During my time at St. Paul's, I gained the English Football Association Preliminary Coaching Badge and worshipped the words of Charlie Hughes' (1973) book, *Tactics and Teamwork*. Despite being over 45 years old, it is still probably one of the finest football coaching books ever printed. Maybe some would now call his tactics outdated, but his mantra was "depth in defence" and "width in attack". These two fundamentals have formed the foundation of my teaching and coaching in football and other territory games ever since.

The accepted and expected form of coaching high school football on a Saturday morning (we had games every Saturday from September to April) was to stand on the touchline and shout instructions to the team. Often it felt like the teacher-coach who had the best football knowledge and the loudest voice contributed as much as the young players on the pitch, who knew that if they wanted to stay in the team, they would follow my instructions. Forty years later, I am very ashamed to confess that this was my first coaching method. But it also reflects how I had been coached and how successful this method proved to be.

As I reflect on my growth as a player, teacher and coach in a variety of sports, I have thought long and hard about how I learned to make in-game tactical decisions. One strategy that sticks in my mind is what I learned from captaining my school and club cricket teams from the tender age of 11. I was selected as captain because I was considered to be the best player; hence I was captain. The coaching culture of youth cricket back in the 1960s was that the players or captain were left to make their own decisions. Looking back, this was a huge challenge for a young captain. It involved making all of the decisions when fielding, moving fielders to different positions, and choosing and changing the bowler without any help from an adult outside of the boundary. We rarely had coaches in those days! The most difficult decision-making was switching the fielding positions at the end of each over without making every fielder run to the same fielding position that they were in when the bowling was from the other end. Unlike any other striking and fielding sport, cricket is played from different ends of the pitch and the fielders are required to move to new fielding positions after each over of six deliveries.

Compare this with softball or baseball where the fielding positions are almost "written in stone" and rarely change. Recently, professional baseball teams have set their field based on the strengths of the batter. Big Papi, David Ortiz of the Boston Red Sox, was such an amazing left-handed bat when hitting the ball to right field, that coaches loaded up the right side of the diamond and outfield. In the early days of the University of Toronto women's varsity fastpitch team, I was Assistant Coach. We reached the final of the Ontario University Championship. We had several good fast ball pitchers, but we chose a pitcher who threw what was called *junk* to pitch the final. Basically, this was slow, spinning off-speed pitches. Nearly every batter from the opposition pulled the ball to left or right field depending if they were right or left-handed and our outfielders did the rest and we won the championship! This was a great example of my knowledge of cricket being transferred to softball. As a cricketer I used to bowl slow off-spin (similar to *junk*) and usually got most of my outs from batters pulling my slow deliveries into the hands of fielders on the boundary.

Returning to the description of my first experiences as an 11-year-old school and colts club cricket captain, the advice that was given to me was to write fielding positions down on small cards and keep these cards in my pocket so that I could look at them when needed. This worked really well and I soon learned to captain the team without even looking at the cards. I feel that this responsibility helped me develop my own ability to analyse the game situation, make informed decisions and become a leader. Taking an interest in cricket coaching and gaining my first cricket coaching award at the age of 16 also helped. Today, the role of being a cricket captain is very different. At many different ability levels, teams now have an array of coaches and tactical experts who discuss the bowling, batting and fielding plans.

Another form of learning that helped me develop into a player who was involved in decision-making, was observing countless matches of many sports and talking with players and coaches who were always keen to help me. Without this support, my growth as an in-game thinking player would have been much slower. Like many athletes of my age, I lived and breathed many sports. Without realising it, I became a student of the game. The more recent phrase is having "Game Intelligence."

The more I listen to coaches from many different sports, especially football managers and coaches from teams in the English Premier League, trying to explain why a performance has not been as successful as they would have liked, the more I hear them say "If only the player or players had made better decisions". One question I have asked many coaches is: "If you could choose only one ability for your athlete or team and given them the choice of being technically gifted, tactically astute or physically commanding – what would you choose?" The answer that I get most often is "The ability to make good decisions at the right time".

One strong memory I have as the University of Toronto women's varsity squash coach, which subsequently shaped my coaching philosophy, was a discussion that I had with one of my players. This player was a good player, but one who lacked confidence. She was playing in a squash tournament semi-final on Saturday evening against a good player and won the match. This put her into the final on Sunday morning. I explained that I could not watch her as I had a previous engagement, but I told her that she had previously beaten the player 3–0 and that if she played like she had played all weekend, she would win. I was fully confident of her ability to win the final. When I saw her on Monday morning, the conversation went like this:

DAVID: "How did you get on?"
PLAYER: "I lost!"
DAVID: "How did that happen?"
PLAYER: "You were not there to tell me what to do."

To hear that was quite worrying and made me think about how I was coaching my players.

Just as I had done with my U12 soccer team, I was good at telling my players how to play against different opponents by analysing their playing strengths and weaknesses. This worked very well, and from 2000 to 2015 we were the strongest varsity squash team in Ontario and Canada. We were good enough to take on some squash playing universities in the USA. But after this experience, I had to ask myself "What am I trying to achieve?" I could tell my players what to do and we might win or lose the match. Or I could develop their own in-game decision-making skills so that they would become better squash players, and risk them losing because they had tried to make their own decisions but were not successful.

In my opinion, this question still haunts many athlete-centred coaches and possibly prevents other coaches from adopting this approach. My decision was to change how we coached, and we focused on developing the players' tactical decision-making skills as well as their technical, physical and emotional abilities. We consciously stopped saying "good shot!" and changed it to "good choice!" The change of vocabulary is significant. "Good shot" is usually said when that shot has won the rally; it is outcome-based. "Good choice" indicates that the player has made a good shot decision regardless of whether or not that shot leads to winning the point; it is process-based.

Practices were devised in which players were faced with a variety of possible shots to play depending on the game situation, the player's ability and their opponent. Mike Way, in his Chapter 18 on squash, makes reference to how he coaches this shot decision-making. It soon became clear that more advanced players could cope with multiple shot choices while intermediate players often struggled with just two choices. However, beginners were usually only capable of making one choice or playing the shot that they had been told to play. As we continued to use game-centred practices, players of all abilities became more comfortable and confident in making their own choice of shots. Sometimes these shots were successful and sometimes they were not.

An important part of the process was to ask the players in a supportive environment about what their thinking patterns had been. Such a discussion between player and coach has to be non-judgemental and non-threatening. The coach must respect the choice of shot made and discuss other alternatives so that it becomes a learning opportunity for the player.

Since 2015 I have become an observer of sport and no longer a coach. I have continued to teach two Canadian National Coaching Certification Programs (NCCP) that are embedded in my two academic Theory of Coaching courses in the Faculty of Kinesiology and Physical Education at the University of Toronto. I am now into my twentieth year of teaching these courses and must have certified nearly 1000 young coaches. The NCCP is the backbone of developing Canadian coaches from the grassroots to international level. My academic coaching and teaching courses have provided me with the opportunity to introduce and educate young physical education and kinesiology students to the benefits of Athlete-Centred Coaching (ACC), Game-Centred Approaches (GCA) to teaching and coaching and Developing Thinking Players (DTP).

The longer I teach these courses, the more certain I am that coaching is all about communication. I try to provide as many opportunities, in the classroom and on the field or in the gym, for students to develop their communication and leadership skills. Academic courses usually require a strong basis of academic research, writing and exams. These skills are important but there are others which coaches need to become proficient; such as organisational skills, sport-specific technical knowledge, the ability to work with others and the ability to communicate their ideas to their athletes and players in a supportive environment.

In each of my courses I include at least one practical presentation and one academic presentation. For example, in my Theory of Coaching Part 1 course, students have to lead a Territory games group coaching session on the field, which is evaluated with visual, verbal and written feedback. For the in-class presentation, they have to present a sport-specific skills and abilities analysis. It is such a worthwhile experience to work with knowledgeable and enthusiastic students.

Co-writing and co-editing this book has also been a great experience and a pleasure. Although I am physically no longer an active coach, I am still involved in coaching and have spoken at length to all the writers of the chapters in this book. This has been a truly outstanding experience! However, the more I discuss and read about coaching, the more sport I watch on television, the more I ask myself "What is the role of the coach in the twenty-first century?".

References

Dench, L.N. (2003). Telling tales in sport and physical activity: A qualitative journey. *The Sport Psychologist*, 17(3), 372–374.

Headley-Cooper, K.J. (2018). The autoethnographic journey of athlete-centred experiences, research and learning. In S. Pill (Ed.), *Perspectives on Athlete-Centred Coaching* (pp. 150–160). New York: Routledge.

Holt. N.L. (2003). Representation, legitimation, and autoethnography: An autoethnographic writing story. *International Journal of Qualitative Methods*, 2(1), 1–22.

Hughes, C. (1973). *Tactics and Teamwork* (1st edn). London, EP Publishing.

Sparkes, A.C. (2000). Autoethnography and narratives of self: Reflections on the criteria in action. *Sociology of Sport Journal*, 17, 21–43.

PART V

How can coaches successfully turn theory into practice?

22

CONCLUSION

Barrie Gordon

The initial stimulus for the book was the realisation that while good tactical decision-making is rightly regarded as a crucial element in sporting success, coaches needed a resource that offers both a theoretical framework for understanding developing tactical decision-making, and practical suggestions of how this could be achieved through their coaching. It is the drawing together of the theoretical frameworks on decision-making and the offering of specific examples of how to achieve this, from a wide range of games and sports, that is the strength of the book.

We would suggest that the book can be used in a number of ways. Coaches of specific sports will be initially attracted to the chapters based on their sport(s) and we hope that these chapters offer useful ideas and activities for your coaching. To gain the most from the book we would suggest that you take the time to read Parts I and II, which offer a firm theoretical underpinning in tactical decision-making. While this can be a challenge for those who are not familiar with this type of writing, we expect that you will find the chapters interesting and informative. The increased knowledge and understanding that you get from these chapters will allow you as coaches to build on your own expertise and knowledge in developing games and activities to challenge and develop your players.

The six authors in Parts I and II offer a number of perspectives based on their personal experiences and interests. Chapter 1, the introduction, sets the scene for the book and identifies a number of commonalities shared by the authors.

Coaches who wish to develop a player's ability to become a better in-game tactical decision-maker need to coach in ways that facilitate this growth. It is important that the coach creates an environment where athletes are empowered to be active participants in their coaching and learning experience. An important aspect of the athlete empowerment process is developing a supportive and non-threatening practice environment where athletes take responsibility for their decision-making and find answers to the challenges that are presented to them. A supportive environment means that making, and learning from, mistakes in practice becomes an integral part of an athlete's development. It is only after athletes become comfortable with this process that they will begin to feel confident about making their own decisions in the in-game environment.

This description identifies a number of key areas that are important for coaches who wish to develop better in-game tactical decision-makers. Empowering participants to be active learners and creating a positive supportive coaching environment are common to all the approaches presented in this book. While there are commonalities, it is also important to acknowledge that there are a number of differences.

Chapter 2 is one example of the different approaches. DTP™ uses modified equipment and rules to allow coaches to develop advanced tactical understanding and decision-making in players, independent of the players' skill levels. The prioritising of the cognitive engagement as a means towards developing game skills is a new approach within Athlete-Centred Coaching and differs from other approaches which tend to teach tactical understanding in parallel with skill development.

Chapter 3 focuses on the theoretical basis for decision-making. The author identifies over 300 different theories in the literature that seek to explain decision-making. While this could have been a little off-putting initially, this has been reduced to 12 that are sport related and then to the two most popular sport-related theories – heuristics and ecological dynamics theory. During the discussion of these theoretical frameworks, important questions are raised for coaches of what constitutes 'good' decision-making. While this may appear a relatively simple question, the study of 25 soccer coaches, (O'Connor, Wardak, Goodyear, Larkin & Williams, 2018) showed it is complicated and challenging, even for highly experienced players and coaches. This question could be an important starting point for any coach who is considering how best to develop good decision-makers.

The remaining chapters in Part II all offer different theoretical perspectives with simple concepts that can be adopted by coaches. The tactical triangle presented in Chapter 4 is an example of a relatively simple concept which has the potential to be useful for coaches. Coaches in any sport can teach this framework and help players develop the three corners of the "tactical triangle" – reading of the play or situation, acquisition of the requisite knowledge to make appropriate tactical decisions, and application of one's decision-making skills to the problem. The use of softball and squash examples in Chapter 5 starts to illustrate how coaches can bring together theory and practice in an accessible way, while Chapter 6 challenges coaches to consider the role of data in facilitating players' tactical decision-making.

Part III offers 13 coaches the opportunity to share their knowledge and expertise on how they develop tactically good decision-makers. Each coach has been asked to present their chapter in a coach-friendly way, giving readers an understanding of their underpinning principles and some easily replicated examples from their own practice. It is anticipated that, having read the relevant chapter, coaches will have sufficient knowledge to use the given examples in their own practice and to allow them to expand on what they had read in order to develop their own games and activities.

While the largest number of sports presented in Part III are from the territorial games classification, we offer examples from all four classifications plus a chapter on combat sports. Sports and games from striking and fielding and target games classifications have generally received less attention than those from other classifications and we are therefore pleased to be able to offer chapters on softball/baseball, cricket and generic target games. As mentioned, the chapter on combat sport is an unusual addition for books such as this.

While all 13 chapters fit under the general heading of games-centred pedagogy and aim to develop tactical decision-making, there are a range of approaches presented by the authors. An example of this diversity can be seen in the degree to which the players are given the freedom to generate their own responses. The DTP™ approach, presented in Chapters 2, 8, 15 and 17, is based on "guided discovery," where the coach creates situations and the players "discover" the options available and can "own" their decisions. In the chapters on squash, ice hockey and netball, the coaches have more initial input, identifying and offering players a variety of choices to choose from, rather like a menu. These coaches also work with their athletes in games and game-like situations, getting them to choose the most appropriate response based on the situation they find themselves in. Another difference among the coaches can be seen in when play is stopped to allow the players to discuss their decision-making. For most coaches this occurs at the natural end of a play sequence, when the ball goes dead, or a point is scored, etc. The coaches in volleyball and squash take a different approach and stop the rally at the point that the player makes the poor decision. These coaches feel that this is the best time to ask a player about the thinking behind a particular decision, rather than waiting until the game is stopped naturally. If there is a delay they believe there is a risk that the thought processes may be lost.

The belief that in order for players to develop good decision-making the coach needs to create a supportive coaching environment was consistent throughout all the coaching chapters. It was also considered important that the coach and player(s) shared a vision, and that the coach took a strengths-based approach with a focus on the strengths and abilities of their athlete(s) when planning tactics and strategy. In discussions with the coaches, it became evident that they all felt that there are some players who find it very difficult to "think for themselves." These players find it challenging when a coach asks them to think about and take responsibility for their in-game decisions. The coaches attributed this mainly to the tendency of some traditional coaches to underestimate the cognitive ability of young players and, as a result, simply tell them what to do. One only has to watch youth soccer to see examples of a coach standing on the touchline constantly shouting out instructions to players. While this direct instruction may win games in the short term, in the long term it runs the risk of producing the type of player who is coach dependent. If players are to become successful decision-makers, then the process of learning how to make good decisions should begin early in the athlete's career, when they first begin to show an understanding of the game.

Thank you for reading *Tactical Decision-Making in Sport: How Coaches Can Help Athletes Make Better In-Game Decisions*. We hope you enjoyed it and found it interesting and helpful, and that it has a positive impact on your coaching and on the decision-making and game enjoyment of your players.

Regards
David and Barrie

Reference

O'Connor, D., Wardak, D., Goodyear, P., Larkin, P., & Williams, M. (2018). Conceptualising decision-making and its development: A phenomenographic analysis. *Science and Medicine in Football*, 2(4), 261–271. https://doi.org/10.1080/24733938.2018.1472388.

INDEX

Page numbers in *italics* denote figures.